Craig Nelson, when he isn't trekking around the world, can be found in the jungle of New York City, where he is one of publishing's most recognised – and vaccinated – figures. He has spent time in locales ranging from the Amazon to the Yucatan Peninsula and plans on making Zanzibar his next trip, if only to round out the alphabet.

'What a phenomenal trip Craig Nelson takes us on! I don't know which made me laugh harder, the outrageous people and places Craig describes, or his hilarious travel antics. *Let's Get Lost* is a gem!' Lily Tomlin

'There . . . is charm and wonder and a genuine excitement for new things seen' *Observer*

'Entertaining stories of travel from around the world in the tradition of Bill Bryson and P J O'Rourke' *The Bookseller*

LET'S
GET
LOST

adventures in the
great wide open

CRAIG NELSON

HEADLINE

First published in the UK in 2000
by HEADLINE BOOK PUBLISHING

This edition first published in 2000
by HEADLINE BOOK PUBLISHING

10 9 8 7 6 5 4 3 2 1

ISBN 0 7472 6407 4

Typeset by Palimpsest Book Production Limited
Polmont, Stirlingshire

Printed and bound in Great Britain by
Mackays of Chatham plc, Chatham, Kent

HEADLINE BOOK PUBLISHING
A division of Hodder Headline
338 Euston Road
London NW1 3BH

www.headline.co.uk
www.hodderheadline.com

For Brenda

A wide world of thanks to:

—Doug Young, Caryn Karmatz Rudy, Jennifer Rudolph Walsh, Claire Tisne and Jay Mandel, the colleagues of dreams;
—The *National Geographic* archives, America's finest travel brochure;
—Chet Baker, for a title I couldn't resist; and
—All the travel agents, operators, translators and guides who've been so patient, kind, industrious, accommodating and muscular in the middle of God-knows-where. They've taught me that there really is no place like home, since, no matter where you go in the world, you *are* home . . .

CONTENTS

WHY ON EARTH WOULD YOU WANT TO GO THERE?

'I don't know where the shame of being a tourist comes from . . . I like to join those lightning tours in which the guides explain everything you see out the window.'

—GABRIEL GARCÍA MÁRQUEZ

When he turned fifty, my father ran away from home. He was a big Texan in a big Lincoln driving whichever way his mood turned, a man temporarily no longer responsible for a wife, a mother, a job, two kids and whatever else was on his mind. Like almost all runaways, he ended up going back after about a year of meandering, but I guess that wanderlust nestles in the blood. As a 'grown-up,' there's nothing I like more than lighting out for the territories and running as far away as possible . . . traveling to places where *nobody* knows my name, where the airport wind sock really is a sock. I have more than my share of

1

foibles and faults, but when it comes to taking a vacation, baby, nobody does it better.

When people hear about my trips, they always assume I'm some Jon Krakauer *Let's climb Mount Everest for fun!* kind of guy. In fact, I'm a middle-class, suburban, pudgy white person who spent twenty-five years thinking cigarettes were one of life's greatest pleasures. Since I've never met a meal I didn't like, at plenty of times I've been the size not included in 'one size fits all,' and to this day I'm convinced that the best exercises to do are sit-ups because, in between, you get to lie down. If you're not a Mama Cass look-alike (and she's dead), you're easily in better physical shape than I am, and probably a lot braver, too.

On my travels, though, I've been threatened by an orangutan in Borneo . . . taught dance steps to Stone Age cannibals in New Guinea . . . climbed a mountain to get an aerial view of Machu Picchu . . . taken psychoactive pharmaceuticals with a Jivaro shaman in the middle of the Amazon . . . gone hunting with the last of the African Bushmen . . . had a run-in with the People's Liberation Army in Tiananmen Square . . . seen the total eclipse of the sun from the roof of an eighteenth-century Mughal fort . . . sailed the South Pacific in a nineteenth-century brigantine . . . and stalked gorillas through the montane forests of Uganda. Whenever I tell my family where I'm off to next, in fact, my mom always has one question: 'Why *on earth* would you want to go there?'

Before I went to Egypt, my friends and family said, 'How can you go there, with all the Arab terrorism?' and before I went to Peru, they said, 'How can you go there, with the Shining Path guerrillas?' and before I went to Indonesia, they said, 'How can you go there, with all those jungle diseases?' I'll never forget the real answer to these questions. One night, I was walking through the small Nile river town of Esna, followed by a mob of every single Esnian under the age of fifteen. I started off down one particular street, when a young girl grabbed my elbow and pulled me in another direction, indicating that the way I was heading was dangerous. At that time I'd just moved to New York City, couldn't afford a decent apartment, and so lived in a slum. My apartment building was directly across the street from 'the Rock,' the Northeast's biggest distributor of crack, cocaine and heroin, the kind of business where the lower-level employees were only allowed to carry Uzis. In Esna, I walked in the direction the little girl wanted me to go, but all I could think was, 'Compared to where I live, how dangerous could it be?'

A similar tale happened to my friend and traveling buddy Brenda, who was getting ready to meet me in Delhi. There'd just been news about a terrorist bomb exploding in the Paris Metro, and when Brenda called her mom to say, 'Well, I'm getting on the plane to India now,' her mom replied, *'Thank God you're not going to Paris!'*

Another reason I've always gone worry-free throughout the Third World is *the travel bubble.* When a Westerner travels through what Wall Street calls an 'emerging market' we're protected by the fact that what we are there to see isn't really a part of day-to-day life, since locals don't live their lives inside of game parks or national monuments or tropical resorts. Even if you are bound and determined to know what, say, Kenya is like for Kenyans, this won't really happen, as Paul Theroux found out: 'In Africa, in the sixties, I had had the vague idea of going native and living in a mud hut, and to that end I left my Peace Corps house and moved to an African township and into a two-room hut. But it hadn't worked. My African students thought it was undignified and my neighbors were afraid of me. Foreigners who moved into huts were either crackpots or spies.'

The travel bubble exists even for backpacking twenty-somethings, whose consumer demands have created a world-wide web of guest houses, cheap restaurants, *Lonely Planet* must-sees and authentic curio emporia selling tire sandals, knit bags and harem pants. In the Third World, you see these backpackers everywhere, and there's nothing quite as inspiring as watching a sincere, authentic English hippie bitch on her gap year abroad trying to get the last ten cents out of a bedraggled fruit–selling grandmother.

Sometimes, the travel bubble isn't all that strong. On the inaugural run of South Africa's Cape Town–Victoria Falls Blue Train luxury line, the waiting passengers snacked on cakes and champagne in the dining car while a horde of very young children, all barefoot and in rags, stared at them through the windows – until someone thoughtfully lowered the blinds.

I grew up in a Texas suburb where everyone had more or less the same clothes, haircuts, cars, houses, hobbies, attitudes, skin color and shoe sizes. It was a very safe, very predictable kind of life (the way most people around the world live, in fact), but it gave me a yen for the exotic. At the age of eight, I learned about Japan, and immediately wanted everyone to take off their shoes when they came inside the house, and eat lunch out of lacquer boxes. I insisted on having paper lamp shades in my room, and taught myself advanced origami, obsequious bowing, and how to use chopsticks – no small feat for someone whose level of coordination can be politely described as 'oafish.' I thought it was the very height of mature sophistication to eat, very fast, with a pair of sticks, and I always finished those meals with a Chinese touch. How could any child not love the fortune cookie, a dessert whose key ingredient is a slice of wit?

After too much relentlessly day-to-day, humdrum living, anybody needs a change, and maybe the answer is to start eating really fast with sticks . . . or maybe it's to run away from home. A good sojourn will immediately get you out of stale patterns and into a whole new frame of mind. Pick the right voyage, and you're guaranteed a bout of introspection, reflection and objective analysis about where you are and where you want to be. In fact, whenever you feel you should make a big change in your life, whether it's telling the boss 'I quit!' or the spouse 'I want a divorce!' or the kids 'You're going to boarding school,' it's not such a bad idea to go abroad before saying any of these things.

Traveling to the back-of-beyond shows you how most of the world makes do, and it gives you a tremendous perspective on your own life. The next time an American mentions how she's a 'survivor' who 'gets by,' I'll offer to take her to visit a woman who lives in a refrigerator box with six diseased kids, two goats, three chickens and a husband who lives 250 kilometers away assembling videocassettes in a U.S. factory, just so she can see what the rest of the world considers 'getting by.' These are the people you'll meet on any trip to nowhere: people who help you remember that there's a world other than the one you know and that, in the bigger scheme of things, maybe you aren't so bad off after all . . .

It's experiences like these that confirm the travel motto I learned from Jacques Cousteau, the inventor of scuba and the creator of such memorable sentences as 'Joos lyke humen children, ze seacow baybeez mus lairn about ze whirl from zair muthair.' Jacques said, '*Il faut aller voir*' – 'We must go and see for ourselves.' Are you really willing to pass from this mortal coil without seeing, for yourself and in person, the Taj Mahal, the Great Pyramid or the Forbidden City? Watching a moist Sigourney Weaver tousle her conditioner-free hair through *Gorillas in the Mist* just does not compare in any way with trampling through the African jungle until, fifteen feet from your outstretched hand, one of the world's remaining mountain apes is forcefully giving you the eye. Did you know that their fur looks just like a mink's? That in many ways, they are far more human than your little sister? That they quite obviously think human beings are a pathetic, boring, loser bunch of gorillas?

Don't think it doesn't matter, that these things will always be there, waiting for you. At this moment, if you want to visit Algeria, Iraq, Iran, Afghanistan, Sudan, Rwanda or Congo (Zaire), to name just a few, you can't; they're all off the visitor map. China opened its doors to Western tourists in 1899 and then, in 1949, shut them all over again and threw away the key. 'If you wanted to go to China, it was too late,' adventurer Norman Lewis lamented. 'You would have to content yourself with reading books about it, and that was as much of the old, unregenerate China as you would know.' Even the vast majority of what I saw on a 'Friendship Tour' of Beijing and Shanghai ten years ago has since been bulldozed away in the name of progress.

The wild places, too, are disappearing in the blink of an eye. Today, luxury tour ships cruise the Amazon, Mount Sinai is getting its own airport, and the New Guinea head-hunters who ate Michael Rockefeller run a curio shoppe with river views. For around $30,000, anyone can climb to the top of Everest, or take a submarine to the *Titanic* at the bottom of the seas. As Redmond O'Hanlon pointed out, 'Jungles are very, very sensual, with a warmth and loveliness that I associate with the feminine. Then there's the pleasure of seeing all these screeching, squawking, brilliantly plumed birds, or hearing gibbons whooping in the early morning. You know it's absolutely special when you're there. And you're thinking: Maybe this won't be around forever. That makes it all the more poignant. You feel like you may be one of the last people in paradise. So, you try to catch it while you can.'

Unlike Redmond's typically horrifying adventure tales of man-eating reptiles and voracious pygmies, my own travels haven't yet involved last-minute escapes from New Guinea cannibals (though I did get to dance with some) or blood-curdling adventures with savage maidens in the jungles of Africa (though one did tongue-click me) . . . they've been about contact.

I've held hands while walking with a Maasai through his Kenyan lands, as well as with a sign-language-adept orangutan and her nursing baby on a tour of the Borneo jungle. As one of the first American tourists in China, I had as many Chinese taking pictures of me as I took of them. It is one thing to gaze, in real life and in their own home, on the upturned face of a young orangutan, and it is quite a different and remarkable experience when they gaze back at you . . . which they will. When you make a connection with a being not at all like yourself, it is a different kind of adventure. You go as a sightseer, but you come home the sight seen.

To make contact, it's very important to open yourself up to whatever cultural idiosyncracies your destination has to offer. An old friend of mine and I were off to visit an alien race on one trip, and I found out that this particular tribe would get very offended if visitors didn't speak their language extremely well. Before going, I taught myself how to say, in the tribe's foreign and convoluted tongue, 'Excuse me, but I am a stupid American who cannot speak French,' which is exactly what I said to the waitress in a grand ice cream emporium on the Ile de la Cité, before asking, 'So, could you just bring us whatever is the right thing to have?' The response was to send over a platter of half-teaspoon-sized scoops of every flavor in the store. My friend and I ate, barely keeping ourselves from licking the plate like cow-pigs when we were done, all the while being stared at by the other customers with that fervor of envy and bitterness that only pure Gauls can muster.

Do you remember learning to read? How all of a sudden you looked out the car window and understood that those strange geometric lines meant 'Stop' and those storybook squiggles meant 'cat' and everywhere you looked there were words, words and more words that now, finally, you could understand? I remember when it happened to me because something similar happens on almost every trip I take, where I have this moment of shocking realization, every time and all over again as if out of nowhere . . . that I can safely go anywhere in the world, and make real contact with people who are completely alien to me in their culture, in their language and in their civilization. That people living in other times and places are as different from us as if they were another species from another planet, but if you try, you really can have something of a relationship with them, you can even become a temporary member in good standing of their society. When that happens, you realize that it isn't just your neighborhood, or your city, or your state, or your country, but all of the earth, every last inch of it, that is home.

In order to have that extraordinary feeling today, though, you need to beat the clock. Let's say you've decided, right now, to take a vacation that gets you more than a nice tan and the chance to finish that new John Grisham. With the sound of 'Born to Run' dancing in your head, you get on a plane and travel to the other side of the globe, arriving at one o'clock in the morning, China time, in Beijing. You're so excited you can barely sleep, so you wake up the next day at the crack of dawn (eating the hotel's 'American' breakfast of scrambled eggs with tomatoes) to rush to the Forbidden City, the centuries-old Imperial capital, which is cheek-by-jowl with Tiananmen Square, the absolute center of modern China. There you are, you think, completely away from it all . . . but in fact, directly across the street from Tiananmen, exactly in the line of sight of the immense portrait of the Great Helmsman Mao Zedong himself, is . . . a Kentucky Fried Chicken outlet.

Let's say you tried a different trip, traveling almost halfway around the world in the opposite direction, this time entering into the very heart of Mother Russia herself, the Kremlin's Red Square. What could be more distinct from our culture than this centuries-old outpost of anti-Americanism? But just guess what would catch your eye amidst those wildly colored onion domes? Sitting directly across the street from the square is merely the ultimate symbol of American life . . . a McDonald's.

The West didn't just win the cold war; we won the Race for

Complete and Total Global Cultural Domination. After making sure that every American city and suburb today looks almost exactly alike – with the same reflective-glass sky-scrapers, tract homes, fast food franchises and national brand stores – now the giants of American business are making sure that every other place in the whole wide world looks just like us, too. You could be traveling through parts of Paris, Rome, Madrid, St Petersburg or even Tokyo, and there'd be the same brown-mirror buildings, the same Planet Hollywood restaurants, the same Gap outlets – and you'd have absolutely no concrete evidence that you'd ever left Des Moines. Travel anywhere today and you'll learn that 'Fall into the Gap' has become a worldwide philosophical creed. We are all wearing Levi's and T-shirts while listening to Celine Dion or watching CNN, and if we've escaped the bonds of poverty and are comfortably middle-class, we can be Japanese or Sudanese or Saudi or Chilean or Greek or Fijian . . . and we are all still wearing Levi's and Ts while listening to Celine Dion or watching CNN.

This global homogenization means 'getting away from it all' requires a whole new level of thinking. If the only difference between where you live and London is a river, a tower, a cathedral and odd police uniforms (and the opportunity to purchase a snow dome with a river, a tower, a cathedral and odd police uniforms inside), then why go there? In fact, why go anywhere? Being near any major Western city today means you can easily get French clothes, German cars, Vietnamese food, Mexican handicrafts and Vermont antiques, and you can pretty easily meet any foreigner you can think of in the bargain. If you're an American and you'd like to travel to the world's largest Polish city, it's pretty easy, since it's Chicago; and if you ever find yourself in the L.A. suburb of Carson, you'll be able to meet more Samoans than there are in Samoa.

There's only one answer: to seriously run away from home. We'll take a trip from the heart of the Amazon to the tombs of Ancient Egypt . . . from the holy Ganges of India to the holy swine of New Guinea . . . from the lost city of Machu Picchu to the Forbidden City of Beijing. We'll be attacked by orangutans in Borneo and kissed by cannibals in Irian Jaya, go on safari through the key spots of Africa's Rift Valley, and crew a square-rigger through the tropical isles of the South Pacific.

If it sounds like heaven, well, it is. Close your eyes; *let's get lost* . . .

CHINA

RED MENACE

'I can't think of anything that excites a greater sense of childlike wonder than to be in a country where you are ignorant of almost everything. Suddenly you are five years old again. You can't read anything, you have only the most rudimentary sense of how things work, you can't even reliably cross a street without endangering your life. Your whole existence becomes a series of interesting guesses.'

—BILL BRYSON

UP CLOSE AND PERSONAL WITH THE PEOPLE'S LIBERATION ARMY

Anyone who's ever been on a group tour almost always returns home with stomach-churning tales of their obnoxious fellow travelers, of people who actually say, 'No Bruno, today's Tuesday, so this has gotta be Auschwitz!' Few, however, have known the pleasures of the ultimate group tour – a group tour arranged by a totalitarian fascist state – which is exactly what my first Third World vacation turned out to be. On this trip, every move we made was tracked by Communist spies, and our tour leader could easily have arranged for us to be executed.

It was all Brenda's fault. Brenda is my most significant traveling companion, a woman of above-average height and curvaceous form with a head for business and a heart for love. We first met over a decade ago in the vacant corridors of a lonely midtown office tower just after a failed corporate merger. At that time, I was dating an illegal alien from Eastern Europe and playing synthesizers as a hobby, and I turned on the TV one night only to bump into a new series about a New Yorker who dated an illegal alien from Eastern Europe and played synthesizers as a hobby. As you might expect, this program was dropped after just one season, but it was a startling moment. I'd always thought my life was just like a canceled sitcom – funny: but not funny enough – and now, here was absolute proof.

Brenda is the kind of big bunny dreamboat who, when confronted by hordes of Indian youths in the middle of nowhere, knew just the right method to bring us all together in a terrific *We Are the World*–esque moment. Under her tutelage, the kids joined us in singing the one song loved by boys and girls all over the known world:

> *A, b, c, d, e, f, g,*
> *H, i, j, k, l-m-n-o-p . . .*

Tragically, we had to sing this hundreds of times over the next two days as urchins followed us everywhere, screaming the alphabet at us with all the fervor their adorable young lungs could muster. Meanwhile, Brenda herself was repeating over and over to me a popular saying from her New Jersey girlhood:

> *Ladies and gentlemen,*
> *Take my advice:*
> *Pull down your bloomers*
> *And slide down the ice!*

When it comes to travel, she and I are two peas. I make noise; she makes nice. Our first trip together was when she casually mentioned, 'Oh by the way, I'm going to China. Wanna come?'

Now, I always wanted to go to Beijing because I like the way you write it with those three little dots all in a row, but in 1990, when Brenda brought up this idea, there were no English language China travel guides, no *Lonely Planet: Xia'n!s* and no *China on Five Dollars a Day*, since the government ran all the Friendship Tours, and you only needed to pick which one you wanted, hand over your cash in person six months in advance, fill out endless forms about your personal life, and get on the plane. You could in fact run around the country by yourself, but the Mandarin *federales* did everything they could to make that very, very difficult.

What happened during our six months of waiting was a little something called Tiananmen Square, where over a million students appeared in the center of Beijing to protest Premier Deng Xiaoping's pace of democratic reforms (meaning there wasn't any), as well as the lack of press freedom, the lack of sexual freedom, and the universities' bad food. A few weeks before we were supposed to go on our Friendship Tour, the Empire struck back, moving the army into the square, killing hundreds (the exact number is still unknown), arresting thousands, and enforcing nationwide crackdowns. The State Department banned U.S. tourists from going, the Chinese dropped our package price by two thirds. Then at the very last minute, State lifted its ban and we went on vacation, learning an important lesson: *Civil disorder can frequently lead to fantastic travel savings!*

I live in New York City, and something that always surprises me these days in how going to JFK airport is such an absolute feast for the senses. You get in the cab, and your nose is immediately assaulted by air-freshener, that same hypersweet odor used in those *Barbie* or *My Little Pony* kiddie colognes. You listen as the driver talks frantically to his countrymen on the cell phone, his voice rising to drown out the tape deck, while out the window you watch the remnant buildings of the 1964 World's Fair go by. So there you are, smelling *My Little Pony*, listening to melodramatic Celine Dion duking it out with staccato Urdu, looking at the dreamy ruins of tomorrow, and you think: This is America.

Our flight to Beijing was an Air China 747 that smelled like old socks, probably because so many of its passengers turned out to be enormous female Chinese volleyball champions, a pack of Oriental Dennis Rodmans. Before liftoff, we watched a remarkable documentary, scored to the dulcet flutes of a Yanni-wannabe, about plane travel for people who'd never been on a plane before. It explained, in excruciating detail, how to get up, how to sit down, how to use a tray table, how to use a toilet, and not to be frightened when the screen drops down to show the movie. We could barely hear the narration, though, because there was a frightful ruckus coming from the back of the cabin. It turned out the crew was running a little import business, but they hadn't tied down their merchandise, so huge boxes of microwave ovens, stereos, computers and bicycles were sliding around on the floor.

On the plane we got to meet our fellow Friendship Tour members. There was an incredibly ancient Chinese woman, Grandma Ling, a Madame Mao look-alike who smiled broadly at everyone, displaying her blindingly reflective steel teeth. There was Leona from San Francisco, who'd be running through China with two tons of duty-free Gucci accessories. There was a Chicago hippie dude attired in the classic T – 'I Survived Earth Day!' – sitting with a group of junior Mafiosi and their girlfriends, who looked like they were on their way to the Catskills but, at the last minute, decided to try China instead. The mobster broads, both with huge piles of hair and augmented cruise-missile breasts, would end up rolling around the Middle Kingdom in short-shorts and skintight Ts. The rest of us tried to guess every morning what outfits they'd come up with next.

There was also The Emperor, a 'professional' photographer who got her nickname since she always pushed her way to the front of any view to get the best shots, inspiring the Chinese to say, 'Who does she think she is, the Emperor?' There was Mr. Elbows, a party functionary, who bullied his way through any crowd (including us) with bruising jabs; we assumed he must be a spy. There was Jacqueline, a real snagglepuss, whose demeanor was perfectly synched to Bette Davis as *Baby Jane*, and who would cause havoc the entire trip, as she wanted to travel solo without paying the single supplement. Within seconds of takeoff, she threw a temper tantrum over being in the smoking section, but just moving to the front of the cabin wasn't enough; Baby Jane felt this insult could only be remedied with a first-class upgrade. Against Chen, our tough-as-nails Cantonese group leader, she didn't stand a chance.

Do you know the kind of boys who are just about to become teenagers, and they're so manic that you want to like them, but you just can't help but wish they were dead? One of these was the centerpiece of the Mormon family, a group who, at every sightseeing stop, played Frisbee and catch (they'd brought their own equipment) because this kid was way too hysterical to be able to enjoy anything about being in China except for playing Frisbee and catch.

Why did they come? This is something about parents today I just don't understand: going on trips completely inappropriate for their children, and not leaving the kids at home with grandma. You can even see it at Disney World, with thousands of moms and dads pushing around babies in strollers, babies who, if Mickey Mouse has anything to do with them, scream in holy terror. Besides the attention-deficit-disordered preteen, the Mormons also had a pair of baby towheads, perhaps two or three years old, who yowled and wailed and sobbed the entire flight. I'm sure they'll cherish memories of China for the rest of their lives . . .

Our next clue as to what this trip was going to be like happened in Shanghai, at immigration control, when it was revealed that Leona had forgotten her passport. It turned out she knew this getting on back in the U.S., but Chen had reasoned that 'If you go back home now, you will not go to China. But if you get on the plane and come, perhaps you will.' We waited for three hours while the authorities drilled this would-be imperialist running-dog lackey, but amazingly, they let her in. We didn't know at the time that this was because the Chinese were desperate, and had plans to use us in their international PR efforts.

It takes twenty-four hours of sitting and standing in lines to get from New York to San Francisco to Tokyo to Shanghai to Beijing, and we arrived at one o'clock in the morning China time, having been assigned roommates by pulling names out of a hat. Don't do this at home. My winning ticket was Uncle Wang, a seventy-two-year-old Taiwanese visiting the mainland for the first time since Liberation in 1949. His favorite expression was 'I'm a *lousy* guy,' and Wang was basically using the reduced-rate group tour to save on travel expenses. He'd skip every sightseeing trip in order to visit his family and friends, and was almost never in the room, but when he did come along for the sights and hear all the Americans exclaim how wonderful everything was, he'd always say the same thing: Forbidden City? 'But you should see the capital of Taiwan!' Summer Palace? 'But you should see the parks in Taiwan!' Great Wall? 'But you should see the walls in Taiwan!'

Just as we'd all gotten unpacked and tucked in and were lying in our Beijing beds too excited to sleep, at three A.M. there was this tremendous uproar in the halls, a big screaming catfight, and we all ran out to see what was going on. Baby Jane was throwing another temper tantrum, as well as all of her roommate's gear into the hall. 'I can't share with someone who smokes and snores!' she hissed, and poor Chen had to calm down both crazed harridans and reassign eight elderly women to make do.

Whenever you go on one of these trips, you always run across plenty of horrible traveling pig-people, but you also see brave, adventurous souls, quiet heroes who are remarkable: eighty-year-old Floridians asking about wheelchair access at the Great Wall . . . twin sisters who'd just returned from camping in Mongolian yurts . . . and of course the women I've traveled with. It's one thing for me, six foot one and two hundred pounds (give or take) to launch myself on the road in one of these strange and mysterious worlds, and quite another for a small woman (whatever her independent means) to do the same. Brenda is fearless, and in China we met another travelin' gal, Melissa, a pharmacist who'd gotten up that morning before everyone else, had her buffet breakfast of scrambled eggs and tomatoes, bought the local rain gear (a milky-white poncho), and had taken off to rent the universal Chinese transportation device, a Flying Pigeon Deluxe bicycle, to meet us at our first stop.

Most Beijing highways are four-lane, the outers for bicycles (packed) and the inners for cars and trucks (empty), and everywhere we went in urban China, thousands of bicycles were always descending upon us with their vast chorus of kiddie bells, a horde of furies from a toddler's nightmare. As Melissa rode surrounded by the great masses, her Flying Pigeon started shaking uncontrollably, and she pulled over, thinking she had a flat. Her tires were fine, however, so she looked at the road. There, just outside Tiananmen, were deep grooves in the asphalt, grooves cut by the wheels of tanks.

Though they obviously want a dynamic tourist industry, the Chinese aren't keen on having foreigners running pell-mell all over their country, and so they've devised a brilliant scheme. Friendship Tours run from eight A.M. to ten P.M. nonstop, filled with attractions no one wants to miss, keeping you with the group and on the go at all hours until you drop dead from exhaustion. If you want to get out on your own, the only answer is to sleep less, which of course we did that first morning by sneaking out of the hotel (a black-and-white concrete high-rise topped by a revolving restaurant) and wandering around the neighborhood, which turned out to be a medieval village.

This village was probably built sometime in the eleventh century, and hadn't changed a whit over the past nine hundred years. With streets laid out wherever the goats had wandered, and black-tile roofs patched with sod now sprouting green weeds, it was one of those back-alley towns of China, a *hutong*, but right on the main drag and in the middle of urban renewal. A grove of bamboo trees waved over the top of a crumbling wall covered in grape vines, and instead of doors, arched entryways would only be covered with thin, frilly curtains, children running in and out screaming with glee.

Men with giant wicker baskets and fifteen-foot bamboo poles tied to their backs came swaying down the street, stopping to stare at us. Bicycle deliverymen, pulling wooden platforms stuffed with extruded coal or red chili peppers or pots of dough, would see us, and fall over (just as in the West where there are hundreds of truck variations, there are a bazillion different kinds of Chinese bike). We'd wander into a dusty noodle store, show a camera, and ask to take pictures. In the split second of raising the camera to our eyes, everyone would vanish out of frame. We found out later that Chinese who'd had their pictures in the foreign press had all been taken in for questioning, and many hadn't yet come back.

Everywhere we looked, cranes and bulldozers and dump trucks were erecting those high-rises that are the signature style of Communists everywhere, stupefyingly ugly things that always look cheap, tatty and unfinished. It was nice to see so much business going on, since the Chinese have endured so many dreadful periods of terrible deprivations; their new motto, in fact, seemed to be: *Get it while you can.* Then we were told that all the *hutongs*, all of the neighborhoods that were Beijing's defining feature for a thousand years, including the one we'd just wandered through, would be bulldozed, and everyone inside moved to those new high-rise apartments.

THE SHOWDOWN

Between the twenty-four hours of transit, Baby Jane's temper tantrum, being too keyed up for our own good, and the fact that it was raining cats and dogs, everyone was groggy and comatose and bundled up in ponchos and umbrellas for our first sightseeing expedition: Tiananmen. The square turned out to be what would happen if you took a hundred acres of Central Park and paved it over with concrete, and then moved the Capitol and the Washington Monument and a bunch of bad sculpture there. Also, post-slaughter, it turned out to be closed to everyone except tour groups. In this huge, raining place, we were the only ones around, except for the People's Liberation Army, still bivouacked on alert and sleeping under the overhangs of the back wall of the Forbidden City.

The square may have been open to us, but they hadn't gotten around to reopening any of the buildings, so we couldn't see inside the Museum of the Chinese Revolution, or the Museum of Chinese History, or the Great Hall of the People, and we especially couldn't see the one thing I wanted to see in all of China: the crystal sarcophagus of the eternally preserved body of Mao Zedong, lying behind a glass wall, draped in a Chinese flag, his face lit by a spotlight, and referred to worldwide as 'peasant under glass.' We were only allowed to look at socialist art and architecture so ugly it was eye-opening, take in the famous mural of a makeup-wearing Mao hanging from the main wall, wander through avenues marked by thousands of crimson flags (limp and sodden in the rain), and run into various members of the Red Army, who'd finished killing college students and were now meandering around on this deserted concrete plain, with nothing much to do. In the heat and wet, I was wearing Bermuda shorts and a T-shirt, while they were in their olive-green wool and polyester uniforms. We looked at each other.

It turned out we'd give the Red Army something more to do than just sightsee. Across the street from the back of Tiananmen, right next to a Kentucky Fried Chicken outpost, there was a horde of people squatting in an outdoor market, eating noodles and watching us. Since Brenda and I were tired of looking at the outside of buildings and bad statues in the pouring rain, we thought we'd go over there. Even in the middle of the capital, a big fat blond American running around saying '*Ni hao!*' (hello) is a big deal, and we were mobbed with people trying to shake our hands and get us to eat plastic bowlfuls of scary, odd-looking things. We spent about two hours with them, speaking a little English and a little Chinese and miming everything else, and then went to get back on the bus.

As only tour groups were allowed in Tiananmen, the People's Liberation Army was guarding its borders, and these teenagers with AK-47s would not let us back in.

I bowed, scraped, kowtowed and pantomimed, but could not get across the idea of *we are with a tour group and our bus is back there*, and they were adamant we not enter the square.

We tried another entryway, and then another, but these were all dead-ends, and we were later and later in getting back to the bus.

We didn't know the tour leader's name or the name of the hotel, we had no Chinese money, and it was still pouring rain and hot as hell.

We went back to the armed teens, mimed driving, pointed, bunched together to look like a group and pleaded what we were told meant 'please' (*doo-ay bouch-ee! doo-ay bouch-ee!*) again and again. After half an hour of this, they finally relented. We ran like hell across the puddles back to the group, only to get a big scolding from Chen and nasty stares from our fellow Friendship Tourists, who, after all, had been sitting in a damp bus for half an hour. Baby Jane, meanwhile, was having trouble with her camera and complaining bitterly that the hotel maids had obviously taken out her perfectly good batteries and replaced them with used ones.

THE DRAGON THRONE

The rain stopped, the sun came out, and we set off for a place no ordinary mortal had been allowed to see for five hundred years. Entering through the Meridian Gate, which has multistoried towers at each side dotted with windows sized for great bows, we passed over a series of white stone bridges spanning 'The Inner Golden River,' to arrive at the vast central courtyard, which looks like concrete, but is in fact layers upon layers of marble carved into bricks. Before us stood building after building, all the same outline as any California ranch house, but with vast rising-sun, yellow-tile roofs spreading over low-slung, fire-engine-red walls and pillars. Then I looked closer to see, at every corner of every roof, a carved parade of animals, led by a man riding a chicken, and I knew I was in a strange and ancient place.

Chinese tour leaders love statistics and math, and so told us again and again that the Forbidden City includes over nine thousand buildings on 178 acres all surrounded by a 33-foot-high wall and a 165-foot-wide moat, and that it would take two solid years to see everything in it, including the House of Crimson Snow . . . the Hall of Tranquillity and Sincerity . . . the Pavilion of Flourishing Literature . . . the Studio of Character Cultivation . . . the Pavilion of Flowing Water Music . . . the Tower of Auspicious Clouds . . . the Hall of Refreshing Mists and Waves . . . They failed to calculate, however, the awesome effect of all this grandeur, all this imperial magnificence, the ultimate power of interior decorating. It left me brain-dead.

Our first stop was the Hall of Supreme Harmony, a dim, immense room shadowed by hundreds of broad pillars painted in shiny gold leaf, centered by the gold lacquer imperial throne (which, like all the others, is really an imperial divan), surrounded by dozens of statues of elephants and cranes, and scores of incense burners. When it came to ornament, embellishment and froufrou, the Chinese ancients beat all comers hands down; the ceiling alone is an eye-popping mass of curlicues, frills, doodads and gewgaws, heavily colored in pine green, carmine red and, predominantly, shining gold, with a centerpiece of writhing dragons suspended above the throne, each with a silver pearl in its mouth.

These aren't vicious reptilian marauders pillaging innocent Dark Age peasants until St George comes to town . . . to the Chinese, dragons are like enormous puppies, playful and wacky, absurd and begging for love. When necessary, however, the beasts can turn viciously protective to slaughter evil people (like Mongols). The ancients were just crazy about dragons and, until about a hundred years ago, many Chinese still believed in them, and still think the outline of their country looks like one. The most famous of them all live at the bottom of the ocean, playing fetch with giant pearls, and jade is thought to be their dried semen.

After a forced march of touring, we wandered around this immense and ancient place, finding ourselves always in off-beat corner side lanes, filled with the dark, the strange, the odd and the beautiful. A screen that was once painted red as cherries, but is now faded to a soft, dense watercolor. A tight, oppressive alley, passing between two three-story-high towering walls. A series of perfectly round moon-gates, leading to a bamboo grove.

Like all great sights of the ancient world, I needed to make some effort to get a sense of what this might've been like when it was filled with people and alive, and not just the empty tourist attraction it is now – when it was the home of the Son of Heaven, the Lord of Ten Thousand Years, the center of the Dragon Throne, a city of silk-quilted armor, helmets of lacquered oxhide, raincoats of woven down, fans of white peacock feathers, robes of screaming-yellow silk, fur and gauze, with cuffs of horse hooves. It was a life of banquets with over one hundred courses, picnic wines chilled by floating the goblets down a mountain stream, medicines of fossilized crab, bear fat and dried vipers, books made from sheets of jade, whips braided from silk, lanterns of goat horn, shade given by baroque saffron umbrellas, men with topknots growing to their knees, and eunuchs carrying their testicles in clay pots, so they would ultimately be buried as whole men. Eunuch candidates would arrive at the City's Castration Clinic, smoke enough opium to make you puke, and then sit on the imperial Beijing version of a potty chair. One stroke of a sharp knife removed their testicles, and only half of these eunuchs-to-be survived.

The palace was festooned with billowing yellow fabrics, the air filled with the chatter of concubines (their hair sprayed into geometric outlines), and the shouts of little boys chasing their mice, turtle and cricket pets. The goal of the concubines was to do whatever it took to bring the emperor to ecstasy, and when they failed in attracting him, they were sent to wander the Garden of Dispossessed Favorites, a haunting spot of ex-beauties and a harsh moral for all you would-be party girls. Trespassers caught inside the Forbidden City were executed with 'The Death of a Thousand Cuts,' where a sword would slice off tiny swathes of your criminal flesh, keeping you alive and in as much pain for as long as possible. When one huge carved stone wouldn't fit through a door, the emperor had it beaten, and whenever he turned moody, a whip would crack and everyone would have to bow down.

It was a life of such immense leisure that one emperor, Kang Xi, spent his days imitating the calligraphy of the Soong poets. It was also a life of such leisure that the Chinese had the time to invent paper, the suspension bridge, cast iron, the crossbow, forged steel, the umbrella, poison gas, the decimal point, porcelain, the stink bomb, toilet paper, the seismograph, phosphorescent paint, the kite, parachutes, the printing press, rudders, the fishing reel, playing cards, the steam engine, wheelbarrows, whiskey and clocks – but then they forgot how to make clocks and, in the opening to the West, had to import fourteen thousand of them for the Forbidden City.

I saw all this, and then, over the next few weeks, got a glimpse at how the rest of China must've lived: generations of peasants barely eking out a living, or merchants taxed to death to pay for all this stuff. I thought that everyone of repugnant wealth, from Bill Gates to Donald Trump to England's Queen Betty, should come have a look. When you see the Forbidden City set against the rest of China, the only conclusion you can reach is: *No wonder they revolted.*

Outside the window, on a marble plain, the Mormons played Frisbee.

TWO WOMEN

Traveling through the Middle Kingdom means learning its history, and the history of Imperial China is an epic of family feuds, betrayals and revenge. One of the greatest stories began in the 1400s, at the height of a battle that had raged for months between the ruling Ming and the Fewe tribe. One of the renegade chiefs, dying, threw the Ming a curse: 'A Fewe woman will bring down your house!' For five hundred years, no Fewe concubines were allowed into the Forbidden City, but eventually his words were forgotten, and one Fewe took her place in history, ultimately becoming the notorious dragon-lady, Empress Dowager Cixi (*see-zhi*), who, as a power-monger, made Nancy Reagan and Madame Mao look like baby dolls.

Cixi was a low-level concubine when her emperor died in 1861, but she was also the only one of the many wives and concubines to have given birth to a son, who'd just turned six. In alliance with the emperor's brother and the senior concubine, she arranged for her son to take the throne, with the three adults serving as co-regents. When the new emperor suddenly and mysteriously died at the age of twenty, Cixi's power was so great that the throne then went to her nephew, whom she adopted as another son, and who at the time was three.

An opera fan and tropical fish hobbyist who protected her scary fingernails with eight-inch-long gold sheaths, Cixi's favorite spot in all the Middle Kingdom was the Summer Palace, where she used money earmarked for China's navy to construct herself a marble pleasure ship that doesn't float. The Summer Palace is a collection of mansions, walkways and gardens, of lily ponds and lotus ponds, of structures called Know-Your-Fish Bridge and the Lodge of the Propriety of Weeding, all set on the shores of the broad, man-made Lake Kumming. After murdering six of his colleagues, Cixi kept her nephew/son under house arrest here, and for a decade the Chinese referred to him as the Prisoner-Emperor. In 1908, as she lay in her deathbed, the Empress Dowager arranged for his murder and appointed in his stead Puyi, who'd become China's last emperor, mostly through Cixi ignoring the public uprisings all around her. The Fewe woman had brought down the house, and the Summer Palace is now a very crowded park where, for a quarter, visitors can stick their heads through holes in a painting to look like Cixi, or ride about in duck boats.

At the palace's exit (just like at the finish line of every Chinese tourist attraction) is a restaurant and a Friendship Store, a mind-boggling spread of merchandise: ten thousand variations of picture postcards next to ten thousand imperial masks next to ten thousand bamboo back-scratchers next to ten thousand carved and shellacked Buddhas next to ten thousand scenic key rings, and on and on it

25

goes until you develop *tchotchke fatigue*. There is always a needle-point department, where you can have a treasured family snapshot reproduced as a giant hand-stitched wall hanging, but where you can also get, in multiple sizes, ten thousand different needlepoint creations of fluffy white kittens playing with a goldfish, looking like no kitten you've ever seen. Like their interior decorating, when it comes to souvenirs the Chinese just don't know when to quit.

At one stop, I bought a red cloth-covered book that wasn't a book; it was bound like an accordion, and unfolded to become a screen of gold leaf with red ideograms on both sides, the one hundred Chinese words for prosperity and long life; an ideal birthday present, beautiful and unique. This, I thought, looking at in later on the bus, will be the perfect gift for almost everyone I know back home; at the next stop, I'll get a dozen. In every store from then on I looked for more of the little books, but never saw another. The exact same story happened with a black lacquer box lined in pink and gold silk; a great present, but we found two, and no more. Every store in China, however, had their own ten thousand needlepoint sets of fluffy white kittens.

We were quite keen to shop for some fab Commie souvenirs, perhaps a poster of 'The Running Dog Traitor Li Po Being Shown the Error of His Ways,' and finally found some pretty, shiny plastic buttons of Mao painted red and gold. We got a lot of them, and would show them off to the other Chinese we met on the trip, not knowing for some time that these were 'accomplishment' badges from the Cultural Revolution, probably the most hated ten years of recent Chinese history. It would be like walking around Berlin in 1946 showing all the locals the really pretty Nazi paraphernalia you'd just picked up for a song. We were told that ardent Red Guards would pin these Mao badges directly into their skin. Eck.

Just think of how you'd feel if your sweet, kind and heroic father suddenly went nuts. Or, if you grew up when George Washington was still alive and, in the last years of his life, he turned evil. This is the troubling position most Chinese today have with Mao, who in the Great Leap Forward and the Cultural Revolution almost completely destroyed China, spending the last ten years of his life engineering a government-backed civil war run by an army of teenagers.

In 1958, Mao announced the Great Leap Forward, which was to circumvent China's having to wait like all other countries to develop industry. A hundred million people were sent from their farms to build infrastructure, hydroelectric dams, irrigation canals and vast communes that merged farming with light industry. The Leap failed miserably when food production collapsed and famine resulted in over twenty million people starving to death from 1959 to 1962. While moderates like Deng Xiaoping and Zhou Enlai tried changing government policy to fix this debacle, Mao insisted on staying the course. In 1965, he publicly complained that the Communist Revolution hadn't achieved its goals, that too much wealth and power still lay in the hands of the elite. Beijing high school students formed an anti-elite club, the Red Guards, which Mao publicly supported, and this trend spread across the country until eleven million teenagers, wearing what looked like Brownie uniforms with crimson neckerchiefs, massed into squadrons and launched the Cultural Revolution.

Egged on by Madame Mao (who might've well been Fewe herself), the teenagers rampaged across the country, painting the streets red, tearing down temples, vandalizing libraries, burning books, destroying anything from Imperial China or foreign countries they could get their mitts on. Some toured their villages and neighborhoods with scissors, 'helping' their comrades avoid looking elitist by cutting off their hair. They held 'struggle sessions' of harassment, making their onetime teachers wear dunce caps and kicking them to death. Thousands were tortured, thousands committed suicide. Deng Xiaoping, who previously had been Mao's handpicked successor, was imprisoned, and his son was paralyzed after being thrown out a window.

It wasn't until Mao's death in 1976, the life imprisonment of Madame Mao, and the return of Deng Xiaoping that the Cultural Revolution was officially declared over . . . and a terrible mistake. The standing of the Chinese Communist Party had been damaged beyond repair, leading to the student rebellions that culminated in the slaughter at Tiananmen. A whole generation of Chinese weren't educated past grade school, and are now both ignorant and bitter. The national economy was completely derailed in a period when Korea, Thailand and Japan saw their economies soar.

All Chinese today are still recovering from those years, living with an ever-present, underlying fear that such chaos and horror could easily happen again at any time.

Brenda, Melissa and I were hoping to get a full out-and-out People's Republic experience – go to a Red Army opera, see Socialist Realism posters, watch gangs of people in Mao jackets, hear the shouts of *zou gou!* (running dog!) and *jieji diren!* (class enemy!), that sort of thing. We kept seeing signs everywhere, banners of red silk written in gold leaf, and assumed they must be exhortations from the chairman. Finally Chen translated, and it turned out that they all said: *Play Lotto!*

DID YOU GET THE BLOOD?

Tootling around Beijing, you always know you're in a foreign country, since everything is slightly off. The moat that circles the original ancient town's line of defense is planted in alternating rows of Christmas fir trees and weeping willows, and it is as odd-looking as it sounds. Between the smoke from the coal (everything in Beijing runs on coal) and the dust blowing in from the Gobi Desert, Beijingers are all infected with lung clots. At least, that's what it sounds like; we heard millions hawking and spitting with a notorious gargling cough that's such a distinctive Chinese habit the government was running an Anti-Spitting Campaign (which failed miserably and was replaced while we were there by the Please-Use-the-Spittoon Campaign). As a protection from all that dust and smog, Chinese youngsters commonly travel with a sheet of gauze draped over their heads, while the non-potty-trained skip diapers and just have a slit in their pants. Muddy plains where grass once grew are unsuccessfully protected by tiny ankle-high fences, and every public spot comes with its own box of comment cards for you to fill out at your peril.

We watched an old woman in traditional silk robes hobbling down the street, balancing herself with a pole. Her feet looked like tiny balls, and we realized she was one of the last of the lilyfeet, a woman who'd been bound and crippled as a child so her husband would have the pleasure of putting her deformed feet in his mouth during sex. In the eleventh century, an empress was born with a club foot, and (like the lisps of Madrid) a trend was born: limping was *classy*. At the age of five, girls would have their feet wrapped in cloth, pressing the toes under the sole and pulling the heel tightly into a fold, the goal being an adult foot four inches long and two inches wide. The smaller the foot, the bigger the dowry, and foot-binding lasted for a thousand years.

One of our more pressing concerns was food – like any tourists, we were eager to uncover authentic Chinese cuisine. What we got wasn't unlike Chinese food in the West, except that where we have mu shu pork with seventeen ingredients, theirs would have three. The Chinese must think Western tourists are all huge gnawing empty pits, since the quantities were just staggering, a parade of waiters lugging over an endless line of bowls and platters, thrown down to spin at the center of the tables on lazy Susans. Just as you think the meal is finished, more platters and bowls appear, always ending with horse-sized chunks of watermelon. Plenty of the overseas Chinese traveling with us would just go nuts, frantically spinning the Susan and using the chopsticks' thick end to dish out as much as they could fit on their plates of the items they preferred. Even with this massive largesse, Baby Jane had a screaming hissy fit when Grandma Ling took the last piece of watermelon before she could get hers.

We were told that the polite way to get a waiter's attention was with *doo-ay bouch-ee*, which is supposed to mean 'excuse me please.' But on the plane, I'd learned that the word all Chinese use is *Ching!* just like the bell at a hotel's front desk. We were told *Ching!* was considered rude, so we sat through three meals yelling out *doo-ay bouch-ee*, and were completely ignored. One *Ching!* however, and the waiters jumped to attention. So much for nuance.

We drove by a common scene, a road accident between a taxi and a bicyclist, and The Emperor pushed us all aside to get to the window. As the bus pulled away she turned to everyone and excitedly demanded, 'Did you get the blood?' I asked her about the professional market for scenes of Chinese car accidents, but she just sneered at my ignorance of the photojournalist's art. Then we drove by another of the only social engineering posters we saw in the whole country: the silhouette of a young couple, with Zhou Enlai pointing out the rising sun of the future, and telling them they'll be really, really happy if they have just one and only one baby. In this particular poster, the baby was blond.

In the old days, the Chinese would've whispered that I was a *gweilo* (white goblin) or a *wei-guo ren* (foreign idiot) or a *dabidze* (big nose), but no longer; it'd be hard to overestimate how much today's Chinese love Americans. Appearing everywhere are Old Duck Tang (Donald Duck), Old Mouse Mi (Mickey Mouse), and the current national hero, Miku Quiaodan (Michael Jordan). The Chinese see practically every Western movie ever made, but they think our titles are dull, and so translated *The Full Monty* into *Six Naked Pigs* and *As Good as It Gets* into *Mr. Cat Poop*. There are 85,000 Chinese Amway sales reps and 130 Chinese McDonald's outlets (with Ronald known as 'Good Uncle'), while just outside Shanghai, the American Dream Park lets Chinese mingle with cowboys and Indians and wander through a re-created suburb. The head of the State Police has just hired a Californian cop to consult with his troops, and the first thing the American did was arrange for them all to watch a screening of Clint Eastwood in *Dirty Harry*. No doubt they loved it; the movie playing everywhere in China when we were there was none other than *Rambo*, which as I remember is about a big muscled white guy slaughtering Asians.

On the way to the Great Wall, the president of the Chinese International Travel Service got on the bus, along with a pack of news service journalists and a photographer. While the photographer took everyone's picture (and was harangued with questions by The Emperor), the journalists would ask, 'Don't you just love being in China?' and 'What is the most beautiful thing you have seen?' and 'What was the nicest thing that a Chinese person has done for you?' We of course all wanted to talk about Tiananmen, but finally Chen looked at us like we were morons and said, 'They cannot say you are sad for the students.' Privately, however, the Chinese would admit that the Party was stupefied over the international reaction, and they didn't seem to know what to do about it. Compared to the vicious blood horrors of the Great Leap Forward and the Cultural Revolution, the leaders thought army tanks running over some college kids in the middle of Beijing was no big deal.

It was such a shock just being in China that we didn't realize at the time what was going on; we thought having the CITS president (undoubtedly a big-time cadre) and the journalists on board was nothing, that maybe this happened all the time. But then we started looking around beyond the fantastic sightseeing items directly in front of our eyes, and we realized that, besides a few errant German hippies, we were the only Western tourists in all of China. As such, we would now be making regular appearances in Xinhua News, the happy foreign friends having a great time. Then we found out that, because no one but us was traveling in the country, the Chinese government had decided that this was a perfect time for rural Chinese to go on vacation and fill up the empty hotels and restaurants and tchotchke shops. So we didn't see the Great Wall and the Forbidden City and the Temple of Heaven and the Xi'an terra-cotta warriors surrounded by hordes of Westerners; we saw them surrounded by hordes of rural Chinese peasants who'd never seen a Westerner before.

The line of demarcation between sightseer and sightseen had completely broken down. At all the tourist haunts, Chinese would pretend to take a picture of the scenery, but then at the last minute would turn and get a shot of us. Everywhere I went, people would stare, not with the rude looks of tourists or zoo-goers, but with a stare that was deeply curious, inquisitive and just this side of erotic. In conversation, many Chinese would absentmindedly and compulsively stroke the hairs on my forearms, since their own bodies were essentially hairless; they didn't even need to shave. Babies would see me and stop crying; children would run over and scream, 'Hello! Hello!' but this was the only English word they knew, so no matter what I said back, they just kept shouting 'Hello! Hello! Hello!'

THE RIBBON DRAGON

Before running off to see the Red Menace up close and in person, I thought it wouldn't be a bad idea to brush up on my Chinese history, so I read a lot of incredibly boring stuff and learned that there is one big, enduring theme when it comes to China's epic past: *trouble with the neighbors*. Again and again, the Dragon Throne has been overrun and ruled by outsiders, and this has happened so often and so consistently that it's no wonder they put up the world's biggest wall.

From many miles away you first see it . . . a white ribbon waving across the tops of soft velvet-green undulating mountains shaped like thumbs. Wanli Changcheng ('The Ten Thousand Li Long Wall') is two thousand years old and was originally built to keep out the Hsiung-nu nomadic tribes (ancestors of both the Mongols and the Huns). When Ronald Reagan visited, he popped off with 'It really is a Great Wall!' What I didn't realize before going is how *wide* it is, a big paved and elevated two-lane highway, perfect for sending chariots, infantry and messengers anywhere along China's endless border. Now its paving stones have been worn smooth with the polish of time, and we walked up and down this glassy surface at ninety degree angles, and it was really, really difficult.

One thing the Chinese don't mention when you visit the Great Wall is that, basically, it didn't work. The Mongols invaded and took over, creating the Xanadu made famous by Marco Polo and Samuel Taylor Coleridge. Polo claimed to have spent seventeen years here because his parents did some never-revealed crucial job for Mongol Emperor Kublai Khan, but his claims have always been suspicious, and he's probably in fact the first of many world travelers who made up stuff (later in life, Bruce Chatwin had his publisher change the designation of all his travel books to 'fiction'). *The Travels of Marco Polo* never mentions foot-binding or tea-drinking – common at the time, and considered wildly strange by Europeans – and doesn't refer to cities by their Chinese names, but by their Persian ones. Even when his book was a huge worldwide, Middle Ages bestseller, his fellow Venetians snickeringly named Marco 'Il Milione' – a thousand lies.

I was too busy being a tourist attraction myself to enjoy much of Wanli Changcheng. Immediately, a woman came up to me and said, 'Are you a movie star? You are so white, and so fat! And your face is so . . . dimensional!' This she meant as a compliment. Every army man there wanted his picture taken with me; rangy farmers would run up, screaming and shaking their cameras, dragging me over to their extended families where I'd be plopped down front and center. It was like being a freakish celebrity cult figure, Elizabeth Taylor crossed with L. Ron Hubbard crossed with the Elephant Man, and it was exhausting . . . and of course I was also thinking: *China is just terrific!*

We got back on the bus and, while waiting for a few of the gals who were making last-minute pit stops (being twenty minutes late from the trouble with the Red Army at Tiananmen had set a dangerous precedent), we bought quilts and jackets through the windows from some of the local talent. Then, a tragedy, when some of the money got into the wrong hands. The rightful seamstress became hysterical, rushing onto the bus, crying and screaming and taking back her merchandise. This ignited Baby Jane, who in turn started hoarsely yelling, 'Protect your valuables! They're letting her come in here and take EVERYTHING!'

In front of the two-humped Bactrian camel ride, where there was a clearing, the Mormons played catch.

A WELL-LEATHERED PANDA PELT

Probably the most dangerous thing I've ever done in my life was to fly from Beijing to Xi'an (*she-ahn*) on China's domestic air service. It was a Russian plane, an Ilyushin 18, and most likely had been rejected by Aeroflot as in too bad a shape for their safety considerations (of which there are none). Inside, the plane was sweltering, at least 120 degrees, 'just like when you open the oven to check on the turkey,' Melissa said. The air didn't move, and it was filled with flies, so the stewardesses came around and passed out tiny fans, which did nothing, and within minutes we were all sweat-soaked. The overhead luggage racks were thin poles of bamboo, and the other passengers turned out to be hundreds of little old Chinese ladies, each of whom had a giant, seventy-pound cast-iron crate which they insisted we lift into these racks. The plane took off, banked fifteen degrees, and the massive boxes crashed to the floor. The ladies screamed in alarm and then, practically in unison, began vomiting noiselessly into thin cloth bags.

At the front of the plane was an original 1950s metal Kelvinator, a huge hulking beast of a refrigerator, and the stewardesses pulled baskets of a mystery meat out of it and hurriedly passed them out, charging their way through the crates. We asked what this was and they said, 'It's a snack! A snack!' The plane had a stopover in Nanjing, landing in a breathtaking series of bounces and skids, and we sat there, sweating all over again, for two hours, while the women pushed their crates back into the racks. We took off, banked, the boxes crashed to the floor, and we finally arrived in Xi'an, surprised to be alive.

Starting in 1100 B.C.E. and lasting for a thousand years, this was both the capital of China and the start of the Old Silk Road, sending its vast array of merchandise out to Central Asia and the Roman Empire, while cooking sassy meals with coriander, curry, cumin, turmeric and chili peppers (which, just like in Mexico, hang in dried strings from the roof beams). Sited in the country's dead center, eighth-century Xi'an was the largest city in the world, with over a million residents; today it is a polluted, industrial place, a Chinese Pittsburgh littered with temples, ruins and stelae (Imperial edicts carved into stone tablets and riding on the backs of erect turtles). Xi'an's air pollution is now so remarkable, in fact, that it's frequently possible to look directly at the sun without harming your eyes . . . but two thousand years ago, it was the city of Chi'n Emperor Qin Shi Huang, who unified the country, abolished the feudal system, built a network of highways (including the Great Wall), made everyone write with ideograms, massacred intellectuals who disagreed with him, and when he died, arranged to have 700,000 workers spend thirty-six years running ovens at 1800 degrees Fahrenheit so that his Imperial corpse would be guarded by eight thousand life-sized clay soldiers and horses . . . the terra-cotta warriors.

This is truly one of the great wonders of the world, something you must run over and see before you die. You walk into what looks like a football field, covered by a seven-thousand-square-yard pine timber roof. Instead of a gridiron, though, there is a naked dirt plain, with rows upon rows of excavated warriors rising up out of red-clay trenches. While most military statues look cartoony, like uniformed Supermen, the terra-cotta warriors are so human and so lifelike that they look like earthen-gray ghosts, an *X-Files* effect, all in perfect formation and ready at any minute to march out of their football field and trample over you. Each face is unique, and originally they were all painted and carrying pikes, bows, arrows and spears, and must've been an even more frightening sight, but the weapons were all stolen fifteen hundred years ago. Eight employees have spent the last twenty-three years mending soldiers with a glue made from shark's lung by matching up separate, broken parts from the site's huge inventory. We weren't allowed to take pictures, and The Emperor pouted so much at this she barely took in the massive, frightening spectacle.

That night, Chen said, 'We have a very special surprise for you,' which immediately made everyone suspicious. The treat turned out to be an 'American' meal of imported canned spaghetti, and Brenda, Melissa and I wordlessly looked at each other, ate almost none of it, and ran out to the street stalls to have magnificent sizzling dumplings in broth, sitting at picnic tables with all the other Xi'anians, watched by donkeys who stood around with their tongues hanging out. We went for a stroll ourselves and saw, on a street corner, a group lazily playing eight-ball on a billiard table, surrounded by onlookers squatting from years of bathroom practice. Our appearance brought a halt to the game and they came over, surrounding us, moving in closer and closer. One was an albino with pink eyes, while another had hair curled into a Wayne Newton bouffant and was teetering on high-heeled sandals. They moved in too close, like a gang of muggers, but we couldn't decide if we should be nervous or not, since the Chinese, obviously, have a different sense of crowding than we do. They kept saying, over and over, 'Come to our shops!' We told them we already owned one of everything made in China, and asked what they thought about Tiananmen.

'They are spoiled!' the man in high heels said. 'We did not have an opportunity for the college. They have nothing for complaints!'

Everyone else fully agreed with him that the students deserved to get what they got. Then another said, quietly, 'We did not know nobody would come now. When will the tourists come back?'

We told them we thought it'd be a few months, but that wasn't the right thing to say; the town was really hurting financially. Even though these Xi'anians were creepy, we felt sorry for them and so went to their stores, which turned out to be filled with pelts. When I asked about a big black-and-white one that looked suspicious, the albino, in a scolding voice, said that it was already taken, and insisted I should consider a hairy yak skin that'd surely be a snap to get through U.S. customs.

Even though eco-people have thrown their full weight behind saving this ultimate living teddy bear, the Chinese population of giant panda is still declining (in the wild, there's about a thousand left), and trying to get captives to breed is about as unsuccessful a human endeavor as has ever been attempted. Every zoo in the world tries, but only around seven litters of *daxiongmao* (big bear-cat) are born every year. It's hard keeping pandas in zoos, since their jaws are strong enough to chew metal, one of the few activities they seem to actively enjoy. As of 1995, you could still buy panda pelts for $20,000 in Hong Kong, Taiwan, Japan . . . and, obviously, Xi'an. I guess there's nothing that sets off a black-and-white bedroom set like a well-leathered panda pelt.

The one thing that's really hard to do in China is feel lonely. We'd be traveling out in the countryside, as far from anywhere else as it was possible to get, but still, every time we looked out the window at the landscape going by, there'd always be Chinese eyes looking back at us. The bus would pull over in the middle of nowhere, and we'd run out to pee, and just as soon as everyone had separated into territories and gotten down to business, we'd all notice the various sets of faces watching.

That morning on the road to Shanghai, Chen announced that the flight back to the U.S. had been overbooked and to make up for it, the government was putting us all up for an additional five days in China *for free!* Since they'd already reduced the original cost by two thirds, this would mean that we'd spent three weeks in China and only paid for the air ticket. Baby Jane wasn't satisfied and started negotiating, trying to rabble-rouse with: 'They should let us stay two weeks more for FREE and then fly us all back to New York FOR FREE!' The overbooking news was really suspicious, since as far as we could tell, we were the only Americans there. Who were all these people suddenly flying to the U.S.? Maybe the Chinese wanted their first tourists to go home raving about the place (we sure did), and maybe they wanted us staying and spending money for as long as possible. Our very last tour stop, after all, was a shopping mall, which the driver announced with, 'Now you can leave all your dollars behind in China!'

THE WHORE OF THE ORIENT

By the time we reached Shanghai, everyone in the group had mild head colds, sniffles and aches, and everyone had a different theory as to why. When you see China in person, you have to give the Commies some credit. There are plenty of poor peasants eking out a living just like everyone else in the rural Third World, but even going far afield, we never saw starving people in rags, which is how plenty used to get by, and even the poorest people obviously had clothes, roofs over their heads and food: the basics.

There is, however, one serious flaw in this workers' paradise (a flaw found all over the Eastern European workers' paradises as well), which was one of our head-cold theories: massive pollution. There's a little town in western China, Badui, just down the Yellow River from the Liujiaxia Fertilizer Factory. One third of all Baduians are either terminally ill or mentally retarded, women are constantly miscarrying or having stillbirths, and many of the goats are turning blind and insane. Everywhere you travel in the Middle Kingdom, you see beautifully fired, geometric charcoal briquettes – responsible for the air quality that kills over one fourth of all Chinese with lung disease, helped by the massive smoking going on. Today, more Chinese land is used to grow tobacco than tea. Between the coal and the diesel needs of its thirteen million people, each square mile of Shanghai is covered by seventy tons of soot every month.

Shanghai is so much like New York City that it was once nicknamed the 'Big Lychee,' and it was once so decadent it was called 'The Whore of the Orient'; so Marlene Dietrich really meant something when she said, 'It took more than one man to change my name to Shanghai Lily.' The most famous gangster of that long-gone era was Big-Eared Du, and since our local guide was also named Du, a man very interested in the various things that one could do with tourists and their money, I was sure they must be related.

The CCP has enacted such a complicated system of currency, salary and profit decrees that every Chinese there is running some kind of scheme to get around the law (the country is now number ten on the 'most corrupt' list kept by *Forbes* magazine). Guide Du had his own scheme going, based on the fact that China has two forms of currency, one for locals (*reminbi*, or RMB) and one for foreigners (foreign exchange certificates, or FECs). There is also a two-level system of prices for locals versus foreigners running through everything the government can get its hands on (and that is everything), so a hotel room for a Chinese would be $14 RMB, and for a foreigner, $53 FEC. Du was using this law to act as a fiscal intermediary for the tourists, converting our FECs to his RMBs and then paying a local price. It wasn't illegal and it wasn't even underhanded, but when Baby Jane finally figured out what was going on, we thought she was going to kill herself . . . especially when she realized that Mr. Elbows, Uncle Wang and Grandma Ling had all been paying dramatically reduced prices over the rest of us for the entire trip.

Shanghai has run out of indoors, so its streets are mobbed with shopping stalls, alfresco kitchens, people playing cards and pool, tea parties, stoop-sitters and aggressive pedestrians. There's lots of shoving and pushing, so Mr. Elbows and The Emperor felt right at home, throwing their weight around as we wandered through neighborhoods of paint-peeled Tudor mansions built by the Opium War-winning Brits (now with five Chinese families living on each floor). The port is chock-full of thousands of freighters, houseboats, sampans and dhows seeming to drift about at random. While Beijingers are pale and willowy, Shanghaians are dark and meaty, and it's here that the caffeine deprivation I'd been suffering through the whole trip kicked in, with blinding headaches and sluggish response. Remember: If you're an addict traveling through foreign climes, don't forget your drugs.

I was keen to see the city's only pet store, and learn how a country that just recently was eating poodles would now sell them in a shop named *These Are Your Faithful Friends*. I'd even looked through the introduction to the book *Pets*, by beloved Chinese author Ding Dong, which explained why people have pets. We didn't have time for *Faithful Friends*, but we did catch the little old men coming to Yu Park at the crack of dawn to hang the cages of their birds high in the trees. There, they chatter and drink tea and play *Go* while listening to the birds singing, singing, singing.

The Shanghai say, *We eat everything on four legs, except tables and chairs*. I've heard you can still walk into certain restaurants and look into a terrarium while the busboy lifts up the top and shakes a stick to incite the cobras to strike and writhe in fury. You pick whichever appears the most energetic and, just in time for the first course, its cobra blood and gallbladder are served in Baccarat snifters. That night, after a dinner of inside-out squid, Chen told us the story of an American tourist with stomach pains who went to a Chinese doctor. The doctor asked, 'Have you eaten anything *strange?*' Du insisted, 'If your Adam and Eve had been Chinese, they would have eaten the snake,' and then told us the latest joke making the English student rounds: 'Do you know what the American flower is? The car nation!' He was stroking my hairy forearm when he admitted, 'Maybe I'll become a Christian. I heard the story, and found it very moving.'

The languages and dialects of different parts of China are so distinct from each other (with Northerners saying Beijing and Southerners saying Peking, for example, though the word is spelled the same), that all movies, performances and TV shows are subtitled. Perhaps this is the reason why Chinese are so fascinated with languages. Vast numbers want to learn English *right now*, which can lead to such moments as when a woman came up to us at the end of a meal, pointed at our drinks, and chanted, 'Cooked? Coke? Cake? Cooked? Coke? Cake?' When trying to leave one hotel, I showed my key to the desk clerk and asked, 'Do I check out with you?' While the clerk mantra-chanted, 'Checkout? Checkout? Checkout?' two other people sitting in the lobby parroted, 'With you? With you? With you?'

The show that night at the Chinese Acrobatic Theater was once world-famous, a wild mix of acts crossing *The Dean Martin Show* with an offbeat circus. The stage was set with Christmas twinkle lights and backfloods dramatically exposing a series of fountains and waterfalls that, in 1960s Las Vegas, were called 'Dancing Waters.' First up was a woman balancing a dinner service for twelve on a chopstick in her mouth, followed by a very old man playing a whining musical instrument which turned out to be a giant rubber band on a stick, followed by extremely clean-cut brothers – 'Pretzel Boys' – performing body contortions with each other that look like something from an outer space alien sex manual. The human worm with no arms or legs demonstrated getting dressed and smoking a cigarette; a panda rode a bicycle, twirled an umbrella, and sat at a dinner table to eat dumplings with a fork; a shih tzu jumped through burning hoops, and a house cat performed on the parallel bars. Two girls in bathing suits cracked whips at each other, while a third jumped in and out of a lasso. The grand finale turned out to be two dozen beautiful women outfitted in Imperial brocade twirling around the stage, wheeling, smiling, waving, not doing, really, all that much of anything, a little more waving, and suddenly they were gone. That's when we realized they were all men.

We started a round of Shanghaian club-hopping with a Malagasy band (looking half Chinese and half Jamaican) playing the reggae remix of 'I Shot the Sheriff' at the Seven Star, then hopped over to Cosmos, where a southern Han all-girl combo dished out 'Satisfaction' and 'Red Red Wine,' repeating the choruses over and over until I thought someone would scream, 'Enough with the wine!' Beneath the spinning disco ball, parents danced ring-rosey with toddlers in the local variant of lederhosen.

Everywhere I looked in Shanghai, there were couples completely enraptured by their sole child, spoiling him and dressing him up and carrying him around, and I'm saying 'him' since that child is always a boy. There are two theories why: that the sex of the child is determined prenatally and all girl fetuses then aborted (a free operation in China) or, within days of being born, girls are tied up in sacks and drowned in the rivers like unwanted kittens.

Having a son is for many Chinese the only form of pension they can get, and when one Party boss in a South China village forced a woman who already had a daughter to have an abortion in her seventh month of pregnancy, it was discovered that the fetuses were twin sons. Her husband responded by going to the Party boss's own house and throwing the boss's two sons down a well and diving in after them, a murder-suicide. When other enraged farmers began regularly attacking their village Party leaders over the one-child policy, the federal government basically stopped enforcing the regulation, which one Chinese demographer called 'more slogan than reality' in the first place. In Shanghai, however, it was very much in evidence, a city filled with unbelievably spoiled brat boys.

We visited the Children's Palace, part of a showplace commune, walking in to find a wall of preschoolers screaming with delight. The teacher calmed them down long enough to be able to sing a full round of 'Darling Clementine,' their English lesson, and I got our ragtag bunch to sing it back, which made them scream and scream again. One very shy little girl came around with a green ceramic tub and, in the manner of Holy Communion, solemnly offered each of us a look; inside was her pet turtle. Out the window, more kids were chasing a flock of very white geese across a very green lawn.

We'd later hear that the CCP had decided to terminate all the communes and revert everything back to individual peasant holdings; within months, the Children's Palace would be abandoned. The Chinese have also decided to build themselves another Hong Kong here, and so Shanghai's old neighborhoods, just like Beijing's, have been demolished, some with a week's notice. They've left a few red-tile roofs standing where the tourists like to go, while across the waters is rising a whole new district, Pudong, with sci-fi Malaysian Lego glass towers. Even the Acrobatic Theater has been torn down, and to get to the beautiful, ancient resort town of Souzhou, everyone now takes the freeway.

We took the train. It was a classic, old-fashioned steamer, the kind everyone dreams about: Victorian service, cloth club chairs, sisal-covered ceiling fans, potted plants, thermos tea service, tablecloths, gooseneck lamps and twin quilts. The landscape flew by: irrigation canals with arched moon bridges, enormous horses and tiny huts made of sod; endless rice paddies filled with farmers of every age and both sexes bent over and slogging through the mud; women using poles to hang two stories of laundry. In the rivers, fishermen teetering on stilts threw their nets, and later, at dusk, men in punts with skeins of birds huddling by a lantern in the bow rowed across flat, icy lakes.

These were the cormorant men, who have raised, by hand, a flock of birds who live in their homes and are worth around four hundred bucks apiece. The cormorants have a string or metal collar around their necks, and go out with the men at dawn and dusk; afraid of the dark, they stay close to the lamps. The birds dive overboard, catch fish, but can't swallow because of the collars, and come back to the surface when their necks are full and spit up the booty. After they've coughed up enough for him, the fisherman takes off the collars and the birds feed for themselves. Especially in a nation that needs a book to explain why people have pets, the relationship between these men and their birds is immensely touching. You see them nuzzling each other, the animals flocking around their guy just like baby geese waddling after mamas.

Brenda and I left first-class to check out the action on the rest of the train, and found a lot of tension. Two cars over was a mob of sullen and hostile college kids, sitting with vigilant, armed People's Liberation Army soldiers. Every time one of the military turned his back, all the kids shook their fists.

Plenty of times while traveling in the Third World, there's a feeling that comes over me – a Bob Hope/Joey Heatherton kind of feeling – the feeling that I should be entertaining the troops. I guess the explanation for this eccentricity is that I'm having the time of my life, and the only thing the locals are getting in exchange is money, and I feel they deserve more, much more. The only more that I have to give, unfortunately, is the all-American and utterly inalienable right to put on a show, all in the best Judy Garland/Mickey Rooney tradition.

In Chinese, thank you is *tse-tse*, which in Mandarin is pronounced *shay-shay*, and I knew this was just the perfect moment to introduce the entire car to a song-and-dance number based on Aretha Franklin's 'Chain of Fools,' which you may recall begins with: 'Shay-Shay Shaaaaaay! Shay-Shay Shaaaaaay!' At first of course they thought we were nuts, but soon enough, Brenda and I got all the kids singing, and the soldiers exited for a change of cars.

THE BUSINESS OF WORMS

'I am sure all of you are wondering right now, How is the excrement managed?' the guide asked in the same officious Madame Mao tone she'd use for the entire journey through Souzhou. She was leading us through a cracked hothouse filled with hundreds of thousands of silkworms slowly crawling and chewing their way through piles of mulberry leaves. We'd long ago lost interest in the worms' sanitary habits; what we were really wondering was, Why did their boiling pupa smell just like three-day-old fish? 'You know, they should take us to a car plant,' whispered Mr. Elbows. 'That's the trouble with these tours . . . they never take you to the really heavy manufacturing places.'

Souzhou is both the Venice and the Hamptons of China, a little country town just off the thousand-mile-long Grand Canal, lined with waterways and surrounded by rice fields, with local boats, the *wapeng*, that look just like handmade gondolas. While we Anglos floated by on a sumptuous yacht, eating luxurious meals and attended to by liveried men in white suits, we looked at our canal neighbors, crammed with potted plants, hanging laundry, cupboards filled with dishes and a half-dozen bicycles, and they looked back at us.

For thousands of years, Souzhou has been the preferred spot for the Shanghai crème de la crème to build vacation homes – weekend retreats of lush, hourly manicured gardens, tiny parks dotted with ponds covered over in patinae of green scum . . . marked with zigzag walkways and bridges . . . shadowed by alcoves of twin bamboo stalks . . . gardens that contain all of nature in a nutshell. The most famous retreat, the Garden of the Master of Fishing Nets, has been poorly re-created with the money of Brooke Astor at New York's Metropolitan Museum, but the locals were very proud of this anyway; they said that their garden now had a *New York cousin*. You should hurry up and see the original, since, if the Chinese notice it attracting enough tourists, maybe they won't tear it down.

A silk factory is part greenhouse (for the propagation of a single plant, the mulberry), part chemical processor (to extract the skin from the pupa), and part worm farm. The final building houses the thread machinery itself, which looks like something out of a Dickens Industrial Age horror tinged with a hint of sci-fi. While trays of bobbing cocoons lead to a giant series of spindles ratcheting into bobbins, all kept threaded by busy young girls, you can easily imagine Charlton Heston screaming, 'Soylent Green is PEOPLE!' One measly shirt requires over a thousand of these cocoons.

The Friendship Tour of this factory ends with a fashion show featuring annoyed, surly Chinese models photographed by lusting Japanese, followed by the remarkable opportunity to shop for silk fabrics, dresses, blouses, shirts, coats and underpants . . . or ten thousand needlepoint sets of white fluffy kittens. There was an immense bin filled with men's boxers and I took a pair over to the main cashier, got his attention and, assuming he spoke minimal English, showed him the package, made a circle around my waist, and shrugged. 'I'm sorry, sir,' he said in a perfect Jeeves English accent, 'but we only have them in *smalls*.'

When we were there, Souzhou was the most famous silk producer in all of China. Today, it is the world's leading manufacturer of computer mice.

Outside, on the lawn, the Mormons played catch.

SOUTH AMERICA

INTO THE AMAZON WITH P.J. O'ROURKE AND A HEADHUNTING SHAMAN (RETIRED)

There are women who freeze in the headlights of a boutique window layered in shoes, and there are men who can spend days looking at meaty shelves of hardware or high tech. Everyone has their hungers that must be filled, and it's travel brochures (such as *National Geographic*) that start me salivatin' like a Pavlov's dog. One day I got a promotional leaflet in the mail for a Peruvian jaunt that combined the heart of the Amazon with the peaks of the Andes, a panorama of thatch-roofed boats, tree-hanging monkeys, spitting llamas and Machu Picchu, that mountaintop Inca city, wreathed in the foggy light of dawn. Hubba-hubba! Brenda and I booked immediately and took off six weeks later.

Why is it that every time you travel south of Mexico, an adventure in chaos begins the minute you hit Miami International? While every other part of the terminal is perfectly clean and open, you arrive at the Central and South American carriers' section to find a maze of circular alleyways that dead-end and lead to nowhere. You struggle onward, desperate to find your ticket booth, lost in a mind-boggling welter of looming banana republics: the friendly skies of Air Poco Loco . . . the welcoming seats of Noriega Express. Our plane to Peru turned out to be on Fawcett Air, and we were all strapped in and high in the clouds when we picked up our guidebooks to learn that Percy Fawcett, the airline's name-sake, was a British colonel who, during the rubber boom of the early 1900s, spent over twenty years searching for ancient pre-Inca jungle cities. Percy's travels ended when he disappeared, never to be heard from again. Instead of a movie, Fawcett the airline had everyone playing bingo for a $100 pot, which was loads of fun until you realized that there you were . . . up in the clouds . . . on a plane named for a traveler who went away and never came back . . . and you're playing a game of chance . . .

Many of my friends say they could never take the trips I do because of having to spend so many hours on a plane. I don't know what they're talking about. In the air, you can eat, drink, sleep, talk on the phone, work on the computer, read books or magazines, have sex in the bathroom, and watch movies and TV. As far as I can see, it's just like being at home.

We arrived in Iquitos baggage claim to find, even at night, that it was hot as hell, and that the Fawcett employees were violently heaving luggage off the broken carousel and onto the cement floor in a Samsonite challenge. Plenty of Iquiteños had arrived with the universal Third World travel accessory – a thin, red-white-and-blue plastic zippered box big enough to hold a teenager – and all of these, heaved onto the concrete, were splitting open and spewing laundry everywhere.

While waiting for our own bags to arrive and explode, I studied the vast Iquitos Airport mural, which features emaciated Amazon Indians prancing about with alligators next to an Inca ruin. Brenda and I introduced ourselves to the other Amazon travelers, a Coloradan air traffic controller couple named Tim and Barbara, and a single gentleman named Patrick O'Rourke, who I understood to be the cousin of noted writer and political commentator P.J. O'Rourke. On meeting him, I suavely mentioned how much he looked just like P.J., but in fact had a much better haircut, and seconds later it became clear that this was P.J. himself in the flesh. It was doubly alarming, not just because I'd put my whole leg in my mouth, but also because I assumed we'd now be spending our Amazon nights discussing global monetary policy, and the question of who do you think is the most important human being who ever lived: Margaret Thatcher or Ronald Reagan?

We were all herded into a big yellow wooden school bus like the kind a down-at-the-heels Partridge Family might own, and there we met Juan Tejada, our constant companion for the next two weeks. Juan had been trained to lead earnest, authentic *norteamericanos* on sincere eco-tours, and we'd run into his more typical clientele in the Miami airport: ten adamantly women-only women, decked out in drawstring cotton pants and faded all-cotton Ts, bralessly trudging along with huge quantities of eco-friendly luggage . . . Amazons on their way to the Amazon. We saw them again on the way home, now stuffed with souvenirs – a butterfly mounted in a box, a vest made from some animal pelt, a walking stick with a suspicious bit of fur dangling from the tip.

Trained for customers like these, Juan would preach to the converted like any disciple of Sting's *Rain Forest Crunch* crusades, and he launched into a vast eco-tirade the minute we got on the bus:

Stretching the same distance as from New York City to Rome, the Amazon River is the world's second largest after the Nile, carrying twelve times as much water as the Mississippi along with five billion tons of sediment. Its basin, more commonly called Amazonas, is almost the size of the continental United States, and is home to over eight thousand species of insects, over one thousand species of birds, and over 25,000 species of plants, all living in delicate harmony. Perhaps cures for cancer and AIDS and every other human ailment will one day be found here. We are traveling through the city of Iquitos, which was primarily built in the early 1900s during the rubber boom and which soon after suffered financial collapse when it was discovered that the rubber trees could be smuggled out of the country and grown on farms by benevolent Sumatrans instead of being hacked out of the Amazon jungle surrounded by electric catfish and angry cannibals.

Juan didn't really say this last part, but my mind couldn't help but wander as Iquitos went rollicking by in the darkness, a city of friendly bars and open-air snack stands and meandering horses and mobs of *tuk-tuks* (motor scooters pulling a trailer with a canopied bench inside). It all looked like a hell of a lot of fun instead of being the lyrical center of the delicate balance of nature that is the fragile ecosystem of the Amazon . . . and it turned out that all the others on board were thinking the exact same thing . . . except Brenda, who was wondering whether or not this trip would fulfill her personal dream of seeing a three-toed sloth.

THEY DESERVED TO GET CHOLERA

Iquitos is once-grand but now down-at-the-heels, a city made and unmade by rubber. During the boom, the locals were so wealthy they sent their laundry to be washed in Paris. It is, in fact, a lot like New Orleans, with a light, airy French colonial architecture of metal filigree balconies and alabaster froufrou . . . but it's painted in Spanish, with baby-doll-pink doors and toxic-blue walls, and streets entirely taken over by *tuk-tuks*, which sound like a herd of toy lawn-mowers drag-racing twenty-four hours a day. 'In this town,' one Amazonian remarked, 'everything is against the law and everything is permitted. If a policeman asks you for a license or a paper, ask him for his authority to ask. He hasn't any.'

We wandered around aimlessly, looking in the windows of a cement grocery-bar to see every wall decorated with a Warhol *Marilyn*, while next door a taxidermy outlet was selling necklaces of toucan bills, baby caiman alligators posed as policemen, and sloths dressed up as North American Indians (no, I don't know why). Ari's Burger, painted in screaming red, black, pink and orange horizontal stripes, was the only really happening place on the main drag by that time of night, so that's where we ended up to get more acquainted and scarf beers. I kept waiting for P.J. to want to talk about all the good things that Nicolae Ceauşescu did for Romania, but instead he turned out to be a pretty great guy, and the five of us hit it off immediately.

The next morning Brenda and I had breakfast surrounded by a coterie of oil company executives in search of a jungle gusher, and then went wandering ourselves in search of the mighty Amazon, which we hadn't found the night before. It turned out to be a block away, in the opposite direction. I was expecting something that looked menacing, sinister, jungly, but in fact the river is broad, flat, with barely a hint of current; it's peaceful, suburban. The shore is lined with little cedar tubs, *peque-peques*, the boat version of *tuk-tuks*, and you see families out on errands together, paddling as a team. There are homes set in small clearings, a few wood buildings with tin roofs, but most with thatch and looking Polynesian. One island was a pasture of gallivanting horses, alert water buffalo and lurking egrets. A long wooden boat then went by, its windows filled with the black-and-red-feathered butts of roosting chickens. Just past Iquitos are jungle towns called Indiana, Los Angeles, Texas, Cheyenne, San Francisco and Travolta – as in John – while this entire neighborhood is referred to by Peruvians as the 'Wild East.' I couldn't help but notice the flocks of vultures constantly swooping above the horizon.

We had a waterside lunch of the local specialty (hearts of palm) in the Iguana Tree Restaurant, dining right next to hanging branches packed with immense, slovenly, spiky-green iguanas. The restaurant keeps tossing them leftover fruit, but you could tell that if any more iguanas tried climbing on, the whole tree would fall over into your lap. The restaurant also features a parrot and monkey zoo, and while we were drinking coffee, a very Inca-looking woman with a baby squirrel monkey curled up and asleep on her shoulder came by to sell us kitschy blowpipes. We were only interested in the monkey, but when she tried to move it to her other shoulder, it screeched bloody murder, like a crazed infant, and wouldn't be budged.

Besides the *tuk-tuks* and New Orleans atmosphere, probably the most distinctive part of Iquitos is the odd neighborhood of Belén, an entire city floating in the river on balsa planks. Belén looks a lot like Venice (if Venice were a Spanish jungle slum), with houses built from two-by-fours and thatch roofs bobbing up and down in stagnant, clay-colored water, many having their children's home roped in tandem with an open-air thatch platform for cooking, drying laundry and sitting around. There are floating stalls of cows and chickens, floating bars, bobbing grocery stores and discos, boats filled with dried fish and produce making their way through the alleys, followed by dugouts, pirogues, barques, rowboats and canoes. Every night, half-naked prostitutes with bow lanterns cruise the byways, canoe taxis driven by five-year-olds search for fares, and younger children play on the porch with parrots and woolly monkeys. There are no property taxes, but you can't run away from home if you live in Belén; you can only *row* away. All it takes is one big storm and the entire town will float down the river, off to Brazil.

Juan and the rest of the gang picked us up in our Partridge bus and we went to see the open-air market, which sells everything you can imagine and more! There's every kind of fruit and flower in the world, monkeys, coatimundis (a South American raccoon), pirarucus (a river salmon that can reach ten feet in length), peccaries (a cross between a pig and a deer), and one stall selling nothing but various kinds of medicinal bark, all of which, Juan claimed, were good for diarrhea. We didn't see any sign, however, of Iquitos's current big business: tropical fish. I guess the locals aren't big on aquariums.

When you were a child, did your parents have a barbecue pit made from a big oilcan sawed in half? Mine sure did, and it is exactly in such a container that ceviche, raw fish salad, gray as death, is prepared and served on the streets of Peru, including in this violently hot and humid jungle town. In prepping for this trip, I had checked in with the paranoid and suspicious U.S. State

Department and Centers for Disease Control on what horrors would await the well coddled in South America, and one of the truly scary announcements, repeated endlessly on both their phone system and their Web site, was about a Peruvian epidemic of cholera. We got to Iquitos, and found out that all this came from a group of tourists who'd eaten street-marinated ceviche out of those rusty oilcans. We could only think: Anyone that stupid *deserves* to get cholera.

If you've never used the Federal Centers for Disease Control Voice and Fax Information System (404–332–4555 as of right now), it's a must-hear, even if you never go anywhere. My favorite part is when a very chirpy, all-American voice rings out: 'Press One for AIDS! Press Two for Malaria! Press Three for Sleeping Sickness! Press Four for Cholera! Press Five for Meningococcal Infections! Press Six for Yellow Fever!'

THE DOUCHE OF DEATH

To get to our jungle camp that afternoon, we five Anglos were loaded onto a big, wooden, thatch-roofed partyboat that launched out on the main highway, the flat green Amazon, which branches into smaller rivers like side streets, and then into streams like alleyways. The boat had a stern toilet, a closet with a wooden plank and a hole in its middle, perched directly over the Evinrudes. It is quite frightening if you're well endowed; P.J. called it 'the douche of death.' Then the boat started pulling deeper and deeper away from civilization and into the jungle, the trees moving in closer and closer, the rivers narrowing into thin, barely passable trickles.

Beneath us swam *pira ranha*, Tupi for 'fish tooth,' the most vicious of them all being the red- or yellow-bellied meat-eating *nattereri* found throughout the continent with 'teeth so sharp and jaws so strong that it can chop out a piece of flesh from a man or an alligator as neatly as a razor, or clip off a finger or toe, bone and all, with the dispatch of a meat cleaver,' as ichthyologist George Myers so delicately put it. Their highest concentration is

53

found in Brazil's Rio das Mortes – the *River of Death* – cleaning out every piece of meat that hits the water, like aquatic vultures. When piranha in a school sense one of their mates is in trouble, they start taking out chunks of him in a cannibalistic feeding frenzy. The Amazonians, however, are far more afraid of the big-scarred, slow-healing, extremely painful lance of the stingray than they are of piranha bites, and in fact Indian fishermen wading through the waters will shuffle instead of step in order to scare off any lurking rays. Ray poison is so strong and so painful that its sting will even make the Jivaro headhunters cry like babies. Learning this made me feel good, since my wallet was made out of stingray.

Before going to the Amazon, you hear the words 'rain forest' and think: lush, tropical, bounty of nature. But in fact no one, not even the most remote and shyest of the Indians, lives all that deep into the rain forest itself; it is too impenetrable, and any attempts at making a clearing and a home are doomed. Everyone instead lives right on the water in a house on stilts with a boat to get around in, and they call themselves *rivereños*, 'river people.' There are no jungle people, since the jungle trees are covered with vines and epiphytes and mosses and every kind of floral parasite, while the ground is a ceaseless bog, with vast stretches underwater much of the year. There are electric eels, toothy caimans, cranky fer-de-lance, camouflaged stingrays, menacing anacondas, masses of piranha, prowling jaguar and hissing, twelve-foot bushmasters, whose poison is so strong that a good, deep bite can render antivenin worthless. This is nature at its most exuberant and explosive, all of it feeding on each other, and whether you're in Amazonas or Congo or Borneo or New Guinea, the equatorial rain forest has one thing it whispers in the ear of every human who dares draw nigh, and that is: 'GET OUT.'

The Brazilians tried shipping would-be farmers out of the crowded city slums and into this vast emptiness, and it was an all-out catastrophe. With soil too thin even for cattle grazing, constant epidemics of plant disease, hosts of tenacious weeds, attacks by browsing wild animals, and no economical way to bring produce to market, this is not exactly a spot for traditional ranchers and farmers to make a living – the Indians who've lived here for eons barely scrape by. The twentieth century may have conquered everything from Everest to the moon to the deep seas, but vast portions of the Amazon wilderness remain untouched.

We arrived at dusk to find our home in the middle of nowhere, a camp of elevated walkways and thatch-covered dormitories lit by warmly romantic hurricane lamps, with a lodge-cum-dining room that was high-roofed and breezy. There, up in the beams, two pairs of macaws – one scarlet, one gold – and a toucan hopped around, eyeing us. Huge bunches of small, overripe bananas hung down from the eaves, and the toucan ripped one up and began to gobble. Tiring of that, he hopped down to the backs of our rattan chairs, and his big black beak made us more than a little nervous. Then, before we knew what was happening, he leaped onto the table and went from glass, to glass, sticking his banana-smudged mouth deep into our drinks. As we watched bits of unidentifiable toucan leftovers float in our glasses, Juan explained that plenty of times guests would turn their backs, and the toucans would drink down their rum and then run around, plotzed.

Amazonistas love their birds, and the kitchen featured an orphan baby toucan that hissed like a snake when strangers approached. Its featherless head made it look just like a very ugly dinosaur. On the roof lurked a pair of jadegreen Amazon parrots, hopping back and forth in their seriously clownish walk, climbing the walls to peer at us through the windows while singing scales and pieces of opera and screaming out their names ('LORRA! LORRA!') and then laughing like asylum inmates. Brenda opened her door to let two macaws walk around and check out her room, which they did, looking for things to chew, and immediately swallowing her camera button. She had to take all her pictures on the rest of the trip using a safety pin.

That night and every night in the jungle, we slept under canopy shrouds of mosquito netting, and I had a nightmare about the Museum of Natural History, a nightmare that I was inside a vitrine, while a ravenous host of bugs of every shape, color and size swarmed over the cage's glass walls, trying to get in. This nightmare turned out, in fact, to be real: I woke up needing to pee, and turned on my flashlight to find a madding host of insects crawling across the outsides of my mosquito netting . . . emerald shiny beetles and hairy spiders, fat roachy beetles and tiny biting flies, thin flying beetles and colonies of doodlebugs, giant red-legged centipedes and big black hornets, and of course, hungry tiger mosquitoes. Like every night, it was pouring rain outside, so I carefully lifted up my netting, making sure none of these vermin could get in my bed, got a poncho and a flashlight, and started walking to the latrines. With each step, creatures nestling by the path scurried away noisily, and I jumped right out of my goddamn skin.

It's eco-embarrassing to admit this but, from then on, at night in the torrential rains, I peed out the window.

Traffic noise in New York City is nothing compared to the peeping bugs, screeching birds and high-pitched whistling frogs of the rain forest. If you're a light sleeper, you'll need to bring earplugs. Dawn comes with the agitated squawking of lovebirds, and I woke up at first light because some damn animal was screaming right outside the window. After everyone else got up and ate, we went on our first jungle hike. Within minutes, I stepped smack dab into a mud bog, sinking two feet. I washed those boots and left them out to dry for a week, but in all that humidity, they never did. Every single day it would rain, a giant warm mist, while every night there'd be pounding thunderstorms. They don't call it the rain forest for nothing.

We hiked by plenty of silk-cotton ceiba trees, with thorny trunks hard as stone and branches covered in epiphytes, especially the flowering bromeliads, beautiful, primitive and parasitic. Living inside these blooms were lady tree frogs who attracted their mates by giggling like psychopathic villains. There were tribes of leaf-cutter ants, hoisting their greenery along a trail, butterflies with owl eyes on their wings, white-faced tamarin monkeys, dripping birds of paradise, giant ferns, sweat bees, a black branch covered in giant white fungus, and a grasshopper as big as a man's hand. There was one tree so completely covered in houseplants that you couldn't even see the bark – it was a nursery of big, drooping cycads, snakeplants, philodendrons and Boston ferns. Always, just out of reach, is the sound of the birds, cooing and yakking and screaming, along with the croak of cicadas and the harsh whistles of the frogs. But these sounds aren't with you, like in other forests; they are muffled and distant, almost as if you're merely remembering them.

Keeping your eyes peeled for wildlife, like hunting, makes you hyperaware of your surroundings . . . even so, I never found a thing. Tim and Barbara, however, discovered a walking stick, a great big one with a missing leg, and Brenda instantly knew the cause: 'Poachers!'

On our walks, Juan continued to explain how this bark, or that root, or this leaf, was good for diarrhea, and he'd also point out the many, many things you could eat in the jungle if you were *really* hungry. He'd show us a snake and say, 'Some people eat this snake,' and we would say, 'What does it taste like, Juan?' and he'd say, 'It tastes something like chicken.' He'd point out a lizard and say, 'Some people eat this lizard,' and we'd say, 'What does it taste like, Juan?' and he'd say, 'It tastes something like chicken.' He'd point out an iguana and say, 'Some people eat this iguana,' and we'd say, 'What does it taste like, Juan?' and he'd say, 'It tastes something like chicken.' Finally P.J. had had enough: 'If all these things taste like chicken,' he demanded to know, 'then why don't they just *eat* a chicken?'

Juan turned especially energetic when he found a tarantula burrow, poking every entry with a stick, trying to get the spiders to show themselves. No matter how much we protested that we didn't care to watch a family of angry tarantulas running amok, he kept at it, but failed to rouse a single one of the monsters. We came home, Juan dejected, only to find a horde of big, hairy tarantulas climbing the barroom screens.

ONE BIG SNOOTY RODENT

The minute we got back, one of the camp kids came over and started pulling on Brenda's hand; he spoke a version of Spanish I couldn't make out, so we followed him, not knowing what would happen. He led us over to an open section of the walkway where a telescope had been set up; he pointed excitedly, and Brenda put her eye to the viewer to find the one thing she'd been looking for all day: a three-toed sloth. I went back to get beer for me and tea for her and the rest of the gang, and we looked through the scope for hours, watching the sloth not moving. Then Juan arrived and let out a piercing whistle (hawks and eagles being the sloth's enemies), and the creature turned an ovoid face to peer down at us with its placid Chinese eyes. I'd never realized before how there's no distinction between where a sloth's neck ends and its head begins; there's no chin, no nape, just a long, hairy tube with a face on the end of it, like a warm-blooded worm.

We wanted our sloth to do even more, and so started making every kind of whistle and grunt a human being can create, like rude teens in a pet store pounding on the terrariums. Very, very slowly, the sloth started moving, while Juan explained that it had six-inch-long fingernails for digging out grubs, that its pelt was a 'bug carpet' of beetles, ticks, fleas and moths, and that it comes down from the trees once a week to take a shit. P.J. assumed this was because it'd been eating all those things that were so good for diarrhea, while Brenda imagined a sloth circus, entertainment for the overstimulated, where every trick took hours to perform.

The kitchen turned out to be the place to hang out and catch all the action. Even though the camp had no electricity, it did have a big Frigidaire, and the cook would dutifully bring in baskets of produce (especially masses of papaya) and carefully place them inside. Like all Amazonites, the staff believed that papaya is a magical fruit that can cure most human ailments and ensure good health, and they think you should eat a lot of it.

Besides the baby toucan dinosaur, the kitchen was also home to a pet mouse opossum, tiny and long-nosed, with pink ears and huge round black eyes, and an acid-blue-and-yellow poison-spitting tree frog carrying tadpoles on his back. Juan finally realized that the four of us weren't here to *ooh* and *ahh* over this frog's caring-and-sharing as he ferried his children about; we wanted to know how the Jivaro head-hunters used the frog's poison in their blowpipes. (After we came home, Abbott Labs in Chicago would announce that they'd successfully extracted a painkiller from this frog that was as powerful as morphine, but without being addictive.)

Out of all the weirdo animals running through this forest, tree frogs take the prize. They are legion, found all over the insides of flowers and the undersides of leaves, they emit a range of creepy, irritating cries, grunts, moos, barks, clicks and whistles twenty-four hours a day, and they have gelatinous, refulgent skin, so strongly colored it looks irradiated. When I'd been planning this trip and showed my assistant Lauren a *National Geographic* survey about them, her only response was, 'Why do you want to go to a place where the frogs spit poison at you?'

The ultimate kitchen pet was Marguerita, an orphan capybara. These are the world's largest rodents, and at 140 pounds, Marguerita looked like a cross between a hamster and a German shepherd. Like hippos, capybaras are awkward and goofy on land, but have webbed feet and can tear through the water; their local nickname is water hog. They are the preferred Easter dish throughout South America, a jungle ham, and on the plains of Venezuela, they are rustled like calves and brought home to mama.

Out on the boat we'd seen Marguerita moving through the water like a shark, and Juan told us how she was very taken with men. One day, two German couples went swimming, and were rolling around in the water, playing romantically. Marguerita watched from the shoreline until she couldn't stand it anymore. She dove in, made a beeline for the women, and bit them on the butt. When the water pig made her dawn and dusk appearances at camp, she'd almost purr when getting stroked by men, but when women tried petting her, she kept inching away . . . one giant snooty hamster.

César, a student of *chiroptera*, was working down the trail, and after dinner we went to see him. He'd strung a net woven from fishing line about six feet up, and it was completely invisible at dusk (which we found out quickly enough by bumping into it). César and his interns were studying population density, so after catching the animals, they compiled observations and let them go; we'd come just in time for a release. First up was a nectar-eater with a big spiked nose and a long skinny tongue; it looked like a sweet little terrified mouse with wings. The next was an insect-eater, and even for a bat it was ugly as hell, with a giant convoluted nose and ears like devil's horns, but it, too, was terrified, and barely moved a muscle until being set aloft. The last specimen was ready for a fight . . . big, vicious, snarling, struggling, showing its jaws and snapping, frantically squirming its wings and sporting a pink *chiroptera* hard-on. This was the Jamaican fruit-eater, and in his honor we created the Jamaican Fruit-Eating Bat Dance, which goes like this:

Put your arms straight out, and wiggle 'em;
Snap your head from side to side;
Gnash your teeth and snarl like the demon;
Shake your body like a roller-coaster ride.

When Juan saw us trying to get everyone in camp to do this dance, he completely stopped with the 'noble rain forest' bit, and from then on it was bungle in the jungle, baby.

The next morning, we were back on the river with a special mission. Thousands of parakeets went screeching above our heads, followed by chattering parrot couples, and peeping chacalaca. In the trees were hawks, woodpeckers and a pair of great horned spectacle owls, while on the shore, cormorants, ibis and egret were prowling around. Our boat was followed for some time by morpho butterflies the size of a child's head, fluttering silky, acid-blue, almost too much to look at. We motored past a pool, black as fresh oil, covered in ten-foot lily pads, a landscape out of *Jurassic Park*.

At sunrise and sunset, there on the water, the Amazon sky arches with hope, peace and beauty; at night, if you are out on the river and the way is clear, you are guaranteed to see the spreading Milky Way in all its lactic glory. In the jungle, however, that same air is heavy and foreboding, a dark, brutal heat and wetness combined with the crush of approaching thunderstorms. It hangs over you, menacing and oppressive, threatening and mighty. At any minute, you, puny mortal, will be drenched, either with rain or with sweat, and only the petulant sky gods will decide your fate.

We were on the river looking for the famed Amazon dolphins, which are pink, and we motored to their favorite part of the Napo River and then, like all wildlife expeditions, waited and waited and waited. Finally Juan mentioned that when the cetacean researchers were here, they'd played jazz to summon the mighty beasts, but our group's jazz expertise was this side of nil, so we tried the music we knew.

Elvis . . .

Nothing.

Billie Holiday . . .
Zip.
Rolling Stones . . .
Forget it.
U2 . . .
Zilch.

Finally, I thought, 'Why not some Judy Collins treacle?' and launched into 'Both Sides Now.' By verse four, humps of pink skin were breaking the surface. P.J. wondered if it was the Joni Mitchell influence and so tried 'Woodstock,' but this caused the animals to dive precipitously. We went back to 'Both Sides Now,' and worked our way through the full Collins *oeuvre* with terrific results; there must have been a dozen pink dolphins surfacing, sticking up their noses and swimming all around us. P.J. observed, 'Well they may be pretty, but they've sure got lousy taste in music.'

One minute it was sunny and cloudless, and the next, a torrent of biblical proportions rained down upon us. After getting completely soaked, we took refuge in the nearest village's meetinghouse, where P.J., Tim and I stocked up on the locals' handmade rum, starting what would become our group tradition: *The Tasting Tour*. We'd repay the hospitality of the *rivereños* while savoring the product of the local stills. Our favorite turned out to be a mix of sugarcane rum and honeycomb drunk by newlyweds . . . a drink named 'break open the underpants.' While we were bartering, the kids showed Brenda and Barbara their pets: just-born bunnies, and tortoises, and preteen agouti (a half-rodent, half-pig kind of thing). One small girl then brought out her very large and very flapping pet bat, holding it by the wings as it struggled to escape, while we said 'aah!' and 'ooh!' It wasn't so hard to appreciate a bat in the same room with you, gnashing its teeth, after just a few of those 'break open the underpants' specials.

The rain cleared off, and the kids started playing soccer, so P.J., being the sporty member of our group, played with them. We changed his name to Pelé O'Rourke, and later he confided he was doing this to catch the eye of the village's comely young schoolmistress, but instead only caught a case of the chiggers. This led to his new theory: You go to the Great Outdoors to commune with Nature, but all you come home with are reasons to scratch.

At various points along the river, we'd bump into people here doing God-knows-what, such as Roger, an ignorant right-winger who trained U.S. troops for Vietnam in his prime but who now led a family of snotty, holier-than-thou Jehovah's Witnesses. The real compelling expat, though, was Linnea, a rail-thin Scandinavian who looked like she just stepped out of an especially angst-ridden Ingmar Bergman epic. Linnea was a doctor who'd come on an eco-tour, saved a boy from a fer-de-lance bite, and now wouldn't leave. She was called La Doctora, and she had a brand-new clinic built by Missouri Rotarians, a clinic suffering from constant problems with mold and tropical rot. Even her microscope kept developing an internal fungus.

What was the Sean Connery movie where he was a doctor in the jungle and discovered the cure for cancer from ant butts in the sugar? That's just what Linnea was like: frantic, compulsive and frightening, saintly and obsessed, admirable, but a little beyond the pale. She'd saved one woman's life by performing a D+C with a tablespoon, but other patients had died from too much antibiotic, and the Peruvian government was giving her trouble with both her medical license and her residency visa. Linnea also had a continuous problem in that all the local boys brought her any wild thing they could catch, from capybara to monkeys to snakes. They thought she'd buy them, since they'd heard that Americans will turn *anything* into a pet.

'GOOD-BYE, ANIMALS!'

About a mile from camp lived the Yagua, Amazon Indians who'd set up a *faux primitif* re-creation of their traditional village for eco-tourists to come visit. There they would get dressed up in grass skirts, headdresses and facepaint, and shoot blowguns for us … but obviously they couldn't wait to get back to their T-shirts and khaki shorts. The Yagua didn't use cash, and so had a trading system where tourists could relinquish their *South Park* and *Simpsons* T-shirts in exchange for jewelry and wood carvings and intricately carved bowls. At first we tried creative bartering, but soon enough the system became clear: one piece of American clothing got you one Yagua item.

There were German tourists there along with us, demanding in their delicate German fashion for the Yagua to blowgun some monkeys out of the trees. They became so fevered with shopping that they stripped to their underpants to trade all their clothes away. The chief, wearing a ratty thatch skirt, tried demonstrating his blowgun abilities, but missed the target again and again. He offered Tim a chance, and Tim nailed it on the second shot. Barbara, meanwhile, was getting away with two Yagua items per Rocky Mountain High T-shirt.

I like going to places where I can use my odd Spanish, which I learned in a Texas high school from an Iberian noblewoman expatriate. My accent is like hers, snooty and prickly, and I used to be fluent, but so many years have passed that I've forgotten huge patches, and so have invented a new kind of Spanish *surrealismo*, where I just say whatever half-remembered vocabulary pops into my head. During one all-nighter in the Andes, I engineered the customers into a skunk-drunk English lesson, those bombed and bleary *campesinos* learning such key American phrases as '*Me gusta comer sus dedos*' ('I want to eat your fingers') and '*Dame un desayuno de huevos y grabadores, por favor*' ('Please bring me a plate of eggs and tape recorders'). In turn, they taught me the key drinking phrase in Peru: '*Esta noche es la noche!*' ('Tonight's the night!').

I decided to use my language method to now tell the Yagua children a story:

> Those Germans and the Coloradans are not like you and me. They are one-half people, and one-half animals. Every morning they come down from their mountain homes, and do you know what they eat for breakfast? They eat cats, and dogs, and even parrots! Watch them, and you will see how strange they are!

The children sat, listening to me, open-mouthed and spellbound. I wasn't sure how much of my odd Castilian accent was getting through to the Yagua, especially since I'd found out that every time I thought I was asking for an ashtray in restaurants I'd instead been telling the waitress to bring me an elevator. But then, as we were leaving, the entire tribe yelled out: '*Adios, animales!*'

THE WITCH GIVES US A DRINK

There was another part of the camp that was truly extraordinary. If your genius architect father built you the world's greatest collection of *Swiss Family Robinson* treehouses and had them all connected with rope ladders and bridges, you'd have something like the Canopy Walkway, which was constructed for scientists and eco-tourists to glimpse the difference in life from the ground to the treetops, about two hundred feet up. Of course it was pretty up in the trees, and if you looked hard enough you could spot birds and lizards and opossum and a few houseplants you hadn't seen yet, but mainly running around those rope bridges was as much fun as anything out of Disney World, especially after you'd combined break-open-the-underpants drinks with the local form of acid.

One of the camp's neighbors was Antonio, a Jivaro *brujo*, a male witch, a shaman. Everyone was thrilled to meet a real-life shaman, while I was thrilled to meet a real-life Jivaro, the cannibals who invented shrunken heads. Antonio offered to give us a cleansing ceremony, and Brenda and Barbara, the only semi-New Agers in the group, jumped at the chance. This ceremony turned out to be Antonio chanting (a chant which is re-created, perhaps by Antonio himself, on the *Microsoft Encarta Encyclopedia* 'Shaman' entry) while he brushed us down with a hand broom made of twigs, which rustled like castanets; between the chant and the rustle, it was really hypnotic. He told Brenda she was a vegan (which was true) and that I was telepathic (which who knows?), and that to excuse yourself to use the toilet in the Amazon you say, 'I have to see a man about a dog.' Then he smoked an entire pack of Marlboros and blew the smoke over every inch of our bodies. Boy did we feel clean!

That night after dinner, I bought some *clabohuasca*, a rum made from 'the vine of life,' *ayahuasca*, the drug Amazon shamans use to approach the divine. If you've ever known a big-time acid freak, these were the eyes Antonio had; seemingly unfocused and distracted; googly eyes, and he explained how he'd been trained:

> I stopped eating animals. And then I stopped eating fish. And then I stopped eating oil. And then I stopped eating sugar. And then I stopped drinking coffee. And then I stopped smoking tobacco. I went on this diet and got real, real skinny. And then I took the *ayahuasca*, which made me throw up everything, so I was clean. And then it gave me visions and sounds, and those things were just as good as lunch. When you have the *ayahuasca*, everything shows you pictures or gives you words, the people, the animals, the plants, the rocks. It's just like going to school.

We of course couldn't wait to try it, even though there was the threat of 'puking to see the future' involved, and so only some of us took the plunge (now of course I can't remember who). After drinking it for some time, I thought, 'This isn't doing *a thing*,' and then a minute later I said, 'Have you guys ever noticed how *beautiful* the ceiling here is? . . . Don't you think the colors of the candle flames here are really different from how they look in the U.S.?' and that's when we realized that now would be the perfect time to run through the Canopy Walkway.

This walkway is tons of fun all by itself but at night, stoked on break-open-the-underpants and *clabohuasca*, it is *totally fabulous*. You run across the rope bridges and climb higher and higher into the air, at the peak seeing a perfectly clear sky above the treetops, the Southern Cross, the Milky Way, and a big fat reclining Orion. I had (and this was true since one verified non-*huasca* drinker saw it) an extended 'so's your mother!' conversation with a bullfrog:

> *Me:* 'Earp.'
>   *Frog:* 'Earp . . . EARP.'
>   *Me:* 'EARP . . . earp earp.'
>   *Frog:* 'EARP . . . earp earp.'
>   *Me:* 'Earp earp EARP earp!'

Frog: 'Earp earp EARP earp! EARP!'

P.J. and Tim, however, were not having such a good time on the walkway, and we had to coax them down. Bummer, man.

A HOME AT THE
TOP OF THE WORLD

Next morning, Brenda and I bid a fond '*adios, animales!*' ourselves and flew off to Qosqo (or Cuzco, which means 'Belly Button of the World') for a week of running around the Andes with our translator, a hearty Robert Mitchum type named Wilbur. In the jungle, Juan had approached us with a torrent of eco-talk, and now, up in the mountains, Wilbur obsessively discoursed in grave detail on his favorite topic: Peruvian agricultural history. He desperately wanted to make sure Brenda and I were fully informed about every aspect of Inca cultivation methods, especially as it pertained to a subject he found endlessly fascinating: the potato. The Inca created terraced farmland, their own topsoil, and developed something like seventeen thousand different kinds of potatoes, and through Wilbur, we learned about every single one of them.

Moving in six hours from Amazon (sea level) to Cuzco (sixteen thousand feet up) hit me with a bad case of *soroche* – altitude sickness – blinding headaches, dizziness and extreme nausea. It was especially uncomfortable, since Wilbur kept nattering on and on about potatoes. Peruvians cure *soroche* with coca leaves, leathery green and resinous, and about as delicious as a plate of wet pine needles. Brenda and I chewed and chewed, but it did nothing for the *soroche*, and we couldn't even get a little buzz going; gnawing pine needles for an hour would've had about as much effect. Since many Andeans chew a pound of leaves a day, however, we knew we must be missing out on something, and so kept lugging troves of leaves with us everywhere.

In the Andes, all the good restaurants have dozens and dozens of plastic bags filled with water (just like the ones you take goldfish home in) hanging from the ceiling. This, they say, keeps away flies, and why this would work I don't know, but it sure seems to. There are branches of eucalyptus in the rest rooms (organic air-fresheners) and stone fences topped with growing cactus plants (organic barbed wire) and various llamas and their relatives trolling around. Today in the U.S., ranchers are stocking up on *guard llamas*, since these animals are so inquisitive that, if they're standing around with a herd of sheep and a coyote shows up, the llama will immediately run over to investigate. The would-be predator, seeing a three-hundred-pound llama charging straight at it, invariably heads for the hills. Llamas were so important to the Inca that their empire extended only to where the beasts (along with their cousins, the fat, dumb, waddling alpaca and the lean, neurotic supermodel vicuña) could be raised.

Besides llamas, the Inca were crazy about mummies, and they kept their entire ruling family of ancestors mummified in Qosqo. The mummies received daily meals, were consulted by oracles, and the entire royal mummy family would be taken out on festive occasions, paraded around town, and brought to revisit the places they'd enjoyed when alive. Being a high-class Inca (even a live one) was a pretty good deal, since the nobility were allowed multiple wives, vicuña wool, chaws of coca leaf, golden earplugs and cloaks made from vampire bat skins.

Leaving Qosqo, we drove straight through the Urubamba Valley, Incaland, with views as beautiful an alpine dream as anything out of *The Sound of Music*. That the Andes were so relentlessly beautiful stunned me, and I looked around, my mouth dropped open, at zooming snowcaps, quilted farmlands, purple fields of quinoa, towns roofed in red-clay tiles and waterfalls meandering down a granite precipice. We stopped for a visit in one of the greatest places ever, Willoq, a village where people still live exactly as they have for centuries. The Willoqians are Quechua, completely uninfiltrated by the Spanish, and they are fantastic looking, with half-tan and half-red skin, broad noses, full lips and tight almond eyes . . . and just like the Inca, they wouldn't dream of appearing in public without a hat. The village is a sea of sombreros and stovepipes, homburgs and porkpies, bowlers, panamas, derbies and fedoras, ski caps, bonnets, pillboxes and mantillas, and even wimples and snoods . . . always framing long, black, tightly braided pigtails and ponytails. The women's bodies are swathed in flowing serapes and big, pleated, flouncy black skirts, and on their backs are papoosed, grimy babies, bundled up and topped with knit-woollen caps. Inside their houses, we drank tea, watched the kids outside playing with ducks and hogs, and listened to the peep-peep-peeping of the *cuy*.

Spit-roasted *cuy*, or guinea pig, has been a key Andean treat since before time began, and every Willoq house is filled with scurrying herds of these shy rodents. It would be as if you kept packs of wild mice running around the floors of your living room. In Qosqo's main cathedral, there's even a giant painting of the Last Supper with Jesus and his disciples preparing to chow down on a platter of fresh guinea pig. Peruvians, though, feel a little queasy about foreigners' interest in this, so you tragically aren't allowed to take a picture, or even buy a postcard, of the *Last Supper with Cuy*. Juan had said we shouldn't even bother going out of our way to eat guinea pig, since it tastes just like chicken.

Machu Picchu, our ultimate destination, is one of those incredible places in the world that I think everyone has a duty to go look at while they're alive, one of those key 'We must go and see for ourselves' locales. It is here that the lazy, broad Urubamba River turns into a mountain torrent, and you walk a rickety wooden footbridge over those waters to catch a bus, which crosses back and forth in switchbacks to get to the top. This ride is the essence of 'vertiginous,' for no matter which side of the bus you sit on, your window is guaranteed to have many lovely vistas of the road's shoulders: sudden drops into a watery abyss.

In practically every picture of Machu Picchu, the backdrop is always this soft, green mountain called Huayna Picchu, and we saw some hearty German grandmothers hitting the trail to climb it, and assumed we should, too. This turned out to be one of the worst ideas I ever had in my life: mountain-climbing, in old, worn-smooth sneakers, lugging cameras and binoculars (and no water) on my back. Yes, once you get to the top there's a staggering view of the ruins, with the city's terraced geometry now made plain. What you climb, however, is the ancient Inca trail, and instead of actually climbing, we had to crawl up on our hands and knees, scrambling over dripping-wet, slippery, giant boulders, for what seemed like an eternity in hell. After we get to the top, completely soaked in sweat (and looking like we just escaped from a South American prison), it started to pour rain. So we had to go back down, again on our hands and knees, sliding and slipping all over the place. Twice, I slid across the wet stone and grass and landed inches from the precipice. Wilbur looked on, horrified, but he waited till we were all the way back down to explain that just a few months back, a Japanese woman had stepped aside to let some other climbers get by, and fell nine hundred feet to her death.

Machu, though, is worth risking your life to see. The archaeology, the ruins themselves, with tightly placed stone walls, thatch roofs, tiny peephole windows, dizzying stairways, aqueducts and farming terraces climbing up the mountains, all now covered in grass, aren't as dramatic or as beautiful as Luxor, or Tikal, or Chichén Itzá, or many other ancient places . . . but the site! Everywhere you turn is a breathtaking view, an entire landscape of refuge and peace, a home at the top of the world.

As we gazed around, breathless, Wilbur would come over to show us various items that fascinated him: some fern leaves, an orchid, a giant red-legged centipede, a dead fer-de-lance. He'd pick up one rock after another and say, 'Hey! This one looks just like a condor!' or 'Look over here! This one looks just like a crab.' None of these rocks looked like any of these things, and, much to his dismay, there were no potatoes.

The next morning, we rode the scary bus to see Machu again, at dawn. The mountaintops were covered in fog, surrounding us in white air. The green peaks would suddenly loom, vague and blurry, into view, their bases entwined with the glinting brown Urubamba, threads of mist drifting below and between the valley floors. We'd see nothing of the city, and then the wind would pick up, and bits would materialize, only to vanish again. It was all twice as mysterious as in broad daylight, and twice as beautiful.

Every archaeologist and cultural anthropologist seems to have a different theory as to what Machu Picchu was during Inca times. Some say country retreat, others coca farm, and still others think it was a religious ceremonial site. When you are there, this last idea is the one that takes hold, for no matter what it may have been originally, today's Machu is indisputably a sacred place. Whatever religion or spiritual practice you may believe, at this mountaintop, you are guaranteed to believe more of it.

EGYPT

WHEN THE BLACK LAND WAS THE FIRST WORLD

Traveling to odd places regularly gets me up close and personal with odd people, both foreign and home-grown. I've run into my share of horrors – like China's Baby Jane – but I've also met plenty of terrific guys and gals, including Melissa, the bicycle-riding pharmacist. A few years after coming home from Shanghai, Melissa decided to go on a round-the-world tour, and she called me up and said, 'You know, one of my stops will be Egypt, and it's just the greatest and you can't miss it, so why don't you meet up with me there and I'll take you around?' I'd never really thought about going back to the Middle East after a trip to Marrakech where it looked like I was going to be murdered, but she made it sound so easy.

To this day I still remember packs of grizzled men in robes chasing us, shaking their fists while screaming in guttural Arabic, along with every detail of *the airlines of the Middle East*. My NYC-Cairo flight followed the Arab tradition of smoking sections on the left side of the plane and nonsmoking sections on the right. The minute the door closed, however, everyone on board (including the kids) started puffing away frantically. By the time our aircraft began its descent, a third of the cabin was lighting one cigarette after another, a third was spritzing themselves with cologne and hairspray, and another third was doing both at the same time. As every speck of air was obliterated, the non-cologne-wearing nonsmokers started gasping, and I could only wonder: How many airplane explosions in the Middle East have been because of terrorists, and how many have started from the combustible union of Aqua Net and Lucky Strike?

I'd taken a ton of books on ancient Egypt with me to prep for this trip, and when I wasn't praying for the oxygen masks to drop, I read all about what we'd be doing and where we'd be going. This turned out to be quite disturbing, since almost every page had some bizarre fact that was impossible to believe. The history, the culture, the religion . . . it all seemed so crazy, so out there. Then I got to Egypt and found out: It was all true.

OUT THERE

Do you remember the end of *Close Encounters of the Third Kind*, when Richard Dreyfuss abandons his wife and kids in order to climb aboard a spaceship and take off for another galaxy? (We can only hope he wasn't running off with those extraterrestrials who abduct pregnant Montana farm girls and give them extensive anal probes.) The success of *Close Encounters* proves just how many people around the world believe it would be peachy-keen to run off with outer space aliens, and I think you might be one of them . . . in fact, I think that you'd do anything for a chance to meet extraterrestrials. There's wonderful news, though, since you no longer have to get pregnant and go lurking around Montana in order to experience the culture of life from another world. You just have to go to Egypt. No matter how strange, peculiar, bizarre and disturbing the habits of outer space aliens may turn out to be, they can't possibly top what was going on fifty centuries ago in the Nile Valley.

The ancient Egyptians didn't call their country Egypt (like we do) or Misr (like the modern Egyptians do) but Kemet, 'The Black

Land,' meaning good soil for crops. If you close your eyes and try to imagine what Egypt looks like . . . don't you imagine sand-swept, dusty, crumbling pyramids, or parched Bedouins leading their camels across the endless dunes? The people of Kemet, in fact, *hated* the desert and called it Teshert, 'The Red Land,' a chaotic, hellish, terrifying place filled with horrible monsters ruled by Set, a god with the head of an unknown, long-snouted animal, big jackal ears, and a forked tail . . . a god who would later become the Christian beast Satan.

The ancient Egyptians thought of themselves as river people. Their lives revolved around the Nile, whose current runs north but whose winds blow south, making it the perfect means of transportation; so perfect, in fact, that at the time of the building of the Great Pyramid, the Egyptians still hadn't come up with the wheel. They just loved boats, designing hundreds of varieties, even developing a barge that was sewn together with string. Kemet was a land of rafts and ferries and tugs and sloops, and even today, no matter where you turn, that big river is there, feeding the landscape with strips of canals and creating, in the middle of nowhere, a lush farmland that's just right for growing the cotton we prefer in our underpants.

The people of Kemet spent a lot of time on boats and a lot of time in the bathroom, since all of them, male and female, children and adults, were wild about cosmetics. Makeup was thought to be magically alive with healing powers, so they wore a lot of it: orange or yellow henna fingernail polish, black kohl mascara and eyeliner, gray lead or green malachite eyeshadow, and red ocher blush and lipstick. Wigs, fake beards and goatees (made from human or goat hair) were extremely popular, while both sexes wore every kind of jewelry they could come up with: bracelets, anklets, armbands, headbands, pierced earrings, chokers, necklaces, pectorals, multiple crowns, rings on their fingers and bells on their toes. At big parties, they wore cones of pressed flowers and grease on their heads (which took all night to melt and run down their faces) to make sure no one could smell any body odor, which they thought was completely repulsive. Young boys were shaved bald, except for one thatch of hair that was woven into a braid like a Chinese topknot, while bald men rubbed their heads with hedgehog fat, and the high priests went about draped in panther skins. Taking all this into consideration, it could be easily said that the Egyptians were the Michael Jacksons of the ancient world.

Their outfits and makeup may have been distinctive, but it's in the religion department where these guys really went nuts, with a belief system more strange and beautiful than anything a science-fiction master could dream up. You're probably already familiar with the more common, run-of-the-mill Egyptian gods, such as the ones with a human body and the head of a jackal, ibis or baboon. The Kemetians also worshipped Taweret, the god of pregnancy, who has the head of a wig-wearing hippopotamus, the tail of a crocodile, the hands of a lion and the body of a fat old woman; as well as fertility god Min, who wears mummy wraps and a feather hat, while flinging a cat-o'-nine-tails and sporting a big erection. Min's sacred plant (and preferred offering) is a head of lettuce. The oddly global worship of cows (much more on this later) is here in the form of Hathor (*hat whore*), the bull-horned goddess of health, who allows reigning pharaohs to nurse from her sacred udders. Like Greek and Roman gods (who inherited the idea), Egyptian deities could manifest themselves as various animals, with bulls, falcons, cows, cobras, vultures and lionesses being the most popular. The system was ridiculously unfair; Thoth, for example, could be either an ibis or a baboon, while poor Sepa could only manifest himself as a millipede.

SPIRITUAL OFFAL

Our trip, like every trip to Egypt, began with a landing in El Qahira, or Cairo, a city whose buildings are the color of old, tired shoes, and whose air is humid, sullen and permeated with a dun-brown talc, a dust that coats everything. You get around in taxis, and I was only too happy to let Melissa do all the dirty work, a half-hour of dramatic negotiations three times a day that could easily drop the price from $3.50 to 75¢. At that time, the metropolitan slaughterhouses were still at the dead center of downtown, meaning that any food source that could walk to its ultimate destination did so, causing unimaginable traffic snarls. Besides doomed herds of goats and cattle, the streets were filled with professional child beggars, most with missing fingers or congenital deformities, as well organized as anything out of *Oliver Twist*.

If you have to go to Cairo, you should at least stay in a palace, and ours was built by the Khedive Ismail in 1869 to put up the international jet set arriving for the premiere of *Aida* and the opening of the Suez Canal. Melissa explained, 'The last time I came to Cairo, I stayed here, too, only then it was filled with unbelievably rich sheiks and their families. I'd go out into the gardens, and they'd be mobbed with the kids driving around in little battery-powered jeeps, with Filipino nannies chasing after them. The Saudi women didn't wear the usual head scarves, they all had Hermès, and if you went into the ladies' room after they'd been in there, the whole place would be a frightful mess, since they just assumed the servants would be coming round to clean out the stalls.'

We rolled around the Corniche, the Champs-Elysées of Cairo, a broad avenue overlooking the Nile, and Melissa offered that if we took a boat ride here, we'd easily find numerous Cairenes in the shadows under the bridges, furtively, busily masturbating. Whether this is from lack of privacy at home or some erotic pleasure at impregnating the Nile, we didn't know, and couldn't figure out a polite way of asking. Instead, we went on a tour of the Khedive's private palace, with a guide whose only professional ability was to wave at the room while saying nothing, like a surly, unattractive Vanna White. He tried rubbing his crotch up against me, and then against Melissa, to improve his tip, but this wasn't a successful strategy and as we left, he cursed us with shaking fists, screaming in that extra-special 'enraged Muslim' style.

Certain Third World vacations come with a secret, surprise bonus: a culture clash of sonic-boom proportions. You the traveler are there to relax, enjoy, forget your troubles – c'mon get happy – while the locals surrounding you are in hot pursuit of what may turn out to be a significant business transaction. To put yourself in their shoes, imagine you're eking out a bare subsistence and only a few bucks away from eviction when there's a knock at your trailer-park door. You open it: Bill Gates has dropped by. What would you do? Since the stakes for Emerging Marketers bumping into a rich foreign tourist are so high, they commonly move in too close, too loud, too fast, and no matter what the intentions, you can't help but feel threatened, and under siege. Soon enough, we'd found ourselves under siege in Cairo.

Apparently, plenty of Egyptians who work with tourists have found that throwing temper tantrums and screaming bloody murder can dramatically raise their tips, and they'd try this trick on us twenty-four hours a day. They made us feel like walking ATM machines or tender, succulent chickens surrounded by starving coyotes. They'd size us up with piercing eyes, as well as think that we, as Unbelievers of the holy laws of Islam, were spiritual offal. After two weeks of harassment, we learned, when asked where we were from, to say 'Russia.' Everyone in Egypt knows that Russians are broke.

Throughout the Middle East, five times a day, we heard one thing. The ancient Moors loved a mournful, minor-key cascade of wailing that in Spain became the soap opera of *flamenco* and in Islam, the call to prayers of the *muezzin*. We'd be lying in our luxuriously appointed hotel rooms, or traveling in a taxi seeing sky-scrapers, neon and billboards for Sony camcorders and Macintosh computers, when all of a sudden there'd be that cry of Islamic devotion, a sound from the dawn of time.

The same minor key can be heard across all of the Middle East, as, for almost a century, the radio waves have been dominated by one person, Um Kulthum, known by millions as 'Souma.' On the first Thursday of every month, she appears on a Cairene stage to sing two songs, each of which lasts for two hours, wailing soap operettas of love. When we saw her passing through the street, and heard men screaming to her, 'Souma, Souma, my sweetheart, my love!' she'd just turned ninety.

The Muslim women robed in black that I'd pass in public knew that I knew that they're married and unavailable, and this relieved them of the need to act modest. They'd flirt and goof off and have fun with me in a way that a single, unveiled woman couldn't, even when they had five-gallon metal cans of water swaying on their heads. Besides the traditional Islamic robes, many Cairenes wore military outfits – boots, camouflage pants, flak jackets – and just as I was thinking this was a fad and started looking for Army-Navy surplus stores, I realized that these were hand-me-downs from the 1960s Levant – not exactly a groovy era of peace and love in this part of the world.

THE ATTIC OF BROKEN NOSES

We took a walk through the Cairo Museum, and this stroll is exactly like a dream, a dream of when your Miss Havisham-ish grandma drops dead and leaves you *everything*. Instead of the careful layout, lighting and captions that are the goal of most museums, here is chaos, darkness and some of the greatest pieces of art ever made buried in piles of crap, lit by grimy skylights, and kept behind glass so filthy they can barely be seen. 'I always tell people who're coming here to bring a flashlight, a roll of paper towels and a bottle of Windex,' Melissa commented as we meandered through this claustrophobe's attic nightmare. Even so, this museum, like the rest of Egypt, is so bursting with wonders that it makes the other great museum Egyptian wings, from the British to the Met, look like garage sales. Step by step, we stood in awe of an endless parade of furniture, jewelry, carvings and coffins, clear evidence that Kemet was one of the richest nations in history.

Plenty of the museum statues have their noses broken, which is no accident, since it was believed that a statue carried the spirit of the dead inside, a spirit that entered through the nostrils, and breaking the nose would supernaturally kill it. If you have a really good guide (which you won't), he'll remember to tell you this, but invariably he won't bother explaining the corollary, a crucial idea to remember while traveling through this alien culture. For the ancient Egyptians, paintings and sculpture (and makeup) were alive, and in fact they had one word to mean painter, artist or sculptor: 'He who keeps alive.'

Besides evading five thousand years of professional grave-robbing, Egyptian antiquities also had to avoid the various Cairo governments which, when the state coffers drooped, felt quite comfortable selling their heritage, as well as marauding Europeans, who took home souvenirs of anything their Egyptian porters could carry. Because of all these vanished antiquities, historians are constantly trying to work around a giant black hole of missing information, and at the core of Egyptology lies a series of profound mysteries. In the Cairo Museum, we saw illustrations of hyenas lying on their backs, their legs tied together, being force-fed chunks of meat, much as the French force-feed geese for foie gras . . . but no one has any idea why they're doing this. Everywhere we went in the country, we saw countless illustrations of pharaohs wearing the double crown symbolizing the unity of Upper and Lower Egypt . . . but nobody has ever found one of these crowns. Egyptologists don't even know, exactly, what the Kemetians looked like. The Cairo Museum is chock-full of statues and friezes with Egyptian females painted ash-white, males crayon-red, while Nubians and other Africans are black as soot. There's plenty of Egyptian artwork, however, with features that are obviously African (such as the funeral mask of King Tut), and to top it all off, there's one sculpture that looks exactly like Elizabeth Taylor from *Cleopatra*.

There is so much missing from Egyptology that it actually takes on a magical quality. On the first floor of the museum, there are two carved stone signs, about two feet high, called palettes, used to commemorate important events. Both of these were made at the same time, around 3000 B.C.E. One has friezes of donkeys, oxen and olive trees, and could have been carved during the start of any Middle Eastern culture. The other, however, is perhaps the most important piece of Egyptian art ever found: 'The Narmer Palette,' named for the pharaoh who first unified the country. Every single element we identify with ancient Egypt is right there – hieroglyphs, cartouches, the bulbous white crown of Upper Egypt, the towering red crown of Lower Egypt, and even a big display of smoting. (Remember how the Bible is always saying 'Hepsebub thus did smote down the Ephysiates, and Jereboabum did smote down the Hodarites, and Rhubarb did smote down the Zobarites, he smote down every one'? All over Egypt there are illustrations of pharaohs grabbing their much smaller enemies by the hair, and bludgeoning them.) No archaeologists have uncovered any previous evidence of any of the elements that suddenly appear on 'The Narmer Palette,' absolutely nothing that shows the evolution of hieroglyphs, astronomy, medicine or the ancient Egyptian religion.

They all just suddenly appear, fully formed, on this one stone, as if out of nowhere, as if dropped from the heavens.

AN AFTERNOON WITH THE FATHER OF TERROR

If Neil Armstrong had landed on the moon and discovered three forty-story-high, geometrically perfect orbs, each built with immense, multi-ton, perfectly carved cubes, wouldn't it be the shock of the world? This is exactly how I felt seeing the Giza pyramids in person for the first time. They are the tallest thing built by human beings until the nineteenth century brought us the *très chic* Eiffel Tower, and if I turned away from the slum next door and the madding hordes of pyramidiots, frantic camel guides, bibelot merchants and fat tourists exploding out of their neon-colored Lycra stretch pants, I could easily imagine when originally there was no Cairo here; only a city of the dead in the middle of the Great Sand Sea. Even as ruins, even with that limestone casing yanked off by Muslims to build their palaces, even surrounded by camel-ride concessions and postcard-vending tents and horse-renting pseudo-Bedouins (every visitor here is forced to ride a camel or a horse or a donkey or some damn thing), the Giza pyramids knocked me out: forty stories of pure unbelievably mathematical razor-sharp perfection. The idea was for the awesome power and majesty of imperial Kemet to make you feel little and puny and insignificant, and boy did I ever, especially after climbing around inside the Great Pyramid through tunnels angled at ninety degrees, in stifling heat, surrounded by zaftig German newly-weds.

How many pyramid theories have you heard? Are they astronomical observatories, architectural almanacs, scale models of the Northern Hemisphere, energy lenses, power mirrors, weather forecasters, baptismal fonts, astronaut launch pads, temples or tombs? All these and more have been theorized, but we still don't know for sure. The tombs of Kemet are covered with painted scenes of daily life, exquisite details of how those living five thousand years ago fished, hunted, sewed, baked, wove, prayed, tanned leather, smithed gold and smote the neighbors. But there are no pictures or texts describing the erection of pyramids, temples, tombs or any other kind of edifice – a quite deliberate silence.

Standing in front of them all and carved out of living rock is the magnificent creation that the Arabs call Abu al-Hawl, 'The Father of Terror.' We know that Egyptians saw sphinxes as the guardians of sacred locations – supernatural watch-dogs with the smarts of a human and the strength of a lion. Originally the Great Sphinx had been painted to look half human and half carnivore, with the headdress rendered in livid blue and yellow stripes, and if you believed that statues have something of a life of their own, it must've been a truly frightful thing. Gustave Flaubert thought the face looked African, and especially seeing it in profile, I had to agree.

Just next door is Saqqarah, a mortuary complex even older than Giza, whose buildings contain the first writings of the pyramid (or coffin) texts: the *Egyptian Book of the Dead*. These are the line drawings, hieroglyphs and epic comic books drawn inside every Egyptian tomb, covering the walls, the ceilings and the coffins. Much of it can be basically explained by two ideas: 'You *can* take it with you' and 'Just in case you forget what to do in the Underworld, we're going to draw the instructions all over your grave.' Other than those two basic concepts, however, we don't really know much about what any of this means.

One pyramid text, *The Book of What Is in the Duat*, appears all over Egypt and is a great example. For starters, Egyptologists can't agree on what, exactly, the *Duat* is. All measurements in the *Book* are given in *schoeni* (no one has yet discovered what a *schoeni* is), and central chapters are written in a language never seen elsewhere, and which has never been fully translated. The story's key plot concerns the dead pharaoh riding a boat that follows the course of the sun after it sets on this world and enters the next, accompanied by various gods, demons and creatures we don't know anything about: a pair of knife-wielding serpents, a duo of fire-spitting cobras, a baboon carrying an ibis, and snakes named 'He Who Swallows the Forms' and 'The One Whose Mouth Is Wiped.'

Another Saqqarah highlight is a tomb for the two men who were

King Niusere's 'Overseers of the Manicurists' – concrete evidence of just how seriously these people took their cosmetics. We don't know if these overseers were brothers, close friends, lovers or whatever, but in their offering chapel, where the surviving family would go to pray and make obeisances in order to get the dead to do good things for them (or at least not do bad things against them), the two men are depicted, as they will be remembered for all eternity, in the manner that Egyptians used to show the greatest possible closeness between two people: their noses touch, and the knots on their belts are so close that they may be tied together.

Would you like it if your grave became a hugely popular tourist attraction, and tens of thousands of people every year came to peer inside your carefully maintained sarcophagus (a word I like, since it's Greek for 'flesh-eating box')?

I know I would.

THE DISNEYLAND
OF THE DEAD

Melissa was keen to go north to the Mediterranean coast where she had never been, and this turned out to be hours of dull train travel through the rice fields of the Nile Delta to get to a North African port town with little to distinguish it from hundreds of others. When its library with a million volumes burned to the ground, it wasn't rebuilt by its Koran–only Muslim rulers, who also did nothing when the harbor lighthouse, one of the Seven Wonders of the World, crumbled and fell into the sea. Alexandria, though, still has something remarkable: the catacombs of Kom el-Shugafa, a concrete example of the collapse of empire.

A wealthy Greek family living in second-century Alexandria decided they deserved to have a burial plot just like the great Egyptian tombs of yore, so they dug a spiral staircase into the ground, with catacombs and visitors' chambers hewn into the rock at multiple levels, and then had all of it decorated with a cartoon version of Egyptian religious art. We climbed, deeper and deeper, into this clammy, fetid hole, which was unbelievably ugly and creepy, completely depressing, and perfect for Vegas. Egyptian scholar John Anthony West was so taken aback by this site that he remarked: 'Egypt, which began with the superhuman Sphinx, the prodigious pyramids, and the pristine geometry of Saqqarah, which survived internal anarchy and foreign domination to produce Dir el-Bahari, the Hypostyle Hall of Karnak and the lesser but still resonating temples of Edfu, Dendera, and Philae, finished here, in Alexandria, in an underground Disneyland.'

Melissa pronounced it a 'must-miss.'

We got back to Cairo to find out that our palace no longer had rooms available until we ourselves threw giant Muslim temper tantrums, when a suite with only one bed came free. With my sonic-boom snoring, Melissa had to go off and sleep in the tub. The next day, we were told by the travel agent that our train to Aswan left from the downtown station, so we went to visit one of Melissa's friends, Vicki, who lived in a spectacular Heliopolis apartment nearby. She offered us the universal beverage of welcome (Diet Coke) while her blond kids (the husband's French) played *Star Wars* with plastic lasers. The apartment was lavish and immaculate, featuring an antique pipe organ, two washing machines, two deep freezes and twenty-four bottles of Chivas arrayed on silver trays, while the public hallways and vestibules (like in many other Egyptian luxury buildings) looked like utter slums.

Hostess Vicki was almost a perfect stereotype of the New York mother. She kept emerging from the kitchen with bigger and bigger trays of pastry and candy, urging us on with, 'Just have one more. Just one!' It was getting late, and we casually mentioned how our next stop was Aswan, and Vicki casually replied that she was quite sure the Aswan train left not from downtown but from Giza, quite far from her flat. After some hysteric phoning we discovered that this was indeed true, but luckily one of Vicki's neighbors was a professional taxi driver, and he agreed to speed us over. We arrived just as the train was pulling in (late, thank God) and paid him extremely well, at which point he started ranting about what cheap bastards we were and cursed us with shaking fists in that 'enraged Muslim' style we'd already come to know so well.

The main Egyptian railroad is a spectacular ride, as it coasts from

Giza to Aswan along the border of irrigation. We looked out one side of the train to see lush tropical farmland rolling by, one giant oasis, green as Florida, while the other side is an absolute, remote, lifeless desert. On the irrigated side are towns and boats and every kind of farmland and domesticated animal, while on the unirrigated side are nothing but sand dunes and mud domes – like wasps' nests – for the dead. The train slowly rolled along all evening, and it rolled along all night, and it rolled along all morning. We were supposed to hit Aswan at ten A.M., which would allow plenty of time to check into the hotel and get me to the airport for a one-thirty flight to Nubia, but that big old train kept a-rollin'. Ten-thirty passed, and then eleven, and then twelve, and then twelve-ten, twelve-twenty, twelve-thirty . . . and the train wouldn't arrive, and of course I was having a heart attack.

Finally we stopped and jumped out and grabbed the first cab that came along. Just outside the airport, the car 'broke down' (later I realized that the cabdriver probably didn't have an entry permit), so I had to run to the terminal in one hundred degrees of heat, kicking up dust, and got in at one, relieved, but not for long, since it turned out my one-thirty plane had already taken off. The ticket agent told me the next plane was sold out in coach so I'd have to buy a wildly expensive first-class upgrade. I explained that since the Egyptian state tourist agency had set up the trip, and the Egyptian state train was four hours late, and the Egyptian state airline had overbooked, it wasn't me who was going to pay for this upgrade. After much suspenseful waiting, the man gave me a coach ticket and I got on the three-thirty plane . . . to find it two-thirds empty. We arrived an hour before sunset, which turned out, after all that trauma, to be absolutely the perfect moment to see one of the greatest treasures of the ancient world.

THE ULTIMATE SMOTE

Abu Simbel is sited in the lands that were once Nubia and, before that, the Kingdom of Kush, which today's nomads call the Sea of Satan. These were the Mexicos of the ancient world, each with a wonderful culture all its own, but completely dwarfed by their bigger, more powerful northern neighbor. You'd think the ancient Egyptians would've felt warmly toward their Southland, since Nubia was the source of *nub* – gold – which they considered the flesh of the gods . . . but there was no good-neighbor policy. Tutankhamen, for one, had pictures of Kushites painted on the bottoms of his shoes so he could perpetually smite and trample them.

The lands of Kush and Nubia are now drowned to oblivion by the Aswan Dam, the ultimate smote. Today, all that's left of these once-mighty kingdoms are the placid sky-blue waters of Lake Nasser, lapping against the yellow desert sands. At dusk, the shoreline is a bronze canyonland, and tucked into what would be an utterly unnoticeable little alcove is the astonishing Abu Simbel, built to show those low-life Kushites and Nubians just who's boss around these parts.

Abu's entry is four stone colossi, sixty-five-foot-high statues of Ramses the Great, with his wives and kids cavorting between his legs . . . while above their heads is a shelf of twenty baboons, worshipping the sun. The entry hall is supported by pillars of Ramses, fifteen feet tall, wearing heavy eyeliner, while the inscribed and painted walls celebrate his military victories (which involve a great deal of smoting) and the ceiling is patterned in china-blue imperial vultures, spreading their wings in benevolent protection. It is completely staggering, but there's more: twice a year, on February 23 and October 23, the rising sun sends a shaft of light straight back through the halls to the final sanctuary, where it illuminates a pantheon of the lords of creation, each of which has been completely mutilated. By whom? We don't know. Their faces now look melted, vaguely human, like indistinct ghosts of the subconscious, waiting there, in moist darkness, for their two days of light.

Almost every guide in Egypt is from hell. They've learned a basic patter to repeat over and over as quickly as possible, throwing out one piece of information after another in a barely intelligible monotone, with whatever enthusiasm they once had for their jobs long gone. Besides their demeanor, much of what they tell you is wrong (or at least old and discredited). Some of the guides were so astonishingly terrible that I couldn't help but think: How did the people who made the flabbergasting thing I was looking at devolve into this person talking about it?

So when I got back to Aswan and we ultimately found a magnificent guide, almost entirely by accident, it was a shock. Ahmad was an educated man, a schoolteacher, who knew plenty of off-the-beaten-tracks, including a late temple that we wandered through completely on our own. Afterward, we trudged across a hill above the city, behind the Aga Khan's tomb, to see a Copt monastery with beautiful frescoes at the edge of a thousand miles of Sahara desert. We walked around to the back – only to find an immense field of shattered pottery and human feces (the kitty litter box of the gods) – scurried back to the nonfeces part, and started ambling out into the sand. The wind was deafening, our feet were sinking deeper and deeper into the earth with every step, and soon enough, we got scared . . . the vista of that Big Empty, the ominous sound of the winds, the shadows of the dunes, rising and falling against the sands, huge and black, and the feeling in our shoes that, at any moment, we could be swallowed up whole . . . well, we saw right away why the ancients thought the desert was a frightening, awful place. In just a few minutes, we'd left civilization and entered the wilderness, and we now turned to go back as quickly as we could.

THE EMPIRE OF SID CAESAR

Besides Abu Simbel, Ramses the Great marked his Greatness with monumental constructions throughout the New Kingdom capital of Luxor, where every one of the pharaoh's statues is graced with a *Mona Lisa* smile. It's no wonder: Ramses was rich as hell, lived into his eighties, reigned for six decades over the greatest empire of his time, and had ninety kids (so why he became a famous condom brand is anyone's guess). He didn't, however, look much like Yul Brynner in *The Ten Commandments*, since he had red hair, a big jaw, a beaky nose and a long, thin face. In fact, Ramses looked quite a bit like Sid Caesar, and we know from his mummy that he also had arthritis, gum disease and beautiful fingernails.

While Giza is a barren yellow Sahara, the Valley of the Kings, on the other side of the Nile from Luxor, is the white side of the moon, a blinding, limestone desert oven. The minute we started walking around over there, a real Lawrence of Arabia–type Arab, in flowing robes, headgear, the whole bit, came up to me with a little sculpture in his hands, whispering, 'An-teek! An-teek!' It was the head of a woman, nicely done, and of course made that morning, but I liked it, so we had the conversation that African nomads have been having for five thousand years: I asked how much, he said a price, I said one fourth of that, he said three fourths, I said one half, and the sale was made; about twelve bucks. He took off and I walked away, convinced I'd find the exact same thing anywhere else for three bucks . . . but in all of Egypt, I never found anything as well made, and never saw that merchant again. I got back to the hotel and washed off the little head's dirt, and it was even more beautiful, charming and mysterious. Just where was this black-market curio shoppe making such terrific stuff? If Brenda had been with us, *she'd* have found it.

Off and away from everything else in this necropolis of secret caves stands probably my all-time favorite Kemet building, 'The Most Splendid of All,' Deir el-Bahari, tomb of one of the most remarkable figures of ancient history, Hatshepsut (*hot shep soot*), and the site where, in 1997, Islamic terrorists murdered fifty-eight tourists. The ground zero of minimalist design, Deir makes the Lincoln Memorial look gussied up. It's a broad and low-slung marble rectangle set against a sheer cliff, faceted with columns that rhythmically follow its background's rocky orthogonal patterns, so perfectly integrated into its surroundings that it looks as if the earth itself disgorged it . . . not unlike the ancient Egyptians' primordial swamp spitting up all of life and creation.

Looking at it, I forced myself to remember that what is now beautifully minimalist was at one time maximalist to the extreme. The clean white desert highway we walked to get to the tomb was originally landscaped with pools, orchards, flower beds and rows of brightly painted sphinx guardians. Every statue and every frieze was coated in the extreme colors that can be seen in bits and pieces all over Egypt, and there would've been dozens of waving flags, banners and curtains. So much of modern design has been influenced by ruins, but don't be fooled. The ancient empires, whether Chinese, Egyptian or Mesoamerican, may have loved solid brute architecture, but they liked a big gooey paint job even more.

Hatshepsut was both the daughter and the wife of a pharaoh, and when her husband died, the heir was a twelve-year-old boy who sought the bright lights of military conquest instead of the ruling life in Thebes. He took off for the territories, while she declared herself co-regent and ceremonially, like all pharaohs, appeared publicly in full beard. Some of her portraits show her as a man, others show her as a woman dressed up like a man, and still others show her as a young boy. E.T., eat your heart out.

THE DAWN OF A
NEW RELIGION

Just a ways down the river is the temple to Osiris at Abydos, enough off the beaten track so that most tourists skip it, which makes as much sense as skipping the pyramids. Abydos is the only temple which has held on to vast amounts of its original paint job, and it makes all the other ruins look ruined ... dead ... while it looks open and ready for business. Plenty of the neighbors, in fact, still use it to worship Kemet's greatest god, and it's as close as you can get to seeing what ancient Egyptian art really looked like. Here, the men are red, the women are yellow, and the gods are sky blue (or not painted at all – invisible), while the ceilings are alive with butter-yellow stars and blood-red vultures. My favorite picture in all Abydos shows Osiris receiving the ankh (the power of life) from the ibis-headed Thoth, while wearing an ostrich-feather-and-ram's-horn crown, topped with a blinding sun disk. Wrapped around the horns are cobras decked out in plumed hats and miniature sun-balls, waving in a protective breeze. Compared to this, those *Close Encounters* aliens are a real snooze.

Every little hieroglyph and painting in Abydos, every piece of furniture, item of jewelry, headdress feather, striped linen pleat and shepherd's crook is so deeply sculpted, with such craft and such artistry, and then painted in such rich, evocative colors, that it is completely overpowering, and within just a few minutes I went eye-blind and brain-numb. The walls tell the story of Egypt's all-time most popular god, Osiris, who was father of civilization, teaching the Egyptians farming, law and religion. Osiris went off to teach the rest of the world, leaving his homeland in the capable rule of his wife, Isis (who was also his sister). When he got back home, his evil brother Typhon tricked him into getting into a box, which he nailed shut and covered with lead and threw into the Nile, in order to marry Isis and take over the throne.

After many adventures, the box was recovered. Isis turned herself into a hawk, flapped her wings, resurrected her brother/husband back to life, and while doing so had a son, born of the virgin womb, who turned out to be the falcon-head god, Horus. Typhon, enraged, hacked Osiris's body into fourteen pieces and scattered them throughout Egypt, throwing the penis into the Nile, where it was eaten by a fish (the Nubians heard it was a catfish and refused, from then on, to eat catfish). Isis found all the body parts (except the penis) and reassembled her husband. With instructions from the gods, she preserved him for all time by creating the first mummy, and brought him back to life once again. Osiris, however, decided to rule not in Egypt but in the Underworld, and left his kingdom to his son Horus, who battled his uncle again and again, until finally becoming the indisputable leader of all Kemet.

The ancient Egyptians worshipped Osiris, Isis and Horus as a holy family, and they thought of Osiris as being just like a good shepherd, taking care of all his followers (in Egyptian art, he's always depicted with a crook and flail). When the dead travel to the Underworld, they are judged by having their heart (a jar) weighed against the laws of the universe (an ostrich feather), and those with good hearts get to go live with Osiris, who rose from the dead, while the bad-hearted get eaten by a crocodile-snouted, lion-maned, hippo-assed woman.

The details may be different (especially the penis-eating catfish), but there's a lot that Kemetians and Christians have in common. The roles of Isis and Mary are almost identical, and there are many parallel rules of living a moral life, even to the point where an Old

Kingdom collection of sages' wisdom is almost word for word the same as the Book of Proverbs. The key underlying beliefs are almost a perfect match, since both Christians and Kemetians believe that mortal humans have within them the spark of the divine and, if nurtured, they can become immortal. That, if you follow the rules and act the right way, you'll have eternal life.

In its final days, the culture of ancient Egypt didn't wither away from the vast corruption of the Ptolemies or the military conquest of the Romans, but from the fevered Christian Emperor Justinian, who demanded the closing of the temples and the excommunicating of the priests – another ultimate smote. It's believed by many that Egyptians took to Christianity so strongly and so quickly because the two religions have so much in common. You can see the final stand of the Kemet priests at Philae . . . the 'underground Disneyland' of the culture's collapse at Alexandria . . . and here, at Abydos, which most tourists skip, you can see a wholly alien culture outlining the key Christian philosophies . . . and a paint job that'll knock your socks off.

THE WHITE SIDE OF THE MOON

Everywhere I went, I was staggered by the artistry of Kemet, the carving and painting and bas-reliefs and friezes, which are all beautiful beyond imagining. Even the walls and walls of hieroglyphs . . . wonderfully etched flying wasps, and fertile cow-girls, and gasping crocodiles, and 'what me worry?' faces, and plump honeybees, and alert hares, and flying beetles, and blooming lotus . . . are all perfectly carved into solid granite, and can be enjoyed for hours. This isn't, however, an art that stirs us inside . . . it is too strange, too bizarre, too alien. To get a stirring of the soul, I had to travel to one more spot, to Egypt's back-of-beyond. That this place is named for Sin, the Mesopotamian god of the moon, is just right, since the land is a naked moonscape where nothing grows but pathetic, desiccated scrub. The prophet Elijah came here to hide from King Ahab and Queen Jezebel, the Holy Family came here to hide from King Herod, and the Israelites were stuck wandering for forty years after making false idols, which shows exactly how nasty the God of the Old Testament really was. The Sinai is so desolate, so rocky, so empty and so hostile that it just seems to continually whisper: *Don't even think of living here* . . .

Besides being the spot where God gave Moses the Ten Commandments and where Muhammad's horse, Boraq, ascended to heaven, Mount Sinai is also supposed to be the hiding place for a dazzling horde of treasure that the Israelites snuck out of Egypt. Between spirit and mammon, the Mount has been a singular attraction for everyone from self-styled Indiana Jones wannabes to Christian and Muslim fundamentalist maniacs, and today there's plenty of both who believe that the mount in Sinai is not the biblical Mount Sinai at all, that the real deal's around the corner, in Saudi Arabia.

Believe it or not, deep down where it counts, it doesn't matter. Even an atheist cannot visit the Sinai's Mount without feeling a movement in the body, a stirring in the soul. Since I'd agreed to go to Alexandria with her, I forced Melissa to come to Sinai with me, and she was completely prepared to hate it. Instead, she wandered across the rocks, silent, pensive, watching.

Instead of soil, or grassland, or even sand dunes – anything soft and welcoming – the peninsula is acre after acre of gravel, boulders, clay and wind-worn buttes, the only visible life a short-cropped, brutish weed. Even the insects are few and far between. Cemeteries are merely a collection of nicely placed rocks serving as cremation markers, and the only people even trying to live here are Bedouins.

Everywhere in the Third World are people who want absolutely nothing to do with the twentieth century – people deliberately living on the other side of nowhere. The Bushmen of the Kalahari, the Dani of the New Guinea Highlands, and the Bedouins of the North Sahara are all far too wrapped in their own culture to have any interest in ours, and that's probably why they're the most interesting people I've ever met overseas. Most Sinai Bedouins today have given up the camel for the jeep and the tent for a stone house, but that's all they want from technology and progress. Big parties, for example, are still celebrated with that highlight of Bedouin cuisine, pots and pots of boiled goat.

On our visit to Mount Sinai's 1,300-year-old monastery, St Catherine's, the monks showed us their burning bush, their well of Moses, their rock where the waterfall popped out, and all the other Old Testament miracles, none of which seemed remotely plausible. How could they be so certain that it was this bush, this well and that rock? Still, there is something here that defies explanation or description. The rush of the wind . . . the mountains' harsh, rocky peaks . . . the clear air that lets you see for hundreds of miles and makes you want to just start walking off into the ether . . . You've found something, though what it is, exactly, you don't know. But there is something here in the middle of nowhere that you can feel in your bones . . . something real, yet intangible . . . something *out there*.

That this is one of the world's true holy places is, to anyone who comes out and sees it in person, unmistakable.

INDONESIA

INTO THE LIVER
OF BORNEO

THE RITUAL HARVESTING OF
A STRANGE, MULTIHUED
SEAWORM

A year after getting back from Kemet, I left a job I'd been in forever in order to go to a little company just starting up, and it was immediately obvious I'd now be working night and day, nose to the grindstone, fingers to the bone. There were four weeks' downtime in between and at the very last minute, I realized: You won't be seeing another vacation moment for a *very* long time. I wanted to really go, again, to the back-of-beyond; to a place where day-to-day American life was as foreign as it could be, and I spun the globe to what would be exactly the opposite side of the world from my home in New York City. There it was: the Malay Archipelago . . . the East Indies . . . the band of Spice Islands that runs along the Java Sea.

A collection of 13,700 utterly distinct atolls masquerading as one sovereign nation, Indonesia is *très* cool, featuring dancing girls in Java, orangutans in Borneo, renegade civil disorder in Timor, dragons in Komodo, Muslim fanatics in Lombok, sacred water buffalo in Sulawesi, holy whip duels in Simba, 'the ritual harvesting of a strange, multihued seaworm' in Sumba, and cannibals in New Guinea. The cat's meow. I looked at all this and could only remember the phrase Brenda uses as her shopping mantra: 'I'll take them *all.*'

Basically, I wanted to hop from island to island, seeing as much as possible in four weeks, and I wanted to set sail in three days. I booked an appointment to get the necessary chloroquine (a malarial prophylaxis) and started researching to find the very best Indonesian travel agency who could set up the basics ASAP. Vayatour in California seemed the most qualified, which was confirmed when they pulled together a remarkably complicated trip in two days' time. The schedule we finally worked out included three days in the ancient Javan capital of Jogjakarta, five days with the proboscis monkeys and orangutans in Borneo, five in luxurious, land-of-a-million-postcards Bali, and five in New Guinea with a tribe of (hopefully) ex-cannibals. To show just what an achievement this was, the day and a half it took to get from Central Java to the Borneo orangutan preserve involved a car ride from Jogjakarta to Semarang, a flight to Surabaya, another flight to Pangkalan Bun, a car to Kumai, a boat to the Rimba Lodge, and another boat to Camp Leakey.

The New York–Frankfurt–Singapore–Jakarta run was with Singapore Air, which turned out to be just terrific, especially the beautiful and fascistic Malay stewardesses who'd poke me in the shoulder and hiss, 'Wake up! It's time to eat!' Like any international flight today, SingAir showed us various bits of data from the cockpit, my all-time favorite being *The Time Screen*, which tells you what time it is where you are, what time it is where you were, what time it is where you'll be, what time it was when you left, and what time it'll be when you arrive, all accompanied by a constantly shifting series of cartoon planes soaring over ever-zooming maps and charts. *The Time Screen* serves to reinforce the sensation that your life, and your affairs, are quite literally up in the air, and instead of feeling informed, the more I looked at it, the more baffled I got.

The only way I can survive a flight like this is to sleep through most of it, and it took me decades to learn how to nod off against a backdrop of fussy babies, bouncing wind currents, squirming teens and Chevy Chase feature presentations. As a sleeping aid, I always remember that, aloft, I'm rendered completely irresponsible and out of control . . . unreachable . . . in transit . . . neither here, nor there. And I take along a U-pillow and a good supply of sleeping pills, just in case.

When awake, I'd leaf through a pile of guidebooks, and could only think of how much I wouldn't get to see. I'd be missing out on those giant, goat-eating dragon lizards of Komodo, whose tails are lethal weapons and whose saliva is highly toxic. I wouldn't get to see the Asmat, those extraordinary sculptor cannibals of the New Guinea swamps, who ate Michael Rockefeller. I wouldn't get to see the Borneo Dayak, entire tribes living in one giant jungle longhouse, whose pierced earlobes, weighed down with enormous gold and brass rings, extend beneath the shoulders. I'd miss the southern Java coast, where enormous sea turtles lay their oily, leathery eggs on black sand beaches at midnight, while locals serve magic mushroom omelets to gaping tourists. I wouldn't get to experience the 'traditional massage by blind men' of Sulawesi, or see that island's Toraja, who create massive roofs on their houses to imitate the ship from another planet that brought their people to earth, whose children keep bees tied on strings as pets, and who worship the water buffalo. (When I hit Sulawesi on a layover, I couldn't figure out why I was so popular with the locals, until one morning, I looked in the mirror on the way out the door and realized I'd spent the whole trip wearing a Chicago Bulls cap – the bull looking just like their sacred cow.) This whole vacation, I soon decided, would be a terrible disappointment of lost opportunity.

While I read the chronicles of Magellan's own Spice voyage (as transcribed by his secretary, Pigafetta), we finally touched down in Jogjakarta, center of the ancient Java Empire. I drove around, watching silk-robed and coolie-hatted peasants laboring in emerald-green rice fields, backed by sandalwood groves and volcanoes shrouded in their own blue mists. These extraordinary shots popped up again and again, and I could only think that Java is one of the few islands left that still lives up to our South Seas dreams. Since it's got 121 volcanoes (plenty of which are active), I saw smoldering cones everywhere, beautiful and deadly, like a Hollywood special effect about to happen, and could only think: *They aren't dormant enough.*

The right-wing military coup that came to power in 1965's 'Year of Living Dangerously' is still around, coining such political slogans as 'Development, Yes, Politics, No!' Unfortunately, because of nepotism, there's not so much development outside the onetime ruling Suharto family, who've all become billionaires. Even though Indonesia is the fifth largest oil producer, the government became so entangled in monopoly schemes that it financially collapsed in 1997 (a collapse even worse than America's Great Depression), and the International Monetary Fund refused to help unless then President Suharto and his family changed their kickback-loving ways, and left office. One of the things that keeps emerging markets from emerging is when the rulers and their cronies take over vast portions of the economy, stifling competition and scaring off foreign investment, and that's exactly what happened here. The youngest Suharto son, Tommy Putra, owns Indonesia's airline and a monopoly on clove production (the vast majority of Indonesians smoke *kretek*-clove cigarettes), while one of his brothers owns the state's communications industry, and a sister has most of the country's toll roads. Other children own the television and radio networks, petroleum processing, food distribution networks, and prime interests in Bali's major resorts, while Suharto's ex-wife, Tien, was so known for getting her cut of the action that she's commonly referred to as 'Madame Tien-Percent.'

As a Westerner traveling solo, I was constantly running into Indonesian families armed with giant baskets of snacks, samples of which they were quite keen for me to eat. The mama would hand over a mysterious food item, and then the entire clan would gather round to watch me enjoy it. Since for travelers, home cooking in emerging markets is a guaranteed one-way ticket to explosive diarrhea, there I was, looking at this thing, trying to figure out whether or not it's safe and, if not, how do I get out of having to swallow? *Everyone's watching you, Carrie.* At one point, I was given something that looked like a tamale, and it seemed well cooked, so I chawed down, only to have the family become hysterical; I wasn't supposed to eat the outer leaf. Inside was some kind of rubbery, Jell-O–like substance, filled with a very spicy, sugary center made out of nuts . . . the culinary version of Chinese nesting dolls. Frankly, I preferred the wrapper.

My favorite food as a kid was, by far, peanut butter, and here in Indonesia it is served, heated and spiced, as a barbecue dipping sauce. I ordered it everywhere, dipping and slurping and reverting to sloppy boyhood. It was certainly more soothing than the other favorite Indonesian dipping sauce, *trasi* . . . fermented shrimp paste.

All this strange food reminded me of how, today, you can go to a restaurant in Houston and eat barbecued chicken, or you can go to a restaurant in Paris and have chicken Provençale, or you can eat in a hotel bar in Jakarta and have chicken with spicy peanut sauce, and if you make a heroic effort, you can eat local, original cuisine, like the gizzard-paste sandwich that all Britons adore. But how different is any of this (except for the gizzard-paste, which I made up) from what you might eat at a restaurant in your own city? If you *really* travel to the back-of-beyond, however, meals can be filled with mystery and surprise. In the middle of nowhere, dinner will be served, and your host will tell you, 'It's chicken!' but you know for certain that this can't be, since you haven't seen a chicken for days and days. So you keep asking what it is, and they just keep saying, 'It's chicken!' and you keep chewing, trying to figure it out (iguana? tree kangaroo? sloth?), but it tastes okay, so you just keep eating . . .

Everywhere in the East Indies I was asked: Are you married? Where is your wife? How many children? Since everyone in Indonesia over the age of fifteen is married, I was considered a circus freak when I said no, and trying to explain being a middle-aged single person quickly became onerous. The enormous temptation was just to tell a white lie and change the topic, but once I'd start down that slope, where would I brake? Soon enough, my first two wives would be killed in a hurricane, and now I lived with spouse number three, eight children and seventeen grandchildren, on a mountaintop in Iowa.

Besides the details of my wife and kids, no one in Indonesia wanted to know anything about life in the U.S. After all, they've seen *Rambo* and *Animal House* on video. What they wanted to know is, where else had I been in the East Indies, and how many reasons could I think of why their island is the best of them all? Soon enough, I was learning how to say things like 'New Guinea is so much nicer than Bali, since you don't have all those noisy, dirty buses and airplanes,' and sounding completely sincere while doing it. Outside of these questions, the Indonesians didn't seem to want to have much to do with me, or with any other traveler for that matter. They were always polite, but distant, and the longer I was in the country, the lonelier I felt.

Like most developing nations, the local Java homeowners have very original ideas when it comes to decorating, and I quickly started thinking that houses with traffic-sign-yellow walls, peacock-green windows, harlot-red doors and neon-blue roofs were completely humdrum. The center of Jogjakarta is a copyright-free zone where the original, more ratlike Mickey Mouse sells an immense variety of products and services, including Ceriping Pedas Bintang Jul Fried Taro Chips. There were bird cages everywhere, since birding, bird-watching, bird-raising and bird-tracking are easily Java's most popular hobbies. Indonesia has fifteen hundred avian species, and in the squabbling markets, you can buy every single one of them. From the Jogja bird market, I was forced to take the ultimate form of emerging market transportation, thrown into a terror so overwhelming it shook me to my very core. I rode a pedicab.

Remember when you were a child, and your big brother made you sit on his bike's handlebars, and the bar was incredibly uncomfortable and there you were, completely unprotected, thrust forward in this wobbly perch, about to die? This is the pedicab sensation, except that instead of riding on a quiet suburban driveway, I was in the middle of Third World urban traffic. As the poor, aged pedicab operator agonizingly rolled my fat butt across town, I was up front and fully exposed to furtive, hungry dogs, thundering oxcarts, aggressive, motorcycle-riding businesswomen, slow-moving teak snack carts, and herds of desperate animals being driven to slaughter . . . and so learned the full meaning of 'adventure travel.'

THE SACRED SPOCK EARS

Every Indonesian island has its own unique culture, and Java is the pot where they all meet and melt. A local Dutch pastor said, 'One hears that Java is 90 percent Muslim, which is a most deceptive truth. For many, religion is a mixture of animism, Hinduism, Buddism and Islam, which does not please the Muslim extremists, who are trying to make Indonesia the Muslim state it has never been.' If you believe in anything whatsoever, it's convenient to believe it in Java. Many villages in this Islamic nation announce their main thoroughfares with waving Buddhist flags and banners, while here and there on the roadside lie carefully arrayed offerings of fruits and flowers, Hindu memorials to the sites of fatal accidents, with certain highways being so extensively decorated that my first thought was: How pretty! After seeing dozens and dozens of these offerings, though, I understood that I, too, could end up memorialized, and those thoughts of *How pretty!* changed to *We're all going to die* . . .

I had an incredible piece of luck hitting Java in the dry season and during the full moon, since I got to see an extraordinary four-night, sixteen-hour performance of the Ramayana, the original Hindu religious drama, staged against thousand-year-old Hindu towers, the ruins lit by ghostly floodlamps. This epic starred young girls dressed as herds of deer and bunnies, boys dressed as apes, and senior citizens portraying devils, all dancing to a percussive gamelan orchestra on stage, while tiny bats feasted on the insects drawn to the powerful theater lights overhead – and the obnoxious audience of Austrians and Australians documented every bit of this sacred performance with flashing Instamatics.

Besides Bali, Jogja is the Spice Islands' key destination for culture vultures. Every night, beautiful, trance-inducing gamelan orchestras were gonging and trilling, a set of very big, very orchestrated wind chimes. Even though they're percussive, gamelans are remarkably soothing, sounding as they do like the haphazard tinkle of the mobiles that hang above every infant's crib. Jogja has armies of *wayang kulit* shadow puppet shows that can last up to twelve hours where, like opera, everyone in the audience is assumed to already know the plot and, like opera, if you don't know it, the show's about eleven hours and forty-five minutes too long.

A host of these performances takes place at the *kraton*, the sultan's ancestral home, a palace that beautifully displays the Javan culture melt: Islamic tilework, Chinese roofs, sacred swimming pools, skinny black chickens, cactus gardens festooned with hollowed-out eggs, dancing dragons, collections of *kris* (wavy-bladed daggers) and lots of intricate paintings of animals with their tongues sticking out. This is still the home of the current Jogja ruler, Sri Sultan Hamengku Buwono IX, who undoubtedly has a great job since, once a year, there's a big ceremony where all the local bigwigs have to come and kiss his knees. Every day, the servants still take the carved leather *wayang kulit* shadow puppets out to air, and talk with them as though they're alive.

Like in many Buddhist countries, Javans believe giant earlobes to be a sign of advanced spirituality. I browsed through the *kraton*'s various royal photo albums to see slight, regal figures looking just like *The King and I* but with immense, protuberant Spock ears, and could only guess at what implements of torture were used to achieve this effect. Were they squeezed into some kind of mold, like the bound lilyfeet of China? Were they pressed with boards, like the head-flattening techniques of the Maya? I couldn't get anyone to understand what I was asking, as they seemed to sincerely believe that the royals were all born with such imposing lobes.

A VISIT WITH THE WILD MAN OF BORNEO

A van, two planes and a cab later, I was in the river harbor town of Kumai, Kalimantan Tenagh, Borneo, the heart of Bugi country. Actually, Indonesians don't say 'the heart' of anything, since the heart isn't considered such a big deal. Instead, they say 'the liver' – the liver of Bugi country. From the fourteenth to the nineteenth centuries, the Bugis were the most feared pirates in the world, the de facto rulers of the Java Sea, traveling without sextants or compasses in their giant, seven-sailed, Viking-like *prahu* across all of Asia, from the Philippines to India. They were so frightening and so barbarous, in fact, that they're the source of our word 'bogeyman.' The *prahu* are still there, but the Bugi descendants, found throughout southern Borneo and Sulawesi, are now ultraconservative Muslims. It's a generational saga just like in the West, where if you're a wealthy conservative pillar of society, your daughter's bound to turn out to be just like Courtney Love.

Is there any place in the world more exotic than Borneo, a land where the birds and the deer bark, where fish can climb trees and catch insects with their spit? Besides elephant, rhinoceros, clouded leopard, orangutan and legions of extremely odd monkeys, this is also home to two remarkably strange and stinky plants. One is the biggest flower in the world, the rafflesia, a gooey, pink-orange bloom that looks as parasitic as it turns out to be, with an odor that inspired its local name: *the corpse flower*. The other is durian, or jackfruit, with a taste that's considerably addicting (something like homemade custard pie), and a smell so vile it's against Indonesian federal law to eat one on a public bus.

The town of Kumai was where all the permission slips for my entry into Borneo and travel to Tanjung Puting Nature Preserve (the orangutan sanctuary) had to be processed by a bureaucracy inherited from Indonesia's onetime Dutch rulers, something of a cousin to India's Raj. The hours dragged by, so I wandered out along the dusty main road, seeing the town's largest building, a whitewashed, tin-embossed, onion-domed mosque, as well as the thatch-covered houses stilted over the water, the burnished teak *prahu*, the aged storekeeper whose smile revealed one remaining tooth, an entire wall decorated in the dripping tongue of the Rolling Stones, and a young girl tending the traditional Borneo mixed flock of black chickens and baby pigs. Kumai was great evidence of the standard Third World rain forest clearing technique: you burn away everything, and then try to plant what you want instead. Jungle soil is so thin and weak, however, that once the original ecosystem is undone, the only thing that grows is a raw, ugly grassland, like something out of the Oklahoma dust bowl. This is then decorated with random ginger plants and, for extra-special locations, a dead tree trunk held in place with guide wires and thatched to provide the kind of shade that can't be grown anymore.

Little by little, word spread through Kumai, and I started noticing growing numbers of people standing furtively in doorways and under awnings, staring at the big white stranger in the sacred water buffalo cap. Suddenly I heard a gruff scream, and turned around to find a young man, just past teendom, shaking his hands at me and yelling. He wasn't angry, he was just confronting, being the aggressor, demanding to know something. Of course, I didn't understand a single word he said, but I'd learned a little Bahasa on that twenty-hour plane ride, and I knew a few things from getting around, namely, that a little bit of humility, politeness, formality and language will take you far.

I heard some guffawing, and turned to see a group of kids in the road, coming from the opposite direction, and moving closer. They were curious, frightened and disdainful, all at the same time, not a good omen. The screamer was moving in as well, and it didn't look pretty. I backed a bit off the road, took a bow, held out my hands to everyone watching, and sang (somewhat in the style of Harry Belafonte's 'Day-O'), '*Selamat da-a-a-a-y, Kumai!*'

This is the very formal way of saying hello in Bahasa Indonesian; it essentially means 'all the best.' Both the screamer and the kids stopped dead in their tracks, and I sang it out again. This time, a goat-herding girl sang it back; the kids laughed and sang it themselves; and I did it again. Now, other watchers joined in, and we sang back and forth. The screamer slunk off, while the kids took my hands and elbows – four of them to each side – and dragged me off for a tour. We dropped by the weavers to see the makings of walls and roofs, the town's prefecture with its fake stuffed orangutan (a sign explained that he was your friend), and a small pen containing two award-winning roosters, before making it back to the nature conservation office, where my guide was waiting with all the forms processed and ready to go.

A SOFT HOOT AND THE SOUND OF SMACKING LIPS

The guide turned out to be Harry, twenty-two years old, married with three kids, a Muslim Bugi descendant and, just like every other Bugi I'd meet, he looked like he'd been dry-cleaned. Here we were, inches from the equator, in the middle of one of the world's deepest jungles, in astonishing heat and humidity, and I never saw a Bugi who sweated, or had a single hair out of place, or had any body odor whatsoever; they were like Muslim Ozzies and Harriets. This kind of thing isn't so unusual in developing countries, and something worth remembering when deciding if a conversation about politics, religion or sex would be a good idea (it wouldn't). I'd later get myself in trouble with Harry by joking that one of the orangutans found him attractive . . . and it turned out he didn't get mad that this joke meant he might have sex with an animal; he was mad because the animal I joked about was a male.

As the captain and two boat boys ran the ship, Harry and I sat on the roof, talking and looking, eating cookies and drinking java; I was the only passenger. The Sekonyer River was the color of rich black tea, and the shoreline, a heath and peat swamp, was densely packed in low-lying spiny palms, like cactus, completely impenetrable and as hostile-looking as a jungle can get. There was a piercing bark, and I assumed it was some kind of wild dog, but then it struck again, overhead, and Harry and I both looked up at the same time to see a pair of hornbills, big as pterodactyls (and looking very much like them), arching across the sky, racing against storm clouds that had suddenly drawn up and were hurrying straight toward us.

The hostile landscape was now giving way to larger and larger groves of big green mangroves, and in the dying light of dusk could be seen small, humanlike shadows scurrying through the branches – some kind of monkey. And then it was only seconds later that we heard a soft hoot and the sound of smacking lips, turned a bend in the river and saw a blur of rusted cranberry – a nursing orangutan, languidly watching us with her big black Walter Keane eyes, while hanging upside down from a tree limb and eating a small green banana.

The storm never arrived; we tied up at Rimba Lodge; I was led to my bungalow (whose walls were decorated with pictures of the local fauna torn out of magazines), unpacked, and went to the restaurant for a drink before dinner, and to meet the other guests. Here and there, the staff would dash off on errands, ferrying laundry, changing a baby, lugging boxes of food and supplies. I sat at one of the veranda tables but saw no one, save other Bugis, who went quietly about their business. I was brought a menu, placed an order, and had a delicious mulligatawny-styled soup followed by grilled prawns with a peanut sauce. Still no other guests. A few bobtailed cats wandered by, and I thought they might be bred this way (like Manxes), so I asked Harry's wife, Irina, if they were special cats, and she said, 'Yes! They are very special!' The cats yowled for my dinner leftovers while, off in the distance, birds called, monkeys hooted, insects buzzed, and a pigeon cried out its lonely, breathless 'Ha! . . . Ha! . . . Ha!'

Finally, I turned to one of the busy stewards and asked him to tell me who else was staying in the hotel. He told me there was nobody else, that for my entire stay, I'd be the only guest, and if there was anything I wanted, just ask. If everyone seemed busy, he explained, it was because the day after I left, the Rimba would be the site of a major scientific conference with various heads of state attending, and they were all making sure that nothing would go awry. That's when it hit me why this experience seemed so odd. Everyone was so busy getting ready for the conference and completely ignoring me that it felt like I was some kind of intruder, who'd wandered by accident into a Bugi village – a village built in the shape of a giant jungle lodge. This lack of contact makes me feel completely alone and isolated, and I started feeling really, really sorry for myself. I then remembered that part of the reason I loved these kinds of trips was that you went to the middle of nowhere, and were put into situations, and had to figure out how to make do. So I made do. I'd always wanted to travel into the *Heart of Darkness*, to be a *Stranger in a Strange Land*, and now I was going to get just what I paid for . . .

The next morning I got up before dawn to get away from the scurrying, noisy hotel staff and go canoeing off by myself, floating silently, listening to the jungle on a blackwater river flowing to the Java Sea. There was still quite a fog over the water, and I paddled away upstream, finally cut off from any humans nearby . . . and the noise was *deafening*. The cicadas were like miniature chainsaws; there were at least thirty different bird screams, chatterings, calls and songs (with one, the bulbul, making a 'Whoop-de-doo! Whoop-de-doo!'). Reptiles were hissing, gibbons were calling out with a cello hoot, and something was making a deep, rough growl that I couldn't recognize and certainly didn't want to investigate. It was an animal traffic jam, a contest to aurally dominate the world, and it was clear as day that early humans, hearing all this, created musical instruments just so they could compete.

SHE THINKS THAT EVERYONE IS AGAINST HER

After breakfast, the captain, Harry, the boat boys and I made off for Camp Leakey, named for the anthropological Louis who'd started Dian Fossey on gorillas and Jane Goodall on chimps. This camp was created by Biruté Galdikas, the third and least known of the three, who'd been in Borneo studying the orangutan for over twenty-five years. It hasn't been easy. Her first husband, a photographer, got fed up with bush living, fell in love with the nanny, and ran off with her back to the U.S. When Biruté's toddler son started acting more apelike than human, it was thought best for him to go live with them as well (especially after he'd started regularly biting the scientists). Between the orphan orangs she found and the locals bringing her abandoned pets, Biruté soon had a houseful of apes, and as enjoyable in a 'barrel of' kind of way as that may sound, caring for big, willful monkeys is in fact something like baby-sitting a family of extremely muscular, extremely stubborn three-year-olds. Besides the massive damage they inflicted on her clothes, furniture and equipment, the orangs loved to suck the ink out of Biruté's pens, and pop their heads through the thatch roofs of her buildings to see if it'd stopped raining.

One rescued ape even attacked one of the camp's workers, as Biruté described in her memoirs: 'I began to realize that Gundul did not intend to harm the cook, but had something else in mind. The cook stopped struggling. "It's all right," she murmured. She lay back in my arms, with Gundul on top of her. Gundul was very calm and deliberate. He raped the cook. As he moved rhythmically back and forth, his eyes rolled upward to the heavens. Gundul was behaving like a normal subadult orangutan male. Nevertheless, his behavior was worrisome.'

Just as Dian Fossey worked all her life against African poachers, Galdikas has battled constantly with both poachers selling baby orangs in Taiwan, and with the Indonesian federal government in Jakarta, where officials overseeing her domain are perhaps being influenced by logging concerns who want commercial entry into the preserve. Indonesian forestry official Abdul Muin said that, 'Her assistants, the ones who do her "research," whatever that is, are not scientists. Sometimes we suspect she is not doing much of anything except making money from tourism. Mrs. Biruté lives in a world of her own.'

The crusades she's taken on to save the orangs' home have frequently left her own scientific research on hold, putting her at odds with both her professional colleagues and with the wildlife charities that are her major source of funding. Earthwatch, an organization that supports natural history research by sending students to study in the field, has dropped Camp Leakey, meaning a loss to Galdikas of around $75,000 a year. One Earthwatch official, Andrew Mitchell, explained that, 'Like Dian Fossey, Galdikas is becoming detached from reality. She thinks that everyone is against her. She has failed to give us adequate reports and accounts. We have asked her for a new proposal so that we can consider funding her again, but she has not produced one. My heart goes out to her. She began as a scientist, but she has become more and more attached to the animals and more involved in conflicts with local people and the authorities. I fear that she is shipwrecking herself.'

Galdikas's posture makes sense, however, in light of recent history. Homesteading Indonesians (and industries) have been burning down the Sumatran, New Guinean and Bornean forests in order to free more land for cattle and crops. Their smoke has gotten so serious that, for months at a time, the islands' schoolchildren have trouble seeing their blackboards. In both Borneo and Sumatra, the last remaining homes of the orangutan, droves of the animals are fleeing their forests and running into farmlands and villages, where they are killed as a crop pest, captured to be kept as pets, or sold into the black market. Some Indonesian women are so taken with their baby orangutan pets that they breast-feed them.

Camp Leakey was very unusual in that Galdikas both studied orangs in the wild, and tried to reintroduce to the jungle those who'd been smuggled out as pets. It was immediately clear, however, that once orangs had a taste of living with humans in a house, they were quite uninterested in foraging for themselves out in the cold, cruel rain forest. Visitors to Camp Leakey got to interact with orangs who were completely tame, as well as flee for their lives from those who were the true Wild Men of Borneo.

SWEET!

As we motored to the campsite through the lands of Tanjung Puting, the trees grew larger and larger until they almost touched each other in arches over the river, and in this dense forest canopy that allowed only brief spots of sunlight to reach the ground, the branches became alive with monkeys. Proboscis monkeys. Slightly larger than the spiders or capuchins of organ-grinding fame, proboscis have, by far, the most ridiculous noses in the animal kingdom, long, Jimmy Durante zucchini beaks that are so peculiar they were once the inspiration for a primitive tribe in *Popeye*. As the boat passes underneath, the monkeys leap back and forth in the trees, whole families scurrying after each other in frantic bursts of feeding and fleeing, hundreds of animals chattering and complaining about our rude trespass, warning each other, grooming each other, and sometimes flinging themselves from branch to branch just for the hell of it. There I was, lying on the roof of my boat, drinking rich coffee and eating delicious cookies, watching thousands of big monkeys jump over my head. *Nirvana*.

In the jungle, it was as hot and steamy as a Chinatown kitchen, but rolling on the river was cool, and soothing. Families paddled by, and we all waved. At the shoreline, crocodiles, hearing the boat's engine, would scurry to the water and dive.

We reached the Leakey docks, tied up the boat, and the minute I got ashore an infant orangutan bounded out of the forest, wrapped itself around my calf, and looked straight up into my face with big baby eyes that said one thing: 'Love me!' Two of the researchers pulled him off my leg, worried I could give him some kind of disease (orangs and humans are 97 percent genetically the same – closer, in fact, than breeds of dogs). Apes are everywhere here, ranging in color from rust red to circus orange, males and females and babies, just crowds of them. I was hoping it would rain, so I could see in person what I'd been entranced by in books – visions of orangs using giant banana leaves as umbrellas – but no such luck. We walked to the central office while staying clear of the hungry nursing female going through the garbage. She found something, tasted it, dropped it to the ground in disgust, and went into the kitchen, where she took the ladle that was hanging on the wall and helped herself to a drink from the water tank. After giving her baby a small sip, she poured the not-drunk water back into the tank, hung the ladle back where it belonged, and went off to sit in the shade and catch all the action. Another orang living here watched the volunteers doing their laundry, and then she joined in, scrubbing wet clothes with soap on the pier, and rinsing them out in a big pink bucket.

It was time for lunch, a feeding for both the tamed creatures and whatever wild men might show up, so I and two visiting animal behaviorists and the camp workers walked over to the feeding station, a platform high enough for the wild orangs to feel comfortable but low enough to make loading the fruit not an overwhelming chore. The garbage-sniffing female turned out to be Frances, who could speak sign language and who walked with us to the site, my hand in hers, the baby holding on to the hairs on the top of her head. When I asked in sign language, 'Who are you?' Frances replied, 'Sweet!' One of the workers obviously had his eye on a future in tourism since as we walked, he gave me an incredibly detailed account of every living thing along the way, from the razor-sharp palms to the unchoppable ironwood to the erect, shoestring leeches waiting for just the right warm-blooded creature to pass by. When you spend your whole life in one particular part of the forest, you get to know every single detail about every little thing on your trail. They are, after all, the neighbors.

At the feeding, we held tightly on to our bags and cameras, since the apes would try to steal them. At first nothing happened, then slowly, inexorably, there was a growing rumble, which turned into an immense amount of thrashing, as the various Wild Men swang through the trees, making their way to the station. From time to time we could hear 'the long call,' a series of grumbles, moans, burbles and burps that ends in a bellow. 'The first time I heard it,' Biruté said, 'I thought I was in the path of a drunken elephant.' It's no wonder they're near extinction; you can hear orangs coming from miles away, the subway trains of Borneo.

The behaviorists tried to lure Frances away from me, to no avail; we'd found each other, and it was destiny. As the infant crawled across her shoulders, idly nursing, Frances used one hand to play with a burlap bag, and the other to keep a careful hold of my own, while her feet, which were just like two additional hands, peeled and sorted her cache of bananas. Up in the trees, there was a big wet smacking noise, the orang method of trying to scare off anything they considered a threat. It was as scary as watching a baby trying to make its first kiss, but we stepped back to let this wild female feel comfortable enough to descend to the platform, where she quickly loaded up with as many bananas as she could carry and stole off into the brush.

There was a giant crash; leaves cracked and branches snapped behind us, and all the feeding orangs took off into the trees. The camp workers suddenly grabbed everyone's arms, and pulled us to the sidelines to make way for an astonishing beast, about 250 pounds, ambling slowly, majestically, over to the platform. While the others had been frantic, nervous as alleycats, this one, a giant, calmly inspected various items of fruit, found one that appeared acceptable, and quietly began to eat, looking here and there, standing on his two hind legs between a pair of trees and posing in splendor, his carmine erectile hairs making him look even bigger than he already was.

Baltsai was the Big Kahuna, the Wild Man ruler of this particular Borneo domain, and boy did he know it, with a demeanor far more regal and commanding than any mere human could ever hope to have. After making sure that all other living creatures were keeping their distance in proper homage, Baltsai calmly ate his fill, watching us watch him, us with admiration, him with imperial disdain. Finished with lunch, he finally lurched off, most likely to climb his favorite nesting tree and take a snooze.

QUIETLY RABID

I thought I could use a little snooze myself, and so went back to the boat. The jungle was unbearably hot, and being out on the shaded river cooled the air a bit. I got my lunch (water buffalo in pepper sauce; peanuts and sticky rice cooked in banana leaf; clove biscuit) and sat on the deck facing the pier, where another creature had found a shady place to eat his own meal. Kosasi was around 175 pounds, and the second largest male orang there after Baltsai. He'd gotten a bar of soap, and was sitting on the pilings under the pier, lathering up his arm and licking the froth. His mouth, dripping with foam, made him look quietly rabid. I assumed he'd stolen it, since it was undoubtedly considered bad form to feed bars of soap to the endangered species.

So caught up in his lather that he ignored me completely, Kosasi and I both went on eating, and when I finished, I laid back and started drowsing in that jungle heat, feeling the rock of the boat, and listening to a gibbon's plaintive hoot. I opened my eyes; Kosasi was still completely ignoring me, busily lathering up and licking . . . but he'd come closer.

I paid no mind, closed my eyes again, rested quietly, but awoke with a start to a sudden *thwack*! on the deck.

I looked up to see Kosasi standing directly in front of me, mere inches away. He gave me a look of *don't even think of trying anything*, and strode forcefully into the cabin. There was a scream and the crashing of dishes as the poor, terrified boat boy lost his lunch. Kosasi reappeared, clutching the ship's garbage bag. He gave me another 'don't try anything' look, and loped off the deck and into the forest. As he ran away with his treasure, he looked back every so often to make sure no one was taking up the chase, his eyes having an unbelievably humanlike appearance of guilt, like a naughty child.

I was stunned, not from fear, but from the very deepest sense of awe. Never before in all my travels had I felt so removed from civilization, so far, far away from our society and our culture, alive and well in another world altogether. It was a world where humans and apes lived side by side, as much neighbors as anyone in the

American suburbs; a world where none of the animals seemed really fearful of people; where everywhere you looked, there was an explosion of life. I'd entered into a kind of Eden, and I was thrilled to imagine that I'd finally reached the end of the line, the other side of the planet, the ultimate escape from our common, ordinary, humdrum day-to-day life.

As events would prove, these thoughts were hopelessly naive.

TEACHING THE CANNIBALS TO DANCE

'The landscape had a gaunt expression, but I could not deny that it had readable features and that I existed in it. This was a discovery – the look of it. I thought: *Nowhere is a place.*'

—PAUL THEROUX

THE TWO-FACED EDEN

You'd think from looking at a map of Indonesia that getting from Borneo to Bali would be a snap, since they're right next to each other, but it turns out that no one in their right mind travels from Borneo to Bali (except me), and the transit turned out to be an endless stream of planes and cars and boats, of spending hours waiting idly for the next vehicle, all accompanied by disturbing meals. Merpati, the local airline, serves lots of things that are wrapped up inside of something else and, like that Java tamale, I could never tell if you were supposed to eat the wrapper or not. Waiting for a boat, a young boy came over and handed me a box, a napkin and a fork. Inside the box was a dish that combined a rice or couscous-type grain with a pork- or chickenlike meat, but it wasn't rice, couscous, pork or chicken, and I could never find out what, exactly, it was. So I ate it.

I finally arrived in Bali and unpacked to find that someone, some-where, had gone through my luggage. They'd ripped the coiled and ready-to-strike cobra I'd gotten in Java out of its padded bag, and had just left it loose in my main duffel. Now it was crushed, its sawdust stuffing scattered through everything. After spending hours cleaning up this mess (and grieving over my beautiful, destroyed serpent), I then realized my camera battery casing was broken, and had to spend hours fixing it with eyeglass-repair screwdrivers. It was one of those 'Why me, Lord?' days, valuable time wasted to take care of idiotic trouble, and I flipped on the TV for company. On CNN, there was a special about an American doctor working in the Amazon jungle, a rail-thin Scandinavian who looked like she just stepped out of an especially angst-ridden Ingmar Bergman epic. There I was, on the other side of the world, watching a TV special on Linnea, the Amazon doctor I'd met in the middle of nowhere.

A tiny spot in the middle of the Java Sea, the island of Bali turned out to be exactly as physically gorgeous and as filled with magic as all our paradise island dreams. In fact, if my sole travel criteria were gasping beauty, dizzying peaks of culture and luxurious wallows of comfort, this would be my number one spot in all the world. Driving around, I soon realized that no *Travel & Leisure* photo spread could ever remotely capture its breathtaking views of piercing-green rice paddies, lush as any golf course, terracing down the mountainsides, irrigated by centuries-old systems of gurgling pools and cascading streams. Town after town went by, each with its own fields of rice, peanut, onion and cabbage, each with its own enclave of majestically feminine rococo Hindu temples, red-clay brick towers ornamented in gods and demons, sprouting thatch crowns and ceremonial silk umbrellas (Bali has more temples than houses). Everywhere are the most beautiful people in the world, the Balinese, so handsome and so lithe they seem descended from silk and orchids. I watched all these extraordinary men and women, most wearing nothing but a sheet, while a temperate breeze lapped against my skin, and felt completely bovine and inadequate.

In the shadow of Bali's sacred volcano, 'The Belly Button of the World,' I watched a dozen women in lurid silk batiks arrive on motor scooters while balancing, on their heads, three-foot-high pyramids of green apples, black plums, white eggs, pink cookies and woven green palm fronds, topped with arching batons of fat yellow flowers. They didn't spill a drop. Behind us rose the black-thatch roofs and see-through struts of the mother temple, whose shape inspires many to believe it was once the locus of a volcano cult. The entryway was festooned in topaz, aquamarine and garnet silk umbrellas, and marked with twenty-foot-high carmine, saffron and bleach-tinted banners, while all the temple's idols (grinning gods and tongue-shooting spirits carved from soft volcanic stone) were dressed up in skirts and turbans. To one side, a gamelan orchestra hammered out its water melodies for three hours, with not one musician using sheet music, since they'd already memorized every note by heart. In front of them raged a centuries-old religious battle, the fight of the Barong (a magical clown-lion played by two men, just like in vaudeville) against Rangda, Lord of Chaos, the widow-witch queen of evil spirits who wears a necklace made from human intestines. The Barong's triumph assured, 150 men appeared to chant themselves into a trance, screaming 'Chaka Chaka Chaka Chaka!' while converging on a white-faced monkey god.

Come to Bali, and you are guaranteed to see all this, and to believe it one of the most beautiful spots on the face of the earth. You're also guaranteed to see that the island is also cursed by its beauty, overrun with drunken and obnoxious German and Australian college kids, pounding through Kuta beach like an *MTV: Spring Break!* horror, careening through quiet, pleasant hill towns on rented motor bikes that they immediately plow into banana trees. Just like in the Hindu neighborhoods of Java, the Balinese leave offerings of plaited palm leaves, fruit and flowers at the site of accidents to placate the evil spirits drawn by the spill of blood, and their drunk-and-driving tourists have turned these offerings into a big business. I saw them everywhere on the sides of the roads, like colorful, delicate headstones.

I was solo, and I had spent weeks not seeing another English-speaking Anglo, and it was heaven, yet it also made me feel really lonely. Bali was popping with Huns and Ozzies, so I tried being sociable, asking them about Western news and travel tips. But it turned out that Bali doesn't attract the normal kind of travelers you meet overseas; instead, it's the preferred spot for trailer park lowlifes, and being there inspires them to act as badly as possible, similar to what happens when a kind, decent Sikh moves to New York City, becomes a taxi driver, and turns into a homicidal maniac. I was consistently snubbed, rebuffed or ignored by these obnoxious descendants of British axe-murderers and Nazi oven-builders, the kind of tourists who inspire the Balinese to carve and paint thousands of identical wooden dancing frogs, to open shops offering *Antiques Made to Order*, and to come up and tap you on the elbows to ask, 'Massage? Where you from? You like painting? You have wife? You wife like sculpture? You want taxi? Clean your nails? Braid your hair? Look my store for free!'

I drove around, amazed by all the beauty, but I also couldn't help but wonder: *Where did all these damn carvings come from?* Originally, the Balinese had nothing to sell: no timber, no oil, no gemstones, no jute, no spices. It only had a local Gauguin – the deeply untalented German painter Walter Spies – who got the island on the Anglo vacation circuit and taught the locals to paint and carve things that chain-smoking Sydney couch potatoes and alcoholic Frankfurtan *hausfraus* might buy, engineering an elaborate new bric-a-brac industry that flooded the island with dancing frogs, banjo-playing fish, praying hands and thrice-life-sized tabby cats, all carved from *real, genuine monkeypod*!

At a midnight *legong* dance performance, where divine nymphs (all preteen) take the movements of daily life and translate them into ritual beauty for the pleasures of the gods, one Antipodean decided that the delicate lighting wasn't good enough for her camcorder, and so turned on a floodlamp, the kind the FBI uses when they hunt mass murderers in the woods. This pretty much ruined the show for everyone else, but her fellow Krauts and Kiwis seemed to think she was perfectly justified, while the Balinese performers kept singing and dancing and playing their gamelans, even though they must've been rendered stone-cold blind. The more I saw of Bali, the more I realized that to them, she was just another tourist, and worth about as much thought as any whining mosquito.

Look closely enough and you'll see that, no matter how many hordes descend on this minuscule island, the Balinese, at all odds, maintain their culture, ignoring whatever horrors the foreigners can dish out. They are, after all, Hindu, and just like in India, Bali's spiritual mother, the culture here takes in foreign invaders, absorbs what it likes, and ignores the rest. Tim Ruth, in *Dreaming of Bali*, rhetorically asked the question:

> What if some Balinese tourists came to the United States? What if they go out to Nebraska and pay a guide thirty dollars apiece to lead them into the cornfields so they could take pictures of a farmer stooping over in the sun? What if busloads of noisy Indonesians kept coming into our neighborhoods and asking, 'Do you know where we can find a good Methodist burial?' . . . Wouldn't that change who we were, and how we saw ourselves?

This is a compelling idea, and might easily apply to any number of Third World countries desperate for tourist business, but it doesn't seem at all apt here. One man, for instance, said, 'My son already knows Lego, but he doesn't make helicopters or cars. He makes temple gates and funeral towers.' There may be lines of tourists mobbing up the flying-fox temple (a cloth-dressed shrine built inside a cave of thousands of squirming, squeaking bats, and covered with their droppings), or at the water temple (a magnificent series of pools and fountains, of towering cascades and brightly painted animals gushing water from their mouths), but regardless of how many Instamatics and Handycams take in those views, the Balinese still worship at them all, and can do so happily while packs of fat Rhinelanders screech in the background. Perhaps the crucial issue that Mr Ruth forgot to take into account with his theory is that the Balinese think they are far better than us, and of course they're absolutely right. A translation at the mother temple told me their story of creation:

> One day, when the world had been born and everything was ready for the arrival of human beings, Brahma and Batara Guru (who were one and the same person) decided to have a contest. They made figures out of clay, and baked them in an oven, to create humans. The first batch was underdone, and came out a pasty, unhealthy white. The second batch was burnt,

coming out black and fried. But the third batch was just right, a beautiful golden brown – the Balinese.

In Bali, we visitors are nothing more than background noise. The key tourist spots of Sanur, Kuta and Nusa Dua are, after all, strung along the island's southern tip, which to the Balinese is the most tainted, spiritually impure location of them all. In the hill town of Ubud, I'd look out my huge, brick, two-story marble-paved bungalow at dawn, to find my picturesque view of a burbling stream filled with stark-naked locals taking a bath. Like every other Balinese getting on with their life, these bathers completely ignored me. With tourist money, Bali can afford to have bigger gamelans, better dancing costumes, and performers making a living. How much of their culture could be maintained if the only ones paying for it were the Balinese themselves?

One primary example (if you're lucky enough to see it) is the island's all-time biggest celebration. Like the Hindu of Veranasi, Balinese believe that the dead automatically go to heaven, so even though the survivors will miss you, your funeral is a *fête* of great celebration, a party to end all parties. When you die, your surviving spouse will bury you, and then spend six to twelve months saving up enough money to give you a proper *adios*, which in Bali means a Brobdingnagian feast for the entire village. At that time, you're dug up, wrapped in white silk, and put into a coffin, which becomes the centerpiece of a parade of yellow-fringed umbrellas, woven frond sculptures, a portable gamelan orchestra, and enough food to satisfy the entire island's population of German and Australian alcoholics. In the parade, your eldest son rides your coffin like a bucking bronco all the way from your home to the cremation site.

While your corpse goes up in flames, the family appears, all dressed in black silk lace, with pyramids of fruit and rice and roast chickens and ducklings and pigs and turtles spread out for display (just as the ancient Egyptians hated the desert that surrounded them, so the Balinese sincerely think the ocean is Hades, and much of their religious symbolism, like those pyramids, refers back to their mountain volcanoes, the home of the gods). Your best male friends then arrive with elaborately woven, bell-shaped baskets carrying big, aggressive roosters with steel blades sewn onto their feet, ready for a cockfight . . . which is over in seconds. One winner explained: 'If good karma, they win. If bad karma, chicken curry.'

When I saw this entire ceremony in the flesh – the gamelan orchestra, the elaborate hand-dancing of the virgin women, the pyramid offerings of fruit and elaborate weavings of palm frond, the priests offering tea kettles of sacred water, the eldest son riding that parade coffin . . . all the guidebook explanations fall by the wayside and I was left with one question: 'What the hell is going on here, where did it come from, and what does it mean?' Like the Tibetans did with Tantric Buddhism, the Balinese have taken Hinduism and made it completely their own, but there are huge gaps in our knowledge of their culture. Much of this is because archaeology is a science of stones and bones, but the ancient island cultures wrote their stories on wood, palm leaf and bark paper, all long since vanished. The Balinese themselves claim not to remember the source of most of their rituals . . . or perhaps this is where they draw the line as far as foreigners are concerned. Today, a cremation is such a big deal that it is always accompanied by hordes of tourists filming every move . . . while the Balinese ignore them all.

Even with its curse as *a place so magical everyone has to go there*, however, Bali is insanely gorgeous, and once I learned how to escape the madding crowd, I found paradise in every inch. In the mornings, I'd watch farmer boys leading troops of brown ducks out to the rice paddies, since after flooding, the fields are alive with insects, and the Balinese use this opportunity to fatten up their flocks. I'd thumb through ancient books made from palm leaves, with ink drawings of monsters who live at the bottom of the seas, and a fantastical script as elegant as the people themselves. I'd find incredible artists still creating fantastic, original work, and shopped so much that, for the first time, U.S. customs made me unpack the box I was bringing home, since it was big enough to carry your grandmother. I'd find a performance far from the oafs and wonder at the music, since metallophones, the centerpiece of the gamelan orchestra, were discovered in prehistoric sites, their bronze bars and bamboo tube amps almost exactly the same as ones made yesterday. There, in a temple entryway bordered with lotus ponds and sacred groves of nutmeg trees, I'd listen to melodies that seemed to leisurely go nowhere, but when I gave the notes my complete attention, they took me straight into a trance. It was music to dream by; the perfect accompaniment to this Valhalla.

Where Bali takes serious revenge on their obstreperous tourists is just outside the hill town of Ubud, in a spot called the Sacred Monkey Forest. You enter by walking past any number of signs in many languages saying, *Don't Feed the Monkeys!* and *Feeding the Monkeys Is Dangerous!* until you get inside the forest itself, where just as many homemade stands are selling plasticene bags of groundnuts. At the center, there is an open concrete square filled with sober college kids who've had enough of the beach, and who are trying to fairly divvy out their snacks . . . but who instead find themselves set upon by hordes of big, ravenous, crab-eating macaques, the same beasts who starred in *The Hot Zone*. Stingy German girls scream in fear as the bigger males jump on their arms and shoulders, trying to make off with bags of food. Australian boys try feeding the babies, only to have their hands clawed by greedy mothers. The macaques try to steal anything that grabs their fancy, from nuts to purses to cameras, and most of the tourists spend their time in the Sacred Monkey Forest defending themselves against an onslaught of marauding simian thieves.

Off in the corners, this time, the Balinese are watching.

TO THE ENDS OF THE KNOWN WORLD

On the other side of Indonesia from Sumatra, Java and Bali is another tribe of people that also ignores its tourists . . . as well as everyone else from the twentieth century. These are the Dani, a neolithic bunch who live in the isolated Grand Baliem Valley, completely sheltered from the rest of the known world by the towering Snow Mountains of central New Guinea. The Dani never saw another human being but each other for nine thousand years, until 1938, when a plane crash-landed in their valley, and the pilot excitedly radioed back that he'd discovered a new 'primitive' people . . . who happened to know all about crop rotation and terraced farming and erosion control. The Dani never used metal until steel was brought there in 1959, and even today they still don't seem to think it's such a great advance over a good stone adze. In fact, the more time you spend with them, the more you realize they don't seem to think much about the rest of the world at all.

Indonesia is split in two – between Java, Bali and Borneo on the one side, and Sulawesi and New Guinea on the other – by what discoverer Al Wallace called a *biogeographic line*, perhaps the strongest boundary on the planet. These lines separate all of life into obvious and distinct spheres of evolution, dividing North America from South, Equatorial Africa from the Sahara, and Europe from India. On one side of Indonesia's line there are slight, thin-haired Asiatic Malays and tigers; on the other, tall, broad-featured, fuzzy-haired Austronesians and marsupial tree kangaroos. If traveling through the Indonesian archipelago means a completely different nature and culture with every island hop, the jumbo split happens the minute you jump over the line to the western half of New Guinea that Indonesia owns, called Irian Jaya (which means 'victorious hot land,' and is it ever).

I arrived at Irian's capital city of Jayapura at dusk, and drove the long road from the airport to town. On the right was beautiful Lake Sentani, with its velvet lumps of islands and fishing villages built on stilts, while on the left were the pens and troughs of the local ranching industry, which specializes in the skin (for shoes, bags and belts) and the meat (for curing Chinese asthma) of crocodiles.

New Guinea is so exactly on the other side of the world from my home that they share time. I'd look at a watch, switch the A.M. and the P.M., and know exactly the hour back in Manhattan. For some reason, this made me happy.

It turned out that Jayapura's best hotel, the Matoa, was sold out, so my reservation was ignored, and I was shuffled off to the second best, a hellhole so egregious I've completely forgotten its name. The shower in my room was a bucket of icy, fetid water, the street noise from the room's windows was deafening, there was so much light coming through the flimsy curtain I might as well have turned on the overhead, and the lumpy, misshapen bed had bugs I'd never seen before crawling all over it.

The plane to get from coastal, swampy Jayapura (where I was) to the lush, montane Baliem Valley (where I wanted to be) sells tickets, but actually getting on the plane itself is a first-come, first-served operation, and they are notorious overbookers. The strategy is to get there when the airport first opens at five to be in the front of the line for the plane, and then wait four hours for takeoff. Even with this trauma hanging over my head that night in Jayapura, I was too much of a wimp to be able to sleep thinking about those bugs, so I wandered outside the hotel to see what's what. The neighborhood turned out to be a strip mall of derelict, patched-over concrete, with a shop selling stuffed bullfrogs playing miniature ukuleles. That teeming street noise was coming from a cloud of aggressive whores and their idle, drunk, taxi-driving boyfriend-pimps, all of whom immediately sized me up for a mark.

At that time of night, there was nothing else to do and nowhere else to go, so I decided to hang with these Malay skanks. After politely explaining that I was too tired for a boisterous round of New Guinea sexcapades (and wasn't interested in experiencing the joys of tertiary syphilis), I introduced them to a fine American singalong. They were obnoxious and I was pissed off, so I taught them how to sing, in English, the quaint lyrics to that Rolling Stones classic, 'Bitch.' They taught me an equally nice song in Bahasa, and we had a fine old time drinking and carrying on in that sweltering, turbid Hades.

It was now four A.M., and time to get packed and ready to drive back to the airport, so I went to the hotel's 'restaurant,' where a waiter brought me 'breakfast,' which turned out to be some kind of meat soaking in some kind of grease with a roll so hard you couldn't bite it, served with 'coffee' unlike anything I've ever put in my mouth before or since. I was the only person in the place (no surprise), hadn't slept all night, and felt like hell.

The waiter was lonely, so he came over to sit at my table. Like everyone else in Indonesia, he wanted to know where else I'd been in his country, so I told him all about Borneo. He also wanted me to explain in detail why Jayapura was the best place of them all, but this was a riddle I couldn't answer.

Then suddenly, his eyes lit up and he asked, 'Do you love Jesus very, very much?'

New Guinea has been overrun with crazed missionaries since the

1950s, busily converting as many heathens as they could get their hands on. I knew what I was supposed to say, but just couldn't do it. Instead, I muttered, 'I like him okay.'

'Oh! Too bad,' the reactionary fundamentalist coffee shop waiter admonished. 'You won't go to the Happy Place when Everything ends.'

'No . . . I'll be left behind with the Buddhists, the Muslims, the Jews and the orangutans,' I said, as though we'd be having all the fun.

'Oh . . . yes,' he replied, overcome with regret. 'The poor orangutans.'

THE SEED OF SINGING

I drove back past the lake and croc ranches, still in darkness, and arrived to be fourth in line for the plane. The airport floor was more comfortable than the hotel had been, and sitting there, keeping my place, I kept drifting in and out of consciousness, as the waiting room mobbed up with eager travelers. Finally, as a storm grew over the Snow Mountains, a mere dozen of us were let on a tiny plane, and we took off through black clouds.

The view was obscured, but every so often there'd be a break, and I could look down to see that the coastal swamps had given way to ragged mountains, and here and there, a tiny, meandering valley with a river and a few huts in it. We broke through in landing to approach a wide, shining-green bowl . . . the Baliem Valley.

I was met at the Wamena town airport by my translator, Yos, a short, stocky and remarkably dour man who was baptized Missouri Synod Lutheran, a peculiar sect spiritually aligned with Jerry Falwell. You meet a lot of strange people on trips like these, but I was still surprised that a tour guide would be so publicly and relentlessly depressed.

I tried joking around with Yos to get him to perk up a little, but he refused to see the humor in anything. When on the trail to town, we had to cross over a handmade suspension (and suspense-filled) bridge of twine. I said that this was designed for thin Dani and not fat Americans, and surely I would destroy it with my massive girth. Yos merely said, 'No! It is plenty strong!' and sternly watched me cross.

He calmed down a little bit when we got to the Pasan Nyak open-air market, where bare-breasted Dani women, in thatch-cord skirts that hung at their hips, were selling orange ginger root, red chili peppers and yellow tomatoes. Every woman's back was draped in a series of net bags dyed in purple and green stripes – *nokens* – made from bark-fiber string, and tied to their foreheads. The women always wear a few at a time, whether empty or filled with yams, infants and pigs. One woman sat with a pig sleeping in her lap, like a kitten. Men just this side of naked walked by, carrying baby pigs on their shoulders, and Yos explained in grave detail how the tree kangaroo pelts for sale (looking like gray, weasely minks) could be made into stylish hats. He got a nice chuckle at what a fool I was passing on the remarkable opportunity to get a magnificent necklace of cockatoo claws, but erupted again when we saw two naked men, wearing giant penis-gourds, walking hand in hand, and I mentioned how this was not something commonly seen in the U.S. 'Every tourist who comes here thinks this means *a very bad thing*,' he muttered. 'Our people are so pure! *We do not practice homosexuality!*'

I checked into the Baliem Palace Hotel, Wamena's finest, and reminiscent of a Motel 6 that's lost its license. Everyone you meet in the Baliem first asks where you're staying, and when you mutter, 'Baliem Palace,' they *ooh* and *ahh* like it's the Ritz. The room came with detailed instructions on how to use a toilet, and the lobby featured a mynah bird chattering away in Bahasa. After unpacking, I went to the hotel's restaurant for lunch, only to meet Hubon, the waiter/maître d', a man with the personality of Carmen Miranda on speed. I'd have to make sure to keep him and Yos separate, or who knows what might happen?

'You are a new one with us! Welcome Welcome Welcome!' he shrieked from across the room. 'Now, what can I get for you on this your first day and a beautiful one it is in our Baliem Valley?' He danced around the table while tapping out a rhythm on his order pad with a pencil. There was no menu. I asked Hubon what he'd suggest, which brought him to an even higher state of rapture:

'Oh Oh Oh! For you, I will arrange for something very *very* special. Wait! . . . I am thinking . . . do you . . . do you like . . . PRAWNS?' Now his eyes were dancing around in counterpoint to his feet.

I admitted that I did like prawns, and within minutes Hubon appeared with a platter of giant Baliem River crayfish, cooked in butter and garlic, and incredibly delicious. Now it was my turn to *ooh* and *ahh*, and from then on at every meal, even breakfast, Hubon would bring over some form of crayfish. I was off in the middle of nowhere, and here, in the restaurant of a ratty hotel, there was food as good as any you could ever hope to have, food so good that, in such a place, it shocks you right out of your shoes. The restaurant was always mobbed with diners (no surprise), but it never ceased to amaze me that no one seemed to notice it was run by a man in makeup and cha-cha heels.

Besides dour guide Yos's dark pronouncements, everywhere we went in the town of Wamena were signs of the four hundred missionaries running through the valley. Men went by in skintight jeans and big necklaces with crucifixes, and on one thatch-grass hut was a giant, eight-foot-high poster of the blond-haired, blue-eyed Jesus.

At first, the missionaries here were successful beyond their wildest dreams, especially since they were armed with penicillin to cure an epidemic of yaws among the children. Also known as frambesia, yaws is a bacterial skin infection that appears as raspberry-shaped bumps. The early converts were so taken with the holy men and their penicillin that they believed if you didn't close your eyes when praying, God would strike you blind, and that going to church on Sundays would make you immune to all diseases.

After an initial rush of success, however, the armies of God suffered defeat after defeat, which is just as visible the minute you leave Wamena town and hit the country road. Out there, the Dani aren't wearing crucifixes; in fact, they aren't wearing pants. The men, who look something like Australian Aborigines, with lean, muscular bodies and faces aged beyond their years, are completely naked, except for a feather in their hair, and perhaps a string necklace, and the one thing they never appear in public without: their penis sheaths, yellow vegetable horns called *horim*.

The men grow a small gourd and, while it develops, they train it to curl and circle with a system of string and stones; the finished product is then tied around the testicles and the waist, with the penis tucked inside. Some *horims* are curved, some are corkscrewed, some are topped with feathers or fur, while most stick straight up into the air, the tops striking somewhere between the navel and the nipples. When a group of Dani get nervous or excited, they subconsciously tap their fingernails against these *horims*, which, in a group, click like maracas. When they come to town, they carry their money in extra-wide penis-gourds, which makes you think twice about asking for change.

The Dani men weren't impressed with the missionaries' penicillin, and they weren't impressed with Jesus, and they weren't impressed with cars or clothes or anything else that arrived from the twentieth century. Their lives, for as long as anyone knows, have always revolved around yams, women and pigs, the pigs being to them like jewelry, a measure of a man's wealth and achievement; today, a full-grown, healthy Dani pig costs $350. The yams originally came from the Americas (and how they got to this middle of nowhere is anyone's guess), while the pigs are so prized that the Dani believe the *etai-eken* – the seed of singing, the soul, found just below the rib cage – exists only in humans and swine. Herds of pigs are running around everywhere in the Baliem, and after a good rain (which occurs daily and nightly), their distinctive porcine odor hits you like a sack of skunks. Even so, the Dani think white people stink, and when the missionaries would show up, they were forced to stand apart, and downwind. These people live with epidemics of respiratory infections, but they believe it's unmanly and unsanitary to blow your nose, cough or spit. They'd rather just drip. When they watched missionaries blowing their noses into a piece of cotton and then keeping it, like a treasure, they thought this was completely disgusting.

The Jakarta federal government is very interested in having the Dani become members in good standing of their modern nation, but the Dani are very uninterested in this. At first, Jakarta thought it was time for the Dani to wear pants, so they airdropped clothes into the Baliem villages, and the Dani sold it all back to the Java immigrants. Then the government decided that it was time for the

Dani to stop living in grass huts, so they built them villages made out of concrete. The Dani tried living in the concrete cottages for a few days, but they found their own huts far more comfortable. Their pigs, however, *loved* the concrete cottages, so the Dani turned them all into sties. Finally, the government thought their diet of yams, berries, grubs, bee larvae, caterpillars, bats, mice and tiny bits of pork was unhealthy, so they taught them to grow rice, taro, corn, cabbage, spinach and dredge fish farms. The Dani are terrific farmers, and they now raise all these things, but they won't eat any of it. Instead, like the pants, they sell it all to the immigrants. The Baliem tribal people may not live well – many die in their mid-fifties – but there are 250,000 of them, and they like things just the way they are.

The first European to write extensively about this valley was Robert Mitton, who fell in love: 'Baliem is as close to paradise as one can get, the only place in the world where man has improved on nature.' He wasn't being lyrical; it is knock-you-out beautiful here. The land is so verdant it fluoresces green; the mountains are topped with a permanent ring of cloud forest; and the basin is dotted with oak-brown thatch huts, the rising plumes of home fires, and purple-green fields of yam. Off in the corners are forests of auracaria, casuarina, oak and chestnut, home to the ostrichlike cassowary bird – red-necked, blue-faced and notoriously moody. At the bottoms of the trees grow pitcher plants, which are fertilized by insects they've ensnared, drowned and digested, and in the branches, clamping tightly to the bark, are plenty of New Guinea's three thousand different species of orchids. Through it all rushes the turbulent, milky-brown Baliem River, filled to bursting with those delicious crayfish.

Yos and I walked to the village of Akima in order to meet Kain (great war king) Werapak Elosarek. The smell of fire, pig and tobacco struck the minute we entered the *sili*, a fenced-in compound of round grass huts built from oak and chestnut beams, with a second-story sleeping loft and a roof of saplings tied over in heavy thatch. For a crisp, perfect one hundred rupiah bill (about one cent, but it has to be a crisp, perfect bill or the Dani will refuse it), the Akimans brought out Kain Elosarek, who was a smoked black mummy, his mouth opened in a scream, and his body seated, which is how all funerals are performed; the corpse is tied to a chair and cremated. We visited with the men in their *pilai*, where everything is burnished red from the smoke except for the fresh, purple yams. Any number of fetish objects, especially pig jaws, boar ribs, black magic stones and big fish (imported from the coast) hung in the rear of the hut, and everyone chain-smoked cigarettes.

We then went to visit with the women in their long thatched shed used for cooking and as a home for the black, insouciant pigs. There'd recently been a death in the village, and the deceased's female relatives had daubed their bodies in yellow mud as a sign of mourning. As Dani do not live to be very old, and the tribes are in constant warfare over various small-town dramas involving pigs and women, so lurking constantly in the Baliem are these spectral mud people. Besides the yellow clay, it used to be a common practice to cut off a few of a young girl's fingers when someone died – young meaning around the age of three. The finger was first tied up to stop the blood's flow, the arm would be hit, hard, to numb the hand, and the finger would be chopped off with a stone blade. The removed fingers were then dried in smoke and buried in a holy place, while the hands were bandaged in grass and leaves and the little girl would show it to everyone, a mark of honor. Though this practice has stopped, there are still plenty of middle-aged Dani women today with an entire hand of missing fingers.

Dani life is harsh, and these women are as tough as a good stone adze. The only tool they use in the yam fields is a smoked and sharpened pig thigh, and if necessary it can become a lethal weapon. If a woman is unhappy with her husband, she will dress up every day and work in the fields closest to an enemy tribe, showing herself off and hoping to get stolen. If a man calls for war and the women don't think it's justified, they'll beat him up. It's a custom not to have sex from the first signs of pregnancy until the child reaches four, but most wives don't think much of this idea. While the men think it's okay for unmarried girls to have abortions (an unmarried girl usually being under the age of twelve), they think it's bad for their wives to do it. The wives, however, don't care to be sexually deprived for years, and so feel free to get as many abortions as they want. As far as the men are concerned, the women think, what do they know?

LONG PIG

All of New Guinea was once a hotbed of cannibalism, and though the government claims that this practice has been stopped, I don't believe it for a second. Just a few years ago, the coastal Yali ate two missionaries, wrapped up their heads in fig leaves and rolled them through the fields for target practice. The Asmat, living in the swamps, believe that having a human head pillow will ward off the evil schemes of malevolent ghosts, and that if you kill an enemy, eat his brains, and wear his jawbone as a necklace while carrying a dagger made from a crocodile's jaw, other people won't bother you so much. Who could argue?

Though no one really knows the fate of primitive art collector Michael Rockefeller, it's thought he was eaten by the Asmat while on a sculpture-finding expedition. The story goes that two Dutchmen, searching the wilds of New Guinea for oil deposits, got into a dispute with the locals and killed two of them before running off. The Asmat believe that justice is done when you perform an eye-for-an-eye on anyone from the tribe what did you wrong, and they believe that all white people come from the same tribe. The next white person to enter their territory was Michael Rockefeller.

Now I don't know about you, but I'm fascinated by cannibals, because they've got a thought process I just can't assimilate. Think: You see someone really good-looking, and your mind (or whatever) immediately reacts: *What a beauty*. Would your next thought be: *Sauce béarnaise?* These are two ideas I just can't put one after the other, but every people-eater can, and does. Each human-meat-eating nation comes up with its own peculiar form of etiquette; Paraguayan cannibals, for example, aren't allowed to eat their immediate family (which would be something like incest), aren't allowed to eat brains unless they're an old man, aren't allowed to eat penises unless they're a pregnant woman, and they aren't allowed to eat any vaginas, ever, no matter what. As I wandered around the Dani villages, I couldn't help but annotate that Barbra Streisand classic:

> *People*
> *People who eat people*
> *Are the luckiest people in the world!*

All this time, dour guide Yos was being a damn sourpuss, so I decided what the hell? I made him ask all the Dani (even though I knew he wouldn't like it): *When was the last time you ate long pig?* 'Long pig' is what they call human meat, and practically every Dani replied in exactly the same, evasive way: 'Oh, ah . . . ah . . . a really, *really*, long time ago.' The way they said this, though, made you think that by 'long time' they meant 'last week.' Though there weren't any human skulls lying around, the more time I spent with the Dani and saw that, except for candy, cigarettes and those one hundred rupiah notes, they weren't remotely interested in anything about twentieth-century culture, the more I was convinced that they'd stuck with their entire traditional way of life, even if some of it now had to be done in secret. After all, they were an unbelievably proud people, so much so that the formal version of their hello is the outrageous boast, *Narak-a-la-ok* – 'I eat your faeces!'

It was time to check out of the Baliem Palace and get to the middle of nowhere's middle of nowhere. As I had my last lunch there, Hubon, seeing my luggage, asked in his most perfect Diana Ross diva voice, 'Will you remember me . . . here?' and then giggled in hysterics. Yos and I piled our stuff into a jeep and took off down the highway, which turned out to be a placed line of boulders that kept us from sinking into the mud. We bounced around for two hours, finally reaching the far corner of Dani territory, and checked into the worst hotel I've ever seen in my entire life.

The Losmen La'uk (Motel Hello Woman) is run by a nasty Javanese-Chinese man named Toukimen. If you have to stay in this territory you have to stay at Motel Hello Woman, and his monopoly made Toukimen about as gracious and hospitable as the Microsoft Corporation. A German tour group of four was also staying here, and when we arrived, Toukimen was shouting at them about something. He turned to us and announced that our prepaid voucher didn't include meals (there was nowhere else to eat), so dour guide Yos had to dig up the paperwork and call back to the agency in Wamena (which I had to pay for) to prove we would indeed get food. Toukimen then had us seated in the alley instead of the dining room with the Germans, so he could cover up that he was feeding them better. While I took video of the toilets and the cook and the wife cleaning the vegetables, I had Yos explain to the innkeeper that I was here to make an American television special, and so would be interviewing everyone who worked at Motel Hello Woman. This got us back into the dining room and the better food.

After lunch, I went for a walk in the cloud forest, which, just like its name, was moist and damp and filled with mosses and ferns. As a Dani family approached, a tiny snake crossed the path, and when the family saw it, they halted dead still and began screaming in terror. Snakes are extremely rare in the Baliem, and the Dani think them all viciously poisonous and terrible omens of bad luck. I tamped my foot, the little reptile sidled off into the grass, and the family, obviously grateful, kept walking.

When I reached the path to the holy Waga Waga caves, it started to pour, and the path's boulders turned wet and slippery. I was pathetically making my way downhill and slipping and sliding around when, out of nowhere, before I even realized what was happening, two big Dani men appeared and picked me up under each arm and carried me really fast down the hill and into the caves. At first I thought I was being dragged off for some nefarious purpose, but then I realized this was their moonlighting business, and it was a great ride. They showed me the sacred rocks while, overhead, flying foxes squeaked and rustled their five-foot leathery wings. I passed out smokes, and then they lugged me back into the forest. In a way, they made me feel honored and well taken care of, and in a way, they made me feel like luggage.

That night, I got to find out just what a pit Motel Hello Woman really was. The communal toilet turned out to be a brick tub of river water, black with silt, and a filthy towel lying on the floor. There was no soap and no toilet paper, and it smelled just like a morgue. My room had paper-thin walls and a bed of plywood covered by a

thin piece of foam, one sheet, and an itchy blanket. At nine o'clock
sharp, Toukimen turned off his generator and we were thrown into
primal darkness; I didn't know this was coming, and so had to crawl
around on the floor looking for my flashlight. An unholy ruckus
(which would last the entire night) started up outside: dogs howled
piteously, there was a ratcheting whistle from the cicadas, and the
nightjars called out in their low *tock . . . tock . . . tock*. Every time
I moved a muscle in bed, the plywood would creak and squeal.
Then it started to rain like hell and I realized the roof was made
of tin, since the rain-drops sounded like a marching band of snare
drums. The minute the rain stopped, the dogs, cicadas, nightjars
and whatever the hell else was out there started up again, including
a dozen boisterous roosters, and I too was now ready to *ooh* and
aah over the Baliem Palace.

At breakfast, Yos and the German guide told us we had some
options to consider. Both our agendas today included a two-hour
hike up the slippery mountains to a brine pool, where women stick
banana fronds into the water, get the fibers completely soaked, and
go back to their villages and burn the plants on a rock. The gray
ash result is used as salt and stored in leaf jars. Or instead, we
could go see the village of Jiwika put on a battle, a festival and
a pig roast, but this would cost an extra twenty bucks each. I'd
already had my slippery hike the day before (and today, with no
sleep, wasn't interested in another), and so immediately voted for
the battle/festival/roast, but one of the Germans, a doctor, was
convinced we were being taken to the cleaners, that this was a
guide scheme. 'Why does it cost so much?' he whined. Yos simply
answered, 'You have to pay for the pig.'

THE MANAGEMENT
OF GHOSTS

Finally everyone agreed to this supplement, and we were all led to
an open field, but there was nobody there. We waited, and waited
. . . and suddenly there was a scream of 'Whoop Whoop Whoop

Whoop!' that came from the horizon, and we looked up to see Kain Yali Mabel, the chief of Jiwika, standing about twenty feet up in a *kaio*, a lookout tower made from saplings bound together with vines, and pointing his loaded bow directly at us. Thirty warriors rushed onto the field, screaming the mournful call of the mountain pigeon – 'Who-week! Who-week!' – and battling with spears, bows, and arrows, the lines of men moving back and forth like on a gridiron, offense, defense, countermoves and even a kind of instant replay.

Before, every Dani we'd seen had his penis-gourd, and her cord skirt, the men adding a feather or furred crown for the hair, and the women's backs always draped with their stringnet bags. For this battle, however, the entire village of fifty people had dressed to the teeth . . . literally. The men's pierced noses and ears held boar's tusks and pig ribs, curved up or down like polished-white Fu Manchu mustaches. They'd coated their faces and chests with pig grease mixed with ash to look as black and feral and gleaming as possible, and many had stuck broad, white ferns into their hair to stick out, like antennae, from the corners of their eyes. There were headdresses of black, swooping bird of paradise tail-feathers and red ginger blooms; armlets of braided ferns and dried pig testicles; bibs and breastplates of cowrie, snail shells and stone worn as armor. Along with bows, arrows and spears, the men thrusted and parried with white egret feather batons and black cassowary feather whisks to confuse and distract the enemy. They looked completely alien, completely primitive and completely fantastic.

At the victory celebration back in the village, we were greeted by Kain Yali with the traditional welcoming puffs of 'Wah! Wah! Wah! Wah!' as now the entire tribe came out to chant, sing and dance. There were robin's-egg-blue legs and orange-ocher clay legs and ghostly white legs; one boy had dotted his torso to look like a fawn, and an elder had so many bird of paradise feathers in his crown it looked like a fright wig. Every kind of penis-gourd you can imagine appeared, many with crowns of feathers or fur. Some of the men had a thin thread around their necks, fashioned from a spider's web, which was guaranteed to keep malevolent ghosts from trying to choke you to death. The women had on their best skirts and bags, dyed in various patterns, and after the men had finished whooping it up, they were the ones, led by a crone, who sang a quiet, beautiful chant, shaking out a rhythm with the batons and whisks, a continuous background music during the rest of the ceremonies:

> *Ah oh ay yah*
> *Sapay yo dago ay*
> *Sapay ya pano ay*
> *Ah oh ay yah*
> *Botay yo dago ay*
> *Botay ya pano ay*
> *Ah oh ay yah*

Two of the men brought out a squealing piebald baby pig, carrying it by the haunches and the ears, and held it, stretched out, while Kain Yali shot an arrow into its lungs. The pig was then put down to run away from death, but he was caught, and he lay on his side, his legs still running frantically, until he died. One of the men then carefully removed his ears, tail and teeth, which would be smoke-dried and used in fetish objects to keep away evil ghosts, while the other singed off the animal's hair over a flame.

A great pit had been dug in the center of the *sili*, and its bottom was covered in green branches to make steam. The men used long sticks as tongs to carry over white-hot rocks from the fire, and they layered this pit with yams, rocks, more green branches and finally, wrapped in leaves, the singed pig. The meal would be eaten by hand, served on banana fronds, cut by bamboo stalks sharpened into knives.

This was of course all done for us tourists, but it also maintained a very serious part of Dani culture during a period when the authorities had banned tribal wars and, therefore, victory feasts. Though I'm sure the wars are still going on secretly (nine thousand years of tradition doesn't end with a few Jakarta-exported cops), the Dani were obviously filled with pride at showing off to us. The proof of this attitude came when they brought out some items we could buy: bows and arrows, net bags, grass skirts, *horims* and digging sticks. Nowhere, however, were the magnificent head-dresses and armbands and batons and whisks and the women's special, more beautiful outfits we'd spent the day watching. Some of the Germans tried bartering for the bibs off their chests and the bones out of their noses, but the Dani weren't interested in selling their real treasures.

The spectacle was of course engrossing and magnificent . . . but I was unsatisfied. The Dani were the most alien aboriginal people I'd ever met in my life. Their pigs stank, the local hotel was a hellhole, their language was too difficult to pick up on a short stay, and they were the ultimate in distant stand-offishness when it came to outsiders. Except for cigarettes, candy and those one hundred rupiah notes, they wanted absolutely nothing to do with me, and I just couldn't stand it.

They'd really knocked themselves out performing the war and the dancing, and were sweaty and tired and starting to wander off, when I came up with an idea. I'd seen an awful lot of American Indian shows growing up in Texas, so I had Yos tell Kain Yali that we have people like the Dani in America, and would he like to see how they dance? The chief allowed as to how he would very much like to see that, so I started a little chant, and a little hopping two-step, and suddenly the entire village converged around me, picking up the chant, clapping and whooping. I switched to another, and then another, and then another, and each time the tribe picked up the song as if they'd known it all their lives. They spurred me on and wouldn't let me stop, making me dance in that torpid heat. The one-way exhibition had now become a two-way party.

After a solid hour, I couldn't do any more, and now I was the one who was sweaty and exhausted, but the Dani had never seen anything like this before (no surprise), and they fell in love. Every single male in the village came over to trade chants and songs and steps with me, one after another after another. Soon enough, I too was covered and smeared in their pig-grease bodypaint. One extremely old man, wizened and on his last legs, kept looking at me, and laughing, and imitating some of my steps, and clapping with glee. This turned out to be Kain Yali's father, who in his prime had sixty-five wives. When two of his sons were caught and killed in a raid, he tracked down the murderers and ate them.

Kain Yali couldn't contain himself; he kept coming over to me and softly chanting 'wah wah wah wah wah,' and we walked around the village, our arms wrapped around each other, the Kain holding on so tightly I could barely move. He kept holding me by the shoulders and kissing me on the ears, his huge penis-gourd digging into my belly. With Yos translating, Yali introduced me to his entire tribe, including his six current wives and infinite number of children. Then, when Yos turned his back for a moment, Yali stuck something in my pocket and looked at me with his fist over his mouth.

I went off to take a leak and in that moment of privacy had a chance to look at what Yali had stuck in my pocket, and was stunned. It was a *ganekhe*, a fetish, one of the village's sacred ye stones, long and black like an extruded egg, and originating from the Papua volcanoes many miles away. It was made to bring good luck, and tied to it were the dried tail, ears and teeth of the pig whose ceremonial death anchored it to the world of the ghosts. The stone was oily and resonant with odor; it'd just been cleaned with sacred grease and fire smoke.

I'd finally found it: the ultimate nowhere . . . the anti-Manhattan . . . and I could come back at any time.

I was, once again, home.

INDIA

UNEARTHLY
DELIGHTS

'It is the land of dreams and romance, of fabulous wealth and fabulous poverty, of splendor and rags, of palaces and hovels, of famine and pestilence, of genii and giants and Aladdin lamps, of tigers and elephants, the cobra and the jungle, the country of a hundred nations and a hundred tongues, of a thousand religions and two million gods . . . [but] it is a curious people. With them, all life seems to be sacred, except human life.'

—MARK TWAIN

ABOUT SNAKES

Many of my friends have strange and remarkable fantasies about travel to the great beyond, and why they themselves would love to do it but, because of some nutty idea they've made up in their heads, won't. When I came home from the Amazon and was babbling about it to anyone who'd listen, one person (let's call him 'Rick') asked, 'Did you see any *snakes?*' 'Well not really,' I said. 'There was a little green boa up a tree and we saw a crushed fer-de-lance, but that's about it.' Rick is pale enough as it is, but he now visibly faded to a ghastly white: 'I could *never* even go on a trip like that with . . . all . . . those . . . *snakes!*' he said. 'What if you're in a boat . . . and it goes under a tree . . . and there's some *huge python* that jumps out of the branches right on top of you?'

Many of Rick's fellow ophiophobes are convinced that the minute you step foot outside the North America-Europe vacation axis, hordes of poisonous deadly man-eating snakes are running around everywhere just waiting to sink their fangs into your tender young flesh. For the most part, their phobia is just that . . . an irrational fantasy . . . but there is one part of the globe that no snake-hater in his right mind should visit. When Alexander the Great conquered this particular territory, after all, more of his troops died from snakebite than from battle wounds . . .

I had just arrived from one of those endless transcontinental flights, and hardly got any sleep the night before, and was trudging to our first destination, the Jantar Mantar . . . a homemade astronomy center, demandingly beautiful and strange, built by the governor of Agra in the mid-1700s . . . a fantastic assemblage of geometric constructions all painted in white, black and brick-red stripes, with various buildings for observing the stars and planets, including a gigantic sundial as big as a house, and an eight-story isosceles staircase leading straight to the heavens.

It was just under one hundred degrees, and my guide was obsessed with less-than-compelling astronomical details, and my head started to spin, so I went over to watch the Mantar's lawnmower (a grazing Brahma bull) and a family of raucous parrots in a broad-limbed plane tree, while a little girl, staring balefully, followed me everywhere, wanting to beg, but not knowing exactly how.

I wasn't really all that aware of what was going on around me because I was still in that mental twilight of international transit, and I was trying to wipe the Delhi grime off my glasses and not really paying all that much attention. I heard this *whisk* and my foot bumped something, and I looked down to find a little rattan basket, filthy and tattered, at my feet. Then there was another *whoosh* and another thud and an identical basket appeared. A man of about twenty came running over, bent down, tossed aside the lids, and vigorously beat the insides of the baskets with a long gourd. He drew back, placed the gourd to his lips, and began making the most godawful racket, while two enraged Indian cobras, hoods fully flared and menacing, rose straight up out of the baskets to their full standing height of three feet, their heads weaving to follow the movements of the snake-charmer's horn with that 'come any closer and I'll bite you' beady-eyed stare of the well-venomed serpent . . . and all this is taking place mere inches from my pale calves.

I later found out that all of India's snake-charmers are descended from one family and share the same name (Nat) and their career choice, it turns out, is an illegal but pretty decent way to make a living, since most tourists tip well . . . not because they're pleased with the show, but because they want the serpents, waving in menace, removed immediately. These fears are unwarranted, however, since every charmed cobra in India has been defanged, and almost every one then either starves to death, or develops abscesses where their fangs have been cut out, usually surviving less than a month in the charmer's care. After man, the cobra's mortal enemy is the peacock, who knows how to strike the serpent at the exact weak spot on the base of its head and then swallow it whole, like spaghetti. Wouldn't it be astonishing to come across a muster of peacock, tails full-out akimbo, throwing back their necks and hungrily downing serpents like there's no tomorrow?

Probably the Indian snake that ophiophobes like the least is the king cobra, since one bite of a full-grown, fifteen-foot king has enough venom to kill a hundred people. They've got the fantastic veromonasal gland that all pit vipers have, a sense organ that's delicate enough to 'smell' water. Kings are completely deaf but have very beautiful iridescent-blue tongues and are great swimmers. Another lovely subcontinental reptile is the spitting cobra, with a spit range of six feet, and enough venom to temporarily blind you.

If you're a big-time ophiophobe but must visit India, perhaps the solution is to manufacture your own supply of antivenin. First, grab a mature king cobra by the back of its jaws until it fully opens its mouth, and quickly and firmly press the fangs against a cheesecloth-covered glass until you can see venom shooting out – a procedure called 'milking the snake.' Then inject a horse or two with a minute amount of the poison, wait three months, and extract the plasma. Now you're more than ready for the jewel in the crown . . .

THE STARS OF BOLLYWOOD

Brenda and I went to India in order to take the Grand Tour, to see pieces of the Mughal (or Moghul or Mogul, but Mughal is now preferred) Empire, a little Raj luxury, and a soupçon, a *Mrs. Dash*, of spirituality. The religion department would include classical India's greatest compound of ancient temples, Khajuraho (something like Cambodia's Angkor Wat), the country's holiest city, Veranasi (something like Israel's Jerusalem), and the total eclipse of the sun.

Because of the eclipse, the vast majority of our fellow travelers to India turned out to be astronomy zealots, each dragging along the kind of cameras and telescopes that, a decade earlier, only *National Geographic* employees were allowed to own. Many of these hobbyists had already spent small fortunes trying to see a solar eclipse elsewhere – they'd been to the Galápagos and Hawaii and Bermuda and New Zealand – and almost all of them had failed to see anything because the weather had turned sour. These zealots didn't care a whit that they were in India, and their conversation for the entire trip was the history of their scientific failures, and the likelihood that our eclipse would also end in cloud-cover, and a celestial extravaganza unseen by human eyes.

We'd be arriving too late for Nagayutk Panchami (the big-time Indian cobra festival) in the reptile-loving village of Shirala, where hordes of locals throw rice at every snake they can find, and small boys parade through town hoisting tied crucifixes of living, thrashing, fifty-pound carrion-eating monitor lizards. We would, however, be arriving in time for Diwali, the Hindu New Year, a Festival of Lights similar to Hanukkah, but with saris and dirt floors painted to look like carpets instead of spinning dreidls and electric menorahs.

Within an hour of getting on the plane, we were thrust into the heart of the subcontinent, since the in-flight movie was Delhi home-grown. Hollywood may produce the world's most popular features and TV shows, but its charms are almost completely ignored by Brazil, Hong Kong, the Middle East and India, the latter having such a massive, Bombay-centered film industry that it's nicknamed

146

'Bollywood.' Bollywood productions are all epics, and they are all a mix of soap opera, musical, action/adventure, romance and suspense, now turned into a new form that has become a genre all its own. The leads are always impossibly wealthy raja heroes with Barry Manilow haircuts, decked out in leather pants and neon-yellow California sweatshirts, consorting with heroines attired in the not quite traditional see-through silk robes, bare midriffs, tiaras and bindi dots (the forehead's third eye), all set against a background of lavish Mughal palaces. Our movie was about a raja who'd mistakenly married the evil, never-before-seen twin of the woman he really loves, and the twin was now controlling him (and the destiny of his entire family) through the use of female genie sex demons. The hero had to win back the love of the good twin (since she thinks he spurned her deliberately) and simultaneously kill all the genies (with his extensive training in the Korean martial arts). There were multiple Busby Berkeley–inspired dream sequences with a cast of thousands, as well as plenty of musical interludes where everyone got to dance like wildly enthusiastic strippers. What's really terrific about Bollywood productions is that, if you don't care for a certain part of the movie, you just wait a few minutes and it changes into something completely different.

We landed and were relieved to find that our Delhi hotel wasn't in the rough part of town, where professional beggars cut off their fingers to look like they've got leprosy and then chase you around, waving their stumpy hands and shrieking (you can always tell a fake, we're told, by looking to see if the earlobes are intact). Instead, we're in one of the pretty suburbs, a place of starkly modern buildings and grassy boulevards and houses for rich people who never go home. But even though we're obviously in a posh neighborhood, the view out my balcony isn't of some lush, manicured polo lawns or dazzling Hindi temple, but instead of a small, sparse tree containing a very large and feral raptor – a big brown hawk, or perhaps an eagle – frantically looking for some mammal to swallow whole. Though the hotel is paved in marble, with a huge restaurant and grounds swathed in fountains, parts of it have been abandoned, and one of those parts is the stairway next to my room, with eaves hosting a large colony of fruit-eating bats, a trio of pigeons, and a dump for ruined hotel accessories. The staff, like many Indian tourist employees, have inherited a panoply of bad habits from their onetime rulers, the British Raj, especially that delightful combination of a stuffy sense of propriety, a gross insistence on following every rule to the letter, and a complete lack of organization.

This is what's left of the British Empire, an era on which the sun has thankfully set, but the blood has yet to dry. Coming through the airport to get on a connecting flight, like hundreds of millions of other tourists? The Air India security forces will try to confiscate your camera batteries, since of course they could be used in terrorist bombs. Want breakfast first thing in the morning when you get up? At five A.M., the Delhi hotel's coffee shop had three customers and six employees, but getting a cup of coffee or tea was tremendously difficult and took forever.

Everyone claims to hate Third World cities, especially New Delhi, but it's the only way to see modern India. Just as you can walk down just about any street in Rome and there's a laundromat next to a Vespa dealership next to a tailor shop next to the tomb of Justinian III, so Delhi is a mishmash of time and culture, the ageless Indra Vedism cheek-by-jowl with farming techniques of three thousand years B.C.E., on top of the Raj, on top of businesswomen wielding cell phones and fax machines. Right at the start, scurrying to baggage claim, we looked out the airport windows to see peasant girls gleaning in the loamy fields, accompanied by water buffaloes the color of wet inner tubes.

This is what makes India so incredible, in every way. If much of the Third World is filled with dirt and poverty, if the vast majority can only eke out a bare subsistence, then India is the most of all these things, the dirtiest, the poorest and the most subsistent. In the middle of all this, however, are constant jolts of beauty and elegance, both in the Mughal and Raj glories left behind, and in the day-to-day passing moments of modern life. As a child, I was greatly impressed by a beer commercial that said you should 'Go for the Gusto!' What this had to do with beer I still don't know, but India is indisputably the place where everyone is *Going for the Gusto!* in every direction at once. The subcontinent is easily the most beautiful and the most squalid place on earth, and therefore, the most human . . . with everything that implies.

Out of a population of around a billion, there're 250 million Indians who're decidedly middle-class, with cell phones and Internet access and stock market and retirement planning and a boom in consumer goods and services (including a local chain of McDonald's that serves lamb-burgers). In Volvos and BMWs and Audis, they're driving to their lunch appointments, passing by us tourists, who that morning were out and about in human-powered rickshaws, a wonderful traveler's conundrum. If you ride in rickshaws (almost universally pulled by men suffering from malnutrition and tuber- culosis), you feel like a giant squamous pig person. If you refuse, thinking it's barbaric, then you're keeping money from a family whose main wage-earner suffers from malnutrition and tuberculosis. Just down the street from our marble-clad hotel, we (and the Audi-drivers) passed by a protester carrying the sign, *BRIDES ARE NOT FOR BURNING!* This referred to the not uncommon practice of men marrying rural women to collect their dowries, and then, right after the honeymoon, the new bride is found dead from a suspicious cooking fire.

Just past the protester, set in a grove of flowering trees and mown lawns, is Raj Ghat, where the father of the country, Mahatma Gandhi, was cremated, the event memorialized by a granite slab of the same deep, black, light-destroying bituminous marble that colors the Vietnam memorial in D.C. Those coming to pay their respects throw handfuls of marigold blooms and, scattered by the winds, these delicate, brilliantly colored orange-yellow flowers mark the site as poignant of loss and longing as any cemetery can be. Our Ghat guide was Mrs Sarya Dalton, a big woman who always shaded herself with an enormous polka-dot umbrella, and who spoke in a charming high-pitched, British-based titter. Mrs Dalton had a gigantic schnoz that she'd pierced, so sticking out of her left nostril was a big, thick gold ring. I was impressed by this. Instead of doing everything possible to downplay it, that ring screamed out: 'Just look at my big gorgeous nose!'

In this solemn place, we met two extraordinary women, Moira and Patsy, who we assumed were sisters since they looked like Doublemint Twins in matching olive-green fatigue outfits and big white hairdos. It turned out instead that they were the best of friends for decades, who traveled once a year someplace exotic and, as shoppers, put the rest of us to deep shame. When we all went to a gigantic Delhi luxury mall, these two were the ones who found, in minutes, the secret room selling illegal antiquities, and had shipped back to their Florida gardens matching life-sized statues of Rajput princes.

When we finally got up the nerve to ask Patsy her business, she replied, 'I'm in citrus,' exactly the way a Texan might say 'I'm in oil,' so we just assumed she owned Sunkist. Together, we spent a day in New Delhi being tracked by a grime-encrusted little girl carrying what appeared to be a half-dead baby, but since no one else looked anything like this (even the most visibly abject poor), we assumed it was somewhat theatrical. Later, we were chased by a family of marionette carvers running down the streets, shaking their puppets at us like voodoo dolls, and that night the assault of beggars and peddlers became so overwhelming that, when our taxi was followed by a particularly enthusiastic group of common street urchins, one Anglo had a complete mental breakdown and started throwing fistfuls of rupees out the window.

In one day, we'd already learned this trip's overriding theme: *In the Land of Beauty and Squalor, you will be set upon by hordes.* One thing you can say about India Indians is that there are an awful lot of them, and we were always surrounded by mobs of energetic beggars, demanding salesmen and wheedling children. At one point later on, a few of us were wandering around an alley, and we got lost. Our translator had been running behind us for fifteen minutes, yelling, 'Please sir! Please madam! Hello! Hello! Hello,' but we had completely ignored his screams, since we'd spent weeks hearing the exact same thing shouted at us a thousand times a day.

A DREAM OF TECHNICOLOR NUNS

The center of India is a desert, Rajasthan, where all the big-time rajas once lived, and where we saw one extraordinary piece of historic beauty after another. In the middle of downtown Jaipur, the Pink

City, the raja built for his harem the Palace of the Winds, a vast façade of almost a thousand red sandstone windows, like a five-story Florida screen porch, but carved out of rock. When the bustle of Jaipur city life became too much for the raja's family, they escaped to their country getaway, the Amber Fort, defensively perched high up a cliff. The locals made sure to get a decent share of our tourist dollars by insisting we ride elephants up the mountain to see it, but there are worse ways to get taken advantage of. The animals are kept in pristine condition, painted and watered and trussed up in silks and howdahs. Should the goliaths turn moody (and considering their tempers and sensibilities, this is guaranteed), the mahouts use fireworks attached to sticks as crowd control. Elephant riding looks a lot better than it turns out to be, since, with every step, the mighty beast sways all the way to its left, and then all the way to its right, and then all the way to its left, and then all the way to its right, and there I was, miles up in the air, in the middle of a desert, seasick.

The Amber adheres to the same crucial decorating scheme that every other great sovereign home employs: *How much stuff can we cram into every goddamn inch?* The windows are decorated with carved rock screens; the walls are inlaid with mosaics of semiprecious stones, enamels and glass; the floors are geometric marble slabs; and the bedroom ceilings are covered with tiny bits of metal, glass and mirror. One Zen-sounding wall is where the ruler makes a showing to hear, once a day, the requests of his people: the Window of Appearances. At night, the lamps are extinguished and a servant will bring in a candle so that you may enjoy the show your ceiling creates: one candle, reflected, becoming the entire night sky, a cauldron of stars.

The palace was overrun with cream-furred, black-faced Hanuman vervets with curling tails as long as their bodies, and a taste for the Indian tourists' marigold necklaces, which they'd snap right off like any common mall thief. While we were watching the monkeys throw themselves across the tops of the sandstone parapets, a troupe of a dozen women stalked deliberately through the courtyard, all dressed in saffron-colored saris, their heads covered in waving silk magenta scarves, everything extensively brocaded in gold and flowing with the breeze. There is probably no entourage of human beings that looks as magnificent as a group of traditionally dressed

Indian women, the harsh sun blazing out the saturated tints of their saris and robes and scarves – butter yellow, baby blue, hot pink, carmine red, shining glints of gold and silver – while the air rushing against their bodies dapples the fabric like a dream of Technicolor nuns.

Outside: the beggars, screaming, waving their stumpy hands.

Inside: the Technicolor nuns.

We survived the back of an elephant only to discover another Indian transportation adventure in store. Camels appear to think themselves our betters, since they keep their noses in the air and, of course, are perfectly happy to spit at us. The Rajasthani boys deck out their beloveds with as much ardor as any elephant mahout, and the beasts trudge through the desert with necklaces and nose garlands, geometric haircuts and parti-colored harnesses, beautiful brocaded quilts and elaborate tattoos. One crusty old magistrate, Judge Ann, was concerned that her camel was getting unhappy since the one behind it kept sniffing its butt, but we reasoned with her that he must like it, since who wouldn't? What these animals did not have, however, were well-padded saddles, and my ride (on a big boy named Hero with two-inch-long eyelashes) involved sliding back and forth athwart the great beast's large and protruding vertebrae, of which the camel has far too many.

It's very common for certain tourists to lose their minds when they travel abroad, and India was no exception. When Judge Ann explained her nickname in court was 'That Bitch,' we all sang the theme song that'll have to be written when her life story is turned into a hit sitcom. Another of our fellow travelers was a voluptuous California dentist who bought a number of paisley pajama-styled Bengal outfits the minute he got to Delhi, and he now wore this flimsy and revealing couture everywhere. Meanwhile, a top-heavy Chicagoan who'd brought along a Santa hat to be photographed atop a camel for her Christmas cards had decided to wear it frequently during the entire trip. The local children would see our white-people-parading-on-camels-in-Santa-hat-and-paisley-pajamas bit and assume: *The circus is here!* . . . but at least out in the middle of nowhere, they didn't assault us with the never-ending song of India: 'Hello rupee? Hello pen? Pen? Pen? Pen? Look! Look! Look! Good price for you!' The caravan ended on a sad note, since one of the boys started wailing inconsolably because he'd been in a fight, and his enemy had retaliated by breaking his goat's leg. We could still hear him crying, far in the distance, as we drove off.

INTO THE BENGAL FOREST

Seeing the 'real India' means hours of driving down town-and-country roads choked with red-clay dust and the smells of too many people and too many animals living too close together, along with one particularly distinctive subcontinental aroma. The main source of the cooking fires here is cow patties, and they contribute a certain naive piquancy to the country's smoky-blue polluted haze. On the village roads, we'd be passed by barreling, claptrap *Beverly Hillbilly* trucks painted in detailed blue-faced Krishna murals strung with carnations and poppy garlands; one had a particularly unique bumper sticker: WISCONSIN: YOU'RE AMONG FRIENDS. Then, in the middle of this desert nowhere, we saw a big billboard: *Frozen Semen Bank*.

On the village outskirts would invariably appear a shopping center of roadside stalls made from tree branches and old bedsheets, and even farther out were salespeople not yet up for buying a stall. In these districts we saw constant shots of beauty and squalor, as the road, covered in clouds of red dust and stinking from manure, would suddenly turn to reveal the extraordinary colors of a woman in orange and saffron silks, surrounded by her red-blood chili-pepper harvest, next to her sister, clothed in scarlet-magenta pajamas, standing in a field of just-tied marigold necklaces, bitter gold and green, in front of a wall painted turquoise and rust. From meeting these villagers, I learned that you can run a plow with two bulls, or a camel and a bull, but if you try yoking together two camels, they'd rather fight than plow. This information is bound to, one day, come in handy.

Finally, we arrived at a gate that opened to reveal the dream of Raj India that everyone has . . . Hindu temple ruins and an arched, domed and crimson lake pavilion appeared along a cliff, while just outside our jeep, a closer look showed that the algae-covered bog isn't filled with half-submerged logs but with crocs, big ones, perfectly camouflaged by the pond's green scum, and patiently awaiting the thirsty herds of barking deer (with their slow-moving fawns) to amble over. Minutes away on our drive were these very deer (a big-eared, permanently spotted version of the North American standard) grazing in the upland's dried, flaxen meadows. A bend in the road took us through groves of rosewood, teak, axle-wood, acacia, pipal, ficus, banyan, mangrove, droopy palm, sandalwood and plane trees, and then brought us back to the lake and a marshland where a vervet sat hoping for litter and handouts, while out of the tall grass arched the white parentheses of egrets, ibises and saras (the human-sized Indian crane, with gray feathers and spindly crimson legs).

This is Ranthambore National Park, legacy of Indira Gandhi's Tiger Project, a magnificent compound that really does preserve that great natural beauty of a pre-billion population India. Indira was India's chief of state for decades, and I can't forget her sad eyes, her Susan Sontag hair stripe, or her tyrannical moods. In Ranthambore, we sat in the open car, waiting, for hours . . . until finally in the tall grass there was a movement, and the guides excitedly hushed their groups of mouthy tourists. We've finally found what every visitor here wants to see . . . a Bengal tiger.

Out in the open, the black and orange pelt of a tiger is about as subtle as a highway caution lamp, but in the waterside tall grass where it waits, just like the crocs, for thirsty prey, the orange perfectly matches the wheaty color of the vegetation, while the black stripes exactly mimic the cross-hatch of the grass's light and shadow. The camouflage of our own quarry was so magnificent that half the jeep couldn't even see the four-hundred-pound animal sitting thirty feet directly in front of us. 'Where? Where!' they keep demanding, and we say, 'See the big tree in the middle of the grove? The curve in the branch closest to us? The bird sitting next to the curve? Look straight down from the bird, and there's her face.' Those who hadn't seen the cat walk into the grass never could see it . . . until she then appeared in open range, big and muscular and fluid, beautiful beyond belief, sauntering across her domain . . .

Between sport hunting, pest control and Asian medical exports, global tiger numbers went from 100,000 in 1900 to 7,000 in 1990, so they aren't exactly a dime a dozen, and they aren't exactly the best neighbors you could ever hope to have, either. In the eighty villages ringing the park, about ten people are killed and another ten are seriously mauled every year. The villagers fight back, shooting the cats with guns or blowing off their heads with bombs placed in dead antelope bait ... and so many dead tigers were found in one season that a district politician announced that the cats must be committing suicide.

Ranthambore is filled with practically everything old India has to offer except for one thing – Indians. Of course there are local drivers and poacher patrols and maintenance workers and guides and administrators, but the park, just like others in practically every Third World country, has no local visitors, and the resources spent to maintain it are entirely for the benefit (as the locals see it) of Anglos. A park's next-door villages will invariably be proud that their country has crocs and tigers and elephants, but wouldn't it be better, they think, for all these goat-eating and rice-stomping animals to go live someplace else? Exactly a year before we showed up, a group of twenty-five elephants came into a small village and found the local-made liquor that had been brewed as part of the Diwali New Year celebrations. They drank it ... all of it ... and went on a rampage, destroying the village as well as the nearby pastures, and making everyone in the area flee for their lives. In the West, we love elephants, but after all, we don't have to worry that they're going to come over and flatten our house and destroy our crops ... and if they did, we'd have insurance.

India's biggest social problem, just like Africa's, is overpopulation, which directly causes its biggest natural resource problem, deforestation, with ranchers overgrazing their herd animals and farmers overcutting for timber and firewood and cropland, leading, in turn, to soil erosion, scarcity, floods or drought and, ultimately, famine. This is the emerging market's key horror today, and the very difficult changes required to fix it (from severe cuts in the birthrate to the redistribution of agricultural resources) have been avoided by every political leader since Mao. Meanwhile, Ranthambore, like every other reserve, is getting smaller, and smaller, and smaller, while the Sahara, the Great Indian Desert, and practically every other prominent Third World wasteland, just keeps growing, and growing, and growing . . .

A DARKENING OF THE SKIES

Just outside the village of Mandewar, far from polluting urban districts (but not cow-patty burners) and so remote that practically nobody there spoke English, our trip organizers created their own village of thirty-five sea-green tents (with carpeting, electric lights and gourmet chefs flown in from Bombay and Delhi) in the middle of fallow pasture. The field's ancient stone walls make a fine spot for hundreds of Mandewarians to rest while enjoying the tourist circus, and while we watch the celestial spectacle that is a total eclipse of the sun, they'll be watching us. We were so out in the middle of nowhere that the hordes here didn't know to set upon us. They only formed into gauntlets, the entire region lined up, to quietly study us going by.

At dawn and at dusk in Mandewar, there was always the sound of hundreds of little girls imitating cat yowls, but this would in fact turn out to be the peculiar screams of the local peacocks (hopefully scarfing down the local cobras). As it was Diwali, the New Year festival of lights celebrating Laksmi (goddess of wealth) and Ganesh (god of commerce), everyone in town was ceremoniously gambling, giving each other presents, and taking milk baths, while every night meant an endless racket of popping, screaming fireworks and the rat-tat-tat explosions of guns being fired in ecstasy.

Besides the racket, however, Diwali is a remarkably beautiful holiday that takes place on the darkest day of the year, featuring hundreds of thousands of miniature terra-cotta oil lamps and candles placed in rows along the parapets of temples and houses, and set adrift on rivers and streams. At dusk, smack dab in the middle of nowhere, a sari-clad beauty approaches, her breasts and face and head scarf glowing in illumination from the tiny lamp she haltingly carries through the streets. The stores paint their dirt floors in remarkable imitations of carpeting, and everyone is carrying on with such fervor that we, who would normally be the number one attraction in such an out-of-the-way place, could quietly walk through town without arousing much notice – at first. When a Mandewarian would look up, notice us and become alarmed, we'd try to get a pleasant idea across by holding our palms around our faces and saying 'Happy!' then making a big smile and raising our hands to the sky and saying, 'Diwali!' Within twenty minutes, the secret was out, and everyone was coming up to us, holding their palms around their faces and saying 'Happy!' and then making a big smile and raising their hands to the sky to say 'Diwali!' We then had to disco-dance with men in suits on the streets, shake hands with every single citizen of Mandewar, and go to visit the home of the only barely English-speaking person there. This family offered us every single thing they had in the house to eat, but we were afraid of Bombay Belly, and kept trying to figure out how to pass without being rude. Finally we posed for a round of pictures, all the while praying that the nervous, trembling grandma (a Mother Teresa look-alike) wouldn't have a full-out heart attack right then and there.

The next day was it, a perfectly cloud-free morning, and to celebrate, an Indian newspaper ran a picture of a hideously deformed girl under the headline 'Was It the Eclipse?' – a story of how the girl's mother, while pregnant, had ventured out during the last eclipse, and here was the result. We weren't pregnant, but we were armed with Mylar glasses that Moira and Patsy had thoughtfully brought along, which was a good thing since the travel company, after setting all this up, generously supplied Mylar Pop-Tart wrappers for everybody else. Wearing these cardboard shiny-mirror glasses, we all looked like crackpots, like your nutty uncle who conducts 'scientific' experiments in the basement.

Total solar eclipses are the result of an amazing coincidence, a coincidence that, of the entire solar system, seems to be ours alone. The sun's diameter is four hundred times that of the moon, while the moon is four hundred times closer to the earth than the sun, and with perfect alignment, the moon can cover all but the great star's corona from our view. About every eighteen months a solar eclipse takes place somewhere in the world, but for some reason the perfect viewing spots tend to be in some deeply inaccessible or mythically rainy, cloudy location . . . to the point where the astronomy zealots would say things like, 'See you in '99 in Mongolia!' Now, however, the perfect spot to view the eclipse was the flat roof of the three-story, seventeenth-century fort of Mandewar, which was exactly where we stood.

We watched as slowly, slowly, slowly, an odd lump appeared in the sun, which became a cookie bite, which became a crescent moon, and the light is a little on the amber side, and all this is blurry behind the Mylar glasses and, to tell the truth, for an hour and a half, it's interesting, but not that interesting; in fact, to tell the truth, it's pretty dull.

But then, like a switch, the sunlight winks out and down, and there's a black-blue stillness, a half dusk, half dawn . . . a flattening, two-dimensional light. The common noise of the Indian animals, from birds to dogs, halts into silence . . . the crescent moon becomes a bare, glowing sliver . . . flocks of birds swoop here and there, erratically, frantic . . . the sun becomes a dying ember, the sky dims again, like that of a great storm coming nigh, but this time, it's the storm to end all storms . . .

Do you know that moment when a woman's having an orgasm and she's shuddering like a great motor and rolling like a broad river and she just keeps doing this on and on and on, like it's never going to end? That's just the feeling that ran through me during Totality.

As the sun rose and the moon set, a series of celestial events occurred that were both beautiful and frightening. First out of the gate was a cosmic spectacle called Baily's Beads or the Diamond Necklace, which really did look like an enormous necklace, since the sun was so precisely covered by the moon that the only light seen from earth was spilling through the cracks of the lunar valleys and craters, forming an astonishing ring of brilliant, twinkling lights. Next came the Ruby Rings, where the sunlight, hidden and no longer blinding to the eye, revealed the star's great corona throwing off five-million-mile-long spikes of gasses in a series of explosive, glowing-red-neon bands. Those rings vanished, and next appeared the classic view, Totality, the pale white light of the greatest fire in creation encircling the deepest black that any human eye can see. A few minutes of the classic moment passed, and then it all happened again in reverse, the Ruby Rings, the Diamond Necklace, the sliver, the crescent, the cookie, the bulge, and everyone was bathed in an ethereal, buttery, golden yellow light . . . and everyone was either deathly silent, or softly crying to themselves, while roosters hesitantly fluttered and crowed.

It took hours to recover from this moment, and I spent that day in silence, avoiding everyone, lost in feeling, praying I could remember the look of every instant and every detail for the rest of my life.

NOT OF THIS WORLD

The more you travel, the more you learn that every country has some spectacular complex of historic buildings or reserve of natural beauty that practically no one outside the region knows anything about. As you're prepping a trip or even while on the road, someone you bump into will say 'You've just got to see this,' and then they'll describe something that sounds remarkably tedious, and you'll make yourself go and stumble in and think: *Why isn't everyone in the world talking about this place?* This is one of the themes of great trips: *the momentous stumble.*

In India, that place is Khajuraho, a vast Brahmin temple complex built in the tenth and eleventh centuries by the Chandellas, a dynasty of rulers who descended from Rajput warriors (the Samurai of India), but who believed they came from the god of the moon. The temples are carved out of pink sandstone, peach-yellow buildings with smoky black pagodas and honeycomb crowns, and every single inch of every single surface is fronted by sculpture and friezes and bas-relief. One section of Khajuraho is basically a 3-D *Kama Sutra*, covered in friezes of every kind of sex you can imagine. Our local guide had some kind of classical art training that made him emphasize craft above all else, so he'd say, 'Look the sculpture, how real the hair . . . the eyes . . . the mouth . . . so like life the hips . . . the breasts . . . ees beautiful!' He was right, of course, but he'd say these things while showing, to grandmothers from Iowa, a big-haired gal with huge tits giving a blow job to a horse.

Traveling in a country where you don't know what you're doing, and you can't talk the language or read the alphabet (and you're gainfully employed, so time is definitely not on your side) means that taking care of day-to-day chores is ridiculously crucial, and having the right guides and translators becomes more important than lunch. Many times, if you are very lucky, you will have a guide who makes you fall in love – a dangerous thing, since then you'll end up being married to a guide. In India, we fell for Sanjay Chatta-Ji, a man who was smart and charming and personable and hospitable and laughed just like Geoffrey Holder, and had a tragic past.

Many years ago, Sri Ji fell head-over-heels, madly in love with a Nipponese girl and followed her back home. India may have a caste system and England may have a class system but the Japanese outdo everyone when it comes to purebred hysteria, since they basically believe there are two kinds of people in this world: Japanese people, and people descended from big hairy monkeys. Chatta-Ji ran up against this attitude the minute he arrived, since it was a firmly held belief of the girl's very traditional father, a prominent Buddhist leader. The father couldn't bear the thought of his delicate flower in consort with this monkey person, so he came up with an onerous scheme to sway the young man from his passion. In order to win the hand of his daughter, the father decreed, Chatta-Ji must spend two years in training to become a Japanese Buddhist monk. So in love was Chatta-Ji that he learned Japanese, converted to Buddhism, enrolled in the monastery, finished his two years of study, and was ordained. When the woman he loved so much (whom he'd barely seen during the two years of training in an alien land) flew out to see the ceremony, her plane crashed, killing everyone on board. Sanjay returned to India and started a new life as a tourist guide, a traveling man perpetually on the road, busily explaining the ins and outs of Hinduism, and not looking back.

If you've been the victim of repeated Hare Krishna airport attacks, you may not hold Hinduism in high regard, but in many ways it's the ideal spiritual philosophy. Just as Indian culture vacuumed up every good idea its invaders ever had, so has Hinduism conglomerated to itself key elements of every other religion, becoming a fantastic mix of folk spirit beliefs, the various cultures who've run through India, and a collection of epic dramas and spiritual essays by some of the greatest storytellers and religious thinkers of all time. Of Hinduism's 330 million gods, Chatta-Ji informed us, there are only two who really matter: Vishnu and Siva (or Shiva). Brenda, hearing this, was quite inspired, writing in her postcards, 'Vishnu were here!' and 'Shiva real soon!' Vishnu's greatest desire is to be your best friend and help you in times of need, but he's also something of a goody-two-shoes, and pretty boring. Siva, on the other hand, combines every aspect of the spirit world into one big hunky Lord (if you go for blue guys). He dances the universe into creation, and will dance it into nothingness at The End. He's an ascetic, forgoing all pleasure, who demands you seduce him, as well as the ultimate force of sex as a procreative power. The Ganges flows through his hair, and king cobras are so terrifically fond of him that they wrap themselves around his body in ardor and devotion. He has a third eye that can burn unbelievers to ashes like a laser beam, wears a necklace of skulls, isn't responsible to anyone for anything, and when you pray to him to come rescue you from some horrible disaster, it's usually because he started it in the first place. In India, he's tremendously popular, easily the all-time Number One beauty-and-squalor guy, but to our Judeo-Christian minds, he's not easy to love (or worship).

One of Siva's many notorious stunts is to appear as a giant pillar of flame whose essence can lead the true believer to eternal life, and the first time he did this was in what is easily one of my top ten places in all the world, the city of Kashi, 'the Luminous,' which soon enough changed its name to Veranasi, and then to Benaras, and then back again (a good thing, since every time I see the word 'Benaras' I think 'bananas'). In a country of the world's oldest living religion, in a country where to say hello means 'I praise the holy within you,' the spiritual center of it all, the Jerusalem of India, is Veranasi. Hindus who die there achieve *moksha*, release from the endlessly dreary and repetitive wheel of reincarnation, of having to be born and die and be born and die and be born and die forever and ever. To expire in Veranasi is to be immediately transported to Siva's home in paradise (well, actually, the Himalayas) and live forever with the Lord of All, his consort Uma/Parvati/Durga/Kali, the kids Sonaswati (with six heads) and Ganesha (with an elephant head), and their mouse, bull, peacock and tiger pets and means of transportation. It is the greatest thing that can ever happen to you . . . a guaranteed entry into heaven . . . and it gives funerals and death a wholly different meaning from anything we can imagine. It makes Veranasi one of the most extraordinary places on earth, as beautiful and unique as Venice . . . and just as sinister.

We arrived at dusk, and Brenda, Moira, Patsy and I gulped down dinner in order to run to the *ghats*, the holy riverbanks with broad, ancient stairways leading straight into the river. The streets were thronged with bicycles, cars, trolleys, oxcarts, goatherds, meandering sacred Brahma bulls and madly busy pedestrians. The jam brought our car to a dead halt, so we just got out and started walking with no real idea what the hell we were doing.

The center of all life in Veranasi is at the river's edge in the *pucca mahal*, a three-thousand-year-old neighborhood with buildings so crowded together there's no room for any kind of vehicle (not even a bicycle), and no sunlight, moonlight or streetlight ever reaches the ground. Traveling through the *pucca* is not for the fainthearted, since the walks are swarming with pavement shops of every stripe – here a vegetable district, there a sari outlet – while screeching over our heads were hordes of big-toothed, bare-faced macaques, vivid green parakeets and red-beaked mynah birds. One street was overflowing with big vats of colored powders, so if I'd suddenly decided to run around India as a naked holy *sadhu* man, here was my chance to start off with all the right makeup. Between the people who spend most of their lives out on the sidewalk and the homes with no curtains on the first-floor windows, the neighborhood threw itself at us, getting too close for comfort, and made us feel like trespassing voyeurs. When we finally realized we *really* didn't know where we were going, a young man appeared, offering instant tourist services. But as we trotted back and forth, following him through the claustrophobic maze of the *pucca*, it became plain he had no idea where we were going, either.

At night, close by the river, the air turns clammy, and as we stumbled through the cramped, fetid alleys, our ears filled with the incomprehensible screams of the arguing Veranasites, we couldn't help but think we'd made some terrible mistake. Finally there was an elevation to climb and our sneakers scuffed against a hillock of sand, and we found the water, and *knew* we'd made some terrible mistake.

The guide had taken us, not to the center of the riverway, but to the far outskirts, where a new, vast concrete structure had just been built. We didn't know what it was, we just wanted to get the hell out of there, and then we saw the twin chimneys looming up, and the guide pantomimed fire, and we were made to understand that this was the brand-spanking-new electric crematorium. Many Hindus were coming to Veranasi and finding out, too late, that they couldn't afford the traditional services. So they'd simply half-burn the body themselves and throw the corpse into the Ganges, causing something of a major health and odor problem. To fix this thousand-year mess, the city finally built this double-barreled spitfire oven the size of a shopping mall parking lot and charged only seventy-five cents, which almost anyone could afford. It was going day and night.

Shakespeare's repellent and ghastly moors are nothing compared to where we ended up . . . pitch dark, the only light a construction lamp from the crematorium, the air damp and malodorous, with giant swarms of flies, like living clouds, circling us. A man, dressed in rags, either spiritually devotee or an out-and-out lunatic, danced a little jig out by the water, and the guide, sweeping his hand across this malevolent diorama, helpfully said, 'We don't have any dead bodies here so you can go ahead and take pictures.' He was quite wrong, for there was a do-it-yourself brigade operating just a few yards away, a batch of industrious Untouchables setting up piles of firewood and playing with matches.

The next morning we made it to the *ghats* well before dawn, and were rowed back and forth in a boat while watching the Hindu sunrise rituals of Veranasi, India's most extraordinary moment. The *pucca* waterfront is a Middle Ages, Middle Eastern spectacle of guest houses for the mourning poor (which look like the ruins of Coney Island), Maharaja-built palaces (putting the splendor of Venice to shame), and temples with pagoda crowns and honeycomb turrets. The billboard of a blue-skinned, lipstick-lipped, bug-eyed cartoon Siva watches over all. One entire riverside temple, its foundation poor, fell into the waters where it lies to this day, a sunken golden dome, a freighter gone aground.

Every kind of person that India can produce shows up here at dawn, doing every kind of thing that can be done in public (and plenty of things that shouldn't). On the line where the ancient steps meet the holy water, there's a group of young boys taking baths in their loincloths, next to a sect's congregation performing their sacred baptismal devotions, next to a group of Brahmin priests with shaved heads wailing away, next to white-draped widows murmuring their singsong chants. One devotee sits at a promontory, completely covered in pale yellow silk, a butter ghost. Naked and painted *sadhus*, smeared with ashes and carrying tridents, linga and human skulls, are inches from coiffed socialites performing their morning gossip session, while an unruly mob of peasants prays in screams and whispers to the rhythmic *ching* of a bell outside a temple that looks like a seaside urinal. These are the devotees of Shitala and Mariyamma, the goddesses of smallpox.

On the boat, the tourists giggled at the sight of laundry, joking that they hope it wasn't *their underwear* being beaten against the *ghats*. The region's silks are famous for their spice colors – cinnamon, chili, curry, saffron, dill – but it's the dress of mourning Hindu widows – ice white – that you see everywhere. Between the orange-reds of the most popular paint on the walls, and the burnishing glow of the rising sun, the devouts are washed over in a peachy light that is exactly the color that every painter of the mystic tries to capture – the glow of living consciousness. The guide said, 'On the right, you may see a live baby,' and I said, 'What?' and he said, 'On the right, you may see the library.' Hundreds and hundreds of candles floated across the Ganges in delicate handwoven leaf boats, while bouquets and garlands of flowers bobbed here and there. Worshippers, mourners and morning commuters plied barges across the water, while the banks teemed with life as it has been lived for three thousand years.

In Veranasi, sixty thousand people bathe in the Ganges daily, and plenty of them drink the water. In parts of the river, the fecal-coliform count (not a good thing) is 340,000 times what's considered safe. Two million Indian children die every year from water-carried diseases like dysentery, typhoid, hepatitis and cholera, while just past the city, the surface of Mother Ganga erupts in bubbles, a sign that raw sewage is naturally converting into methane gas. A few years ago, the municipal government tried to improve the situation by importing 29,000 turtles and letting them loose into the water, hoping they'd eat whatever flesh might be floating about. Today, the turtles are all gone, and it's assumed they've been eaten themselves.

Mid-river, there's one building as distinctive to this part of India as the vast crematorium: Mukti Bhavan. The House of Salvation was built by a wealthy businessman as the Roach Motel of Hinduism. The Bhavan charges no fees, and its only guests are certifiably dying Hindus. You can check in, but you can't take medication, you can't get food, you can't bring luggage, and you have two weeks to die. You will, however, expire in Veranasi and be guaranteed *moksha*. It's said that if you die on the other side of the Ganges, you'll come back as a donkey.

Your corpse will then be carried through the streets wrapped in a cotton sheet (red for boys, white for girls). If you are well-to-do, the parade will end at Manikarnika Ghat, where Siva and Parvati decided to stop being the only gods in town and created Vishnu, whose giant stone footprints are still there. The cremation platform is marked with a blackened tower and hundreds of fishing poles holding baskets of wicker oil lamps – sky lanterns – that arc over the river, lighting the way to heaven for the recently burned (who can be seen from the half-dozen columns of white smoke rising). Now it's the lowliest of the low, the caste of Untouchable Doms, who take over, keeping the sacred fire going, making sure the corpses are fully cremated, sprinkling offerings of camphor, butter, sandalwood and mango leaves for families who can't attend. Huge stacks of firewood are everywhere, and the actively working Doms are dressed in black rags and covered in soot and ashes, with skin like Appalachian coal miners. If there's no elder son to do the final honor of releasing the soul, the Doms crack open the skull and poke through the ashes for any leftover valuables, especially dental work. At the sound of the skull crack, instead of applauding, all Indians nearby will shout out, 'Va va!'

The king of the Doms is the Dom-Raja, the universal bogeyman of India who makes his living from the dead, and lives in a circus-colored mansion right on the water . . . but not particularly close to the rising smoke of Manikarnika Ghat. The Doms do not get along with one particular sect who believes that it is a holy, purifying act to eat human flesh, a sect who pulls off chunks of the dead and feeds, right in front of the mourning families. The work of the Doms isn't easy; it takes three hours to burn an adult-sized body. 'We don't burn small children,' one said. 'The children are still innocent and do not need the purifying flames. We take the bodies to the middle of the Ganges, tie them to stones, and cast them in.' Even after the city crematorium opened, running day and night, the Doms make a good living. Cremation fires have been burning continuously in Veranasi for two thousand years.

It is the ultimate in the Land of Beauty and Squalor. Baptisms, ablutions, prayers, baths, laundry, funerals – every aspect of life is right here and right now in Veranasi, piled up on top of each other, a big heaving stripe of human life in all its ways and means.

ABOUT MONGRELS, MONGOLS, AND MUGHALS (OR MOGULS)

Why is it that humans have such endless fantasies about ancestry and being purebred, like dogs? Even democratic 'classless' Americans want to be *Mayflower* descendants, or at least rush out to get *People* magazine's latest Princess Diana cover story. Let's face facts: the British royal family is nothing but a bunch of Huns, and we human beings, everywhere, are all packs of mongrels.

Just like Egypt, Persia, China and every other great empire of the ancient world, India was invaded on a regular basis for four thousand years, and what we think of as 'Indian' today is actually a mix of Aryan, Persian, Scythian, Arab, Mongol, Turk and Afghan (who have nothing to do with the blanket or hound of the same name, just as the French won't take credit for their fries and toast). In each case, India sucked in whatever the invaders had to offer and made it 'Indian' – until the next invaders showed up.

Four thousand years ago, the Aryans (a Mongol bunch who most likely looked half Russian and half Chinese, and certainly weren't the blond-haired, blue-eyed Volkswagen lovers of Hitler's dreams) took over. The only reason we know this is that suddenly India had Sanskrit, horses you could ride, castes, chiefs named 'raja,' the basics of Hindu belief, and the beginnings of what would become an enormous worldwide fad: the worship of cows. The Aryan cow sentiment was so tremendous that in the Vedas (the Aryan Bible), 'clan' is translated as 'cowpen,' and 'going to war' means 'searching for cows.' Their key religious rite was the soma sacrifice, which involved a hallucinogenic beverage of vast importance to ancient Middle Eastern cultures, where desert lifestyles clearly favor escapist drug use.

The subcontinent was taken away from the Aryans and ruled by Ghurs and Turks, until finally a whole new bunch of Mongols showed up and took control in the 1500s, led by Babur, Khan of Fergana. This Fergana must've been just an incredible place, since after winning India, Babur concluded 'Hindustan is a country of few charms. Its people have no good looks . . . of genius and capacity none . . . there are no good horses, no good dogs. . . . We traversed [their gardens] with a hundred disgusts and repulsions.' Babur did, however, begin the Mughal Dynasty, which would put its stamp on the subcontinent like no other family before or since. The Mughals would rule over India for nine generations, they'd take beauty and squalor to bold, new heights, and they'd leave behind some of the greatest art the world has ever seen – a major reason why Brenda and I wanted to go to India to see for ourselves in the first place.

Unfortunately, the Mughals were also one of the most evil and disgusting bunches you could ever hope to meet. After Babur's death, one of his sons had the other blinded through the elegant technique of having the eyes repeatedly stabbed and then the ocular cavities filled with salt and lemon juice. The family warred over the succession, plunging India into repeated civil war, until Akbar, a fourteen-year-old, pushed out all the others and claimed the throne. Akbar's favorite sport was night polo (played by having the balls set on fire), but he never could be bothered learning to read and write. Instead, he had scholars research whatever he needed to know, and then had artists paint illustrations of crucial information – creating a whole new art form. Akbar became the patron of illuminated manuscripts, and the astonishing watercolors we think of as Indian masterpieces were first created during his reign.

An illumination usually took one month to complete, so it was especially astonishing to us to get to India and see so many of them, remarkably accomplished and still, after all these years, glowing with color. The artist would sit cross-legged at a miniature easel, surrounded by clamshells filled with water, binding glue and pigments (ground-up gold, silver, minerals, soil, crushed lac insects and even animal urine), along with a set of quills made from kitten hairs, some of only a single shaft. The painting's basic elements would've been sketched out in advance, much of it drawn from life, and commonly traced on gazelle skin. Astonishing depths of color were created by applying variations of pigment again and again, basically following the same method used to make enamel. The Akbar painters became so accomplished, in fact, that when the Mughals acquired artwork from other countries, they'd commonly have court artists redo portions in the better, Indian manner.

Besides painting, Akbar loved architecture, and when an oracle casually mentioned that maybe he should consider moving his capital city to the middle of the desert, the emperor jumped at the chance, creating the astonishing Fatepuhr Sikri. Remember in kindergarten, when you'd fold up a piece of paper and cut little snips out and when you unfolded it, there was a snowflake? That lacy style is exactly the look of this imperial city – except instead of folded paper, it's carved from red sandstone, an extremely colored red sandstone. Think: sidewalks, minarets, balustrades, cupolas, defense walls, open pavilions and balcony awnings – an entire city carved out of stone and colored dried-lipstick-red. I think it's easily the most incredibly beautiful and just-this-side-of-insane place I've ever been. During its day, with its vast size and great beauty, Fatepuhr put London to shame, but within a mere twelve years, Akbar found out just how difficult it is to have a big imperial city in the middle of a desert, and moved back to Delhi, leaving behind a shimmering ghost town, perfectly preserved.

On the road leaving Fatepuhr, we were half lucky and half not in meeting a man and his livelihood – a leashed and muzzled 'dancing' bear. The man made the animal open its mouth as wide as possible to appear fearsome, but all this accomplished was to display that the poor creature's teeth have been yanked out. I'm quite fond of bears, since they are personality-wise a combination of dog, cat and raccoon (a very large dog, cat and raccoon), and it's wonderful to, in the middle of nowhere, come across a dancing bear, but it's another emerging market tourist dilemma: you're glad to see a dancing bear, and, really, you're sorry life is like that.

One thing you can say about those Mughals: they really knew how to live. Their favorite kind of wool was woven from *shah tus*, hairs collected from Himalayan thornbushes where mountain goats had scratched their chins. They'd execute loved ones by forcing them to daily drink a big bowl of *kawa*, a mix of wine, spices and opium, commonly taken as an aperitif before dinner or, in stronger doses, to relieve pain and heal memories. When Akbar the Great passed on, there was another family struggle, this time involving alcoholics and opium addicts, lasting for two generations. Peace arrived with Akbar's grandson, Shah Jahan (Ruler of the World), who would create one of the greatest works in the history of civilization.

It is time, dear reader, to grant your humble narrator as much pity as you can muster, for his next job is completely impossible, a duty that's horrible beyond all understanding. Think: how would you describe the best meal you ever ate . . . the most wonderful person you ever met . . . the best sex you ever had . . . the most beautiful sight you've ever seen . . . in such a way that the person listening would really feel it for themselves? I must now try to make you feel that way about what is easily the most beautiful building ever erected, an edifice traveler Paul Theroux believes is the only one to have a soul, and I have to accomplish this even though it's a building you've already seen at least a hundred thousand times in photographs and movies and television shows – you've seen it so often, in fact, that you probably think there's no reason at all for you to go see it in person.

But, oh my God, is there a reason. Many who first get their glimpse of it full-on in the flesh start shaking, or crying, or just go completely silent, stunned at trying to take it all in.

As you drive up, you get small glimpses of the ovoid, nippled top (a big Persian trend at the time), ghostly white against the gray skies of India. The building itself is set inside a compound designed so that your entry becomes a theatrical journey, with much walking through gates and across walls and through gardens and around buildings before, finally, it looms up right there in front of your face.

The first thing I realized when confronted by this tomb was how seriously familiarity can breed contempt. Just like Giza's pyramids or even Niagara Falls, the Taj Mahal is so much bigger in real life than you expect that it's part of the shock. Hewn from the same white marble that's so popular with every memorial from Jefferson to Tiananmen Square to Hiroshima (but being in a country where so much of the color is dried red buildings and dark green trees and black dusty roads), this skin seems whiter than the others; it's the bleached white of a movie star's smile, and just like a movie star, it reflects whatever is directed against it.

The skin's color changes all day long, being gray and watery at dawn, too white for its own good at midday, and pink-blood-tinged at sunset. There is a tremendous lightness to the design of the minarets, the archways, the balconies and the trio of domes . . . a weightless, spun-sugar, helium-balloon spaceship that could lift to the skies at any minute and never again be seen by human eyes. Those of us coming to India with Western bias are accustomed to Middle Eastern art that's dogmatic and belligerent, an art of Afghani scimitars and Ayatollah sneers and Saddam rifles and fat black-shrouded women. The Taj is as Middle Eastern as you can get, but it's the polar opposite of what we know . . . something so delicate, so pretty, so eternally feminine, it is mesmerizing.

Shah Jahan built the Taj as a tomb for the favorite of his three queens, Mumtaz, who died giving birth to their thirteenth child in 1631. When his own health began to fail in the later years of his life, there was another battle for the throne. The winner, Aurangzeb, was not Jahan's choice, and he immediately imprisoned his father in Fort Agra – giving him a distant view of the Taj for nine long years. Today, Shah Jahan's prison quarters in Agra is the Taj gift shop, run by a man descended from eight generations of *sadhus*, each of whom took a holy oath of silence and spent their lives carrying around chalkboards (we studied each of their portraits, to notice that the clothes never changed, but the chalkboards did). The most recent *sadhu* is the shopkeeper's brother, and as seen in his photograph, he keeps his holy vows by sealing his lips with extra-strength duct tape.

Aurangzeb ignored his father's dying wish to have his own Taj, this one in black marble, built across the river with a bridge eternally uniting him and Mumtaz. Instead, Jahan was interred with his beloved in the white-as-ivory marble palace while the new emperor became a Muslim devotee. Between the Hindu majority not caring for his religious dogma and the district nobles not caring for his tax or army assessors, the family's power collapsed. When Aurangzeb's son, the last of the Mughals, lost India to an invasion by the Shah of Persia, one of the treasures taken back to Teheran was the very symbol of the family dynasty . . . the Peacock Throne itself.

Hindus believe in a relationship with art that's far more involved than our own, something called *samadhi*, which means the merging of the listener and the music, the dancer and the dance, the seer and the seen. I always understood the concept, but I didn't feel it until I saw, up close and in person, the Taj Mahal.

FLOATING ABOVE THE ROOF OF THE WORLD

Since we are all mongrels, many of the world's great places are the crossroads where mongrelizing can really work its magic, and one of the greatest crossroads of them all is the Kathmandu Valley of Nepal. A tossed salad of India, Tibet, China and Persia, the Newari people of Kathmandu tend to be incredibly handsome (as opposed to so-called purebreds like the Prince of Wales), and may look like any of their surrounding nationalities, or like a whole new kind of person altogether – a pan-Asian. This is in fact the culture of Nepal, to combine everything around them into something new, something Nepalese, something for everyone.

Even though a local ecologist claimed, 'We say there are now three religions in Nepal: Hinduism, Buddhism, and tourism,' socially, the country is one of the many emerging markets that just isn't emerging. The kingdom's economy is stagnant, the life of rural Nepalese one of the poorest in the world (with few living past the age of fifty), and, though everyone can vote, the vast majority are illiterate and

171

so can only take part in civic duties through illustrations. Nepalese voting booths symbolize the political parties with a sun for United Marxist-Leninist and a tree for Nepali Congress – so if you were voting, which would you prefer for prime minister: a tree, or the sun? Commonly, the tourist bubble keeps you from really seeing the effects of these issues, but there was a man I can't forget who, in Kathmandu, followed us for some time. From the waist up, he was so muscular and so good-looking he could easily co-star in Arnold Schwarzenegger's next big action movie. From the waist down, however, he was crippled from birth defects and made his way through the streets of the city using heavily gloved hands to push himself on a small wheeled sled, the kind American warehouses use to move around the merchandise.

In the valley, we stayed in two hilltop resorts, one with a view of the mountains, the other with a panorama of the city. It was a shock to see that Nepal looks more like Bali than India, with the same golf-course green of terraced rice paddies interspersed with villages . . . but here they were ringed by the towering snowcaps of the Himalayas (for which you should use the fecund British pronunciation: *he-MAL-yas*). Every moment in the countryside, I looked at that mountain range, distant, white and foreboding, in awe at the roof of the world. This vertiginous ring, purple in the mists, always gave me a feeling of safety and comfort in Kathmandu, a visible barrier to the unknown terrors that await beyond.

The terrors awaiting within are plenty enough, such as learning, intimately, from the smells of the food market, why burning incense is such a wonderful Asian custom. One district, Thamel, still has Freak Street, where all the flower children in the 1960s came to seek enlightenment and *bhang*. When King Sri Sri Sri Sri Sri Birendra assumed the throne in 1975, he tried getting them all to leave by illegalizing drugs and offering free transportation out of the country. It didn't work, and today, one fifth of Kathmandu's teenagers chase the dragon (smoke heroin), and the hippies are still there. In fact, they've procreated and lured in fellow grunge Eurohippies carrying the faith, and this mass has formed an entire counterculture panhandling village of hippie grandparents and hippie divorced moms and hippie infants. If you really miss the spirit of the '60s, just come to Thamel and find out exactly why you shouldn't. The perseverance and determination of Freak Street denizens to get you to give them money makes the children of India look like well-meaning amateurs.

Down the road from Freak Street is a house with windows lined in grinning skulls, home of the sacred preteen, the living goddess, the virgin Kumari, who is selected in a process similar to how Tibetans find their reincarnated leaders. As a youngster, the girl must correctly identify clothing and jewelry belonging to the previous Kumari, then she must sit in the temple in the middle of the night, surrounded by buffalo heads dripping with blood, while men dressed as demons attack her. If she never shows fear, she's The One, who thereafter never leaves her sacred home except to appear at festivals, where her feet must never be allowed to touch the ground. The minute she begins menstruating (or bleeds from a cut), her service is ended, and she leaves her prepubescence of being worshipped and completely taken care of by servers and retainers, to become a common wife and mother. Frequently, this doesn't go well, as by now the girl's spoiled rotten, plus there's a Nepalese legend that marrying an ex-Kumari brings you bad luck and an early death. We waited in her courtyard forever, with no cameras at the ready, and finally the living goddess made herself known to us: a sneering, petulant brat wearing a great deal of makeup. She looked at us with utter disdain and contempt for about five seconds, and then ran off. Get it while you can, babe.

Kathmandu is a medieval city of wood and straw, of clay tile roofs and mud-daubed walls, the Indo-Chinese version of a Chaucer stage, filled with packs of mangy, rabid, wild dogs, and witches who steal human bones from the crematorium and write your name on them as an eternal curse. It is brick-paved square after brick-paved square of golden pyramids and black cube towers with spindly wooden tiers, and temples dedicated to killer gods and monkey gods and elephant gods and lion gods and reborn gods, as well as the god of nearsightedness and the god of toothache. Everywhere we turned there were laughing stone lions, purple griffins, crocodile faucets and albino ceramic elephants to bring good luck, which Nepal could surely afford.

One of the valley's greatest assets is the result of a national tragedy. When the Chinese invaded Tibet in 1950, the country had six thousand active monasteries; by 1980, it had thirteen, with many of the religious orders fleeing to Nepal and creating a Tibet-in-exile, a sister community to the government's Tibet-in-exile in northern India. If you still don't believe that it's a Mongol world and we just live in it, consider that, when the Tibetan Yellow Hat sect converted the chief of the Mongols to Buddhism in the 1500s, his descendants, two hundred years later, returned the favor by giving them rule over Tibet. It is the chief Yellow Hat – the Dalai Lama – who's still the spiritual leader we know today.

The Tibetans in Nepal naturally congregate near two Buddhist *stupas*, or holy monuments, both of which are thought to be around a thousand years old, and both of which are straight out of the dreams of Indiana Jones. Their peaks are a facade of Buddha eyes, which are supposed to look peaceful and beneficent but, quite frankly, look surly and wrathful, like an omniscient high school principal: '*I'm watching you*.' Both are outlined in a strangely heavy mascara, and look almost exactly like the ancient Egyptians' eye of Horus, which is alarming, and both are wearing umbrella hats, which doesn't symbolize schizophrenia but Nirvana.

One *stupa* rises from the top of a steep hill, and the entire climb has been turned into a pilgrim's progress, marked with resting spots for contemplation and candy-colored Buddhas. It also features three hundred aggressive rhesus monkeys, evil monkeys, wingless versions of the *Wizard of Oz* monkeys, who steal watches, purses, hats, food, anything they can, for no reason other than their relentless pursuit of evil, which they've been doing for over two thousand years. I watched as one rhesus noticed a child eating some candy and so ran over to yank the treat out of the kid's mouth. At the top of the climb, there's the monument, the eyes, the flags, the prayer wheels, all surrounded by a vast circle of stalls – the terrific Nepali version of a shopping extravaganza.

The other Buddhist holy spot, Bodnath, is a giant white dome with a circular stairway leading to the glaring Buddha eyes at the top, stained with the droppings of butter offerings and, according to legend, created through the efforts of a woman who became a millionaire from working as a goose girl. Everywhere are prayer wheels (which Brenda claims look like dreidls-on-a-stick), spun to invoke mantra chants and protect from psychic evil. High above are strings of prayer flags, paper laundry lines that send out messages by waving in the breeze, doused in juniper incense and tinted to represent the five elements of the world. By staggering traveler's luck, we wandered into a Tibetan ceremony, getting to hear fifty monks chanting in that basso profundo muttering, accompanied by blaring yak horns and the rolling clank of giant metal prayer wheels. *Nirvana*.

Kathmandu Airport may not be the number one nutty-and-scary place to get on a plane, but it's easily in the top five. As we walked in, the security guard said to Brenda (a perfectly respectable-looking woman), 'Madame, do you have a bomb?' What is more frightening is to see the group headed for Everest base camp; waddling, obese, too-rich-for-their-own-good North Americans who look like any well-fed, underexercised family you might see sauntering about Minneapolis's best shopping mall. It was exactly these people who'd necessitated a state-run cleanup of the Everest trail, a cleanup that produced eighty truckloads of garbage.

Today it costs around $30,000 to climb Everest, and over 150 have died trying; the last three thousand feet of elevation, in fact, is called the Death Zone. At base camp, several times a day, the singing and chanting of the Sherpas is drowned out by the pounding roar of an avalanche, and when you want to brush your teeth, first you have to defrost the toothpaste. For your ultimate climb through the Death Zone, you have to start at midnight and spend twelve hours climbing a wall of ice in the dark at temperatures of thirty degrees below zero. I got an inkling of what this is like just by trekking the Himalayas, where a festive mountain walk brought me into the Thin Air Zone, whose reduced oxygen slowed me to the trot of a little old man.

'This year as we expected, there's again the specter of bodies on the route,' said David Breashears, who'd gone to the top in order to make an IMAX movie and who'd now become a self-described Everest addict and was returning in the aftermath of the *Into Thin Air* carnage. 'After we went up last year, Bruce Herrod died, and the reports from the Indo-Soviet ascent have him attached to the fixed rope on the Hillary Step. It doesn't appear that they took the effort to remove the body, so that task will probably fall to us, if we get up there. We thought we were through with that last year, so once was enough, but we also have requests from the families to do what we can . . . Looking at the slides of Rob that we took later on, only for his family's use and our analysis, there's some kind of arm or elbow of some kind protruding a few feet from him. Jan Reynolds, his wife, has asked if we could move his body off onto the Kangshung face side, so he won't become slide number twenty-five in people's slide shows in years to come.'

When Edmund Percival Hillary (a beekeeper by trade) and Tenzing Norgay reached the highest point in the world in 1953, they took snapshots, and ate mint cake. Their historic success caused Hillary and Norgay to lead the kind of culture-mingle mongrel life that's in the future for us all. Sir Hillary became a patron of the Sherpa people, while Norgay's children were all educated in the U.S. The two men have been asked repeatedly which *individual* made it to the top first, and for forty-five years, they've always maintained it was precisely a joint achievement, an achievement first reported to the newswires by Welsh journalist James Morris, who had his willy snipped and became famed travel writer Jan Morris, who, before going on a journey, always packs two things: tea, and 'a decent marmalade. The worst of American civilization, the worst thing,' she says, 'worse than the electric chair . . . is grape jelly.'

You can only imagine, watching the Everest-bound as they queue up in the Kathmandu terminal, that every single last one of them is going to die, and the more I looked, the more I knew that we were doing the right thing, as we, too, were going to the top of the world . . . but we were going to fly over it in a plane.

Everest's identity as earth's peak wasn't recognized until 1852, when the Survey of India measured it. The Himalayans, however, obviously knew it all along, since in both Tibetan (*chomolungma*) and Nepali (*sagarmatha*), the mountain is named 'Goddess Mother of the World.' The one problem with going there by plane is that weather conditions have to be just right, and commonly, at an elevation of 29,000 feet, they aren't. After five hours of sitting in that scary airport, though, we were cleared.

The panorama of the Himalayas is as beautiful a series of mountains as anywhere in the world, cragged and primordial, blinding-white, pristine. The sightseeing plane tilts back and forth to make sure you get a clear view of every crevasse, and boy do you ever.

On the Everest summit, it was sixty-five degrees below zero, with a wind speed of 150 miles an hour, and barely enough oxygen to breathe. In the plane, it was seventy-two degrees, steady as a Cadillac, and our trip was narrated by a beautiful Nepali who spoke bell-toned, mildly accented English, and who could pronounce all the mountain names, like Kanakoram and Kanchenjunja.

The sky was aching blue, the snowcaps too white to look at. As we passed over the Goddess Mother of the World, that killer wind drew up, like a cyclone, causing a flurry, a white halo, a corona of snow, to arch around and behind the center peak. It was an absolutely perfect moment and we watched, silent and breathless, a vision straight from the soul of our Himalayan dreams.

AFRICA

COW CULTS
OF THE
SUB-SAHARA

'Going up that river was like travelling back to the earliest beginnings of the world, when vegetation rioted on the earth, and the big trees were kings . . . This stillness of life did not in the least resemble a peace. It was the stillness of an implacable force brooding over an inscrutable intention.'

—JOSEPH CONRAD

DARK CONTINENT

There's one part of the world that I always wanted to visit, even though it made my imagination run wild with apocalyptic horrors. Between *Tarzan*, the nightly news and Sally Struthers, I thought I already knew everything there was to know about Africa: the starving lions and crocodiles lying in wait . . . the famine-drenched infants with stickbone arms and bloated abdomens . . . the giant raw elephants, skinned and detusked by rampaging poachers . . . the clouds of tsetse flies, their stingers engorged with the poisons of sleeping sickness and malaria . . .

Plus, I hate tents. You have to do a lot of camping on safari and, for reasons known only to God, I was an Eagle Scout as a teen and camped enough to make you just want to puke.

What horror stories have you heard about the Dark Continent? Did you know that Gabon isn't having a population explosion, like every other country in the sub-Sahara, because one third of all Gabonese women have AIDS? In the past decade 400,000 Angolan refugees fled to Zaire, 200,000 Zairian refugees fled to Angola, thousands of Burundians fled to Rwanda while thousands of Rwandans fled to Burundi, all of which culminated in a genocidal slaughter of over one million people. In a mere nine years, Benin went through ten attempted (and five successful) coups, twelve governments and six constitutions. In Liberia, the guerrilla leader Prince Johnson didn't just cut off the ears of President Samuel Doe before Doe was tortured to death in 1990, he made a video, which has circulated throughout the country and can be bought by anyone on the street. Journalist David Lamb, after living there for many years, commented: 'Africa is no longer part of the Third World. It is the Fourth World . . . Two decades of African independence has provided one invaluable lesson: progress is not inevitable.' When one of Muhammad Ali's bodyguards returned to the U.S. after the Ali–Foreman bout in Zaire, he said, 'Thank God my grandaddy got aboard that ship.' He meant a slave ship.

So this is what I learned from books and *Tarzan* and Sally Struthers and the nightly news . . . but what did I find out when I went to Africa to see for myself?

That it is Eden. I stood on the back bench of a Range Rover, my head and shoulders sticking out the roof port, my hands gripping the rollbars, our guide pulling across a rut track, bobbing and weaving, a roller coaster with a view like no other. We were north of the Serengeti, in the Kenyan Maasai Mara, just after the Long Rains, and on a ridge named Kechua Tembo, we looked one way to see all the colors of our Serengeti dreams . . . sea after sea of golden, softly waving chaff, marked with dusty paths and dotted with sparse, flat evergreens. On the other side of Kechua, however, were fields of Technicolor golf-course green, as verdant a grassy bloom as anything in Iowa or Kansas . . . and out of the golf course tramped a herd of elephants, the mothers enveloping their babies . . . followed by a troop of olive baboons, the infants riding shotgun

. . . and taking the rear were two hormonally besotted ostriches, madly twirling in circles for the favor of their mates. We turned right and drove a few minutes to a pack of leaping impala . . . went left to a pool of bobbing hippo . . . pulled over the hill to watch giraffe nibbling the thorny acacia, and neck-wrestling in benignant combat. We passed a grove of trees and spied lakes the color of cigarette ash, crowded with algae-eating, gawky flamingos, suddenly taking off, a pink ribbon waving in a Kodachrome-blue sky.

Long before you were born, a volcano erupted and covered a swath of the Rift Valley in carbonite ash, which hardened to a soil hostile to almost all bushes and trees but not to the grasses, not to the tender young shoots beloved by herbivores everywhere. This pasture took over, creating a paradise for browsers, which, in turn, were a feast for the carnivores who love them. Tanzania's Serengeti and Kenya's Maasai Mara, the world's biggest lawn, is thought to currently have 2,000,000 gnu, 400,000 zebra, 500,000 gazelle, 100,000 impala, 50,000 buffalo and 4,000 lions. These numbers are a huge drop from the vast hordes that used to thunder across the African veldt, but still . . .

How magnificent is it? After the first two days, I got depressed thinking how Brenda and I would only get to be there for three weeks, and then for months after coming home, I was lost in mourning at being here, and not there. This isn't unusual; Africa has ignited everyone from Teddy Roosevelt to Karen Blixen to 'Chinese' Gordon to Beryl Markham to Ernest Hemingway, and it's a place that, in the eyes of history, has always been the fruit no foreign Eve can resist. Europeans and Arabs, Indians and Indonesians came to conquer in the name of business, while homegrown dictators turned a cottage industry into the slave trade and invented a whole new form of government – the 'kleptocracy.' It is a continent of madmen pursuing disgusting abuses of every sort, and it is easily one of the most extraordinarily beautiful spots the world has to offer.

I'd spent hundreds of hours putting this safari together, doing the background research, looking through every expediter, from the self-help trucks of Guerba to the liveried service of Abercrombie & Kent, finally settling on Alana Hayden at Born Free Safaris in North Hollywood. She specializes in the entire continent, from Morocco to the Cape, has been in business for twenty-five years, runs the winner's prize trips for *Wheel of Fortune*, and when I explained we needed a private safari through the entire Rift Valley, she pulled out all the stops. It was an incredible effort that paid off in spades; an overwhelmingly beautiful trip that combined an overview (for me, the first-timer) and *spécialités de la maison* (for Brenda, who'd been before).

Brenda is the kind of person who loves all living things, and has designed a diet to match these interests. First, she stopped eating meat, and then she gave up chicken, and then anything with dairy in it, and then the fishes, until now she's out-and-out vegan with only the faintest of egg whites included. It's very Zen, and I don't have the heart to tell her that I can clearly hear the radishes scream every time she bites into their tender, young flesh. You probably already know the big-time vegan rules:

> Don't eat anything with a face;
> Don't eat anything that can run away from you;
> Don't eat anything that yearns for its mother;

but no matter how much you love all living creatures, there's one thing that every tourist coming to Africa wants to see – a Kill – and loving Brenda was no exception.

We want to see lions, cheetahs and leopards, and we want to see them *eat* something. You'd think from all those 'claws and jaws' TV nature specials that the wild cats are just bagging one vegetarian after another, but in fact it's hard to see action in the field. I really wanted to see a cheetah bring down a white-bearded gnu, since gnus are so obviously stupid you can only feel they should be devoured. Think of a giant bisonlike creature with huge horns that can really inflict damage and the brain power of a chickadee – sort of like the bull version of your star high school linebacker. Just looking at them makes you want to throw a steak on the barbie.

We found out later that tourists expect Kills to be picturesque, nicely edited events just like those wildlife specials, but instead commonly turn out to be gruesome and horrifying scenes that the sightseers remember – often in their nightmares – for the rest of their lives. One woman was desperate to see a Kill, and unbelievably enough, a lion brought down a gnu right in front of her . . . but she cried so hard the driver had to take all her pictures. Another time, a group waiting to see their Kill were having drinks at a luxurious resort in a beautiful open-air lounge. An impala ran in, followed immediately by a pack of ravenous wild dogs, who tore at the antelope from every direction and killed it in front of their eyes in an excessively bloody, grisly, guts-spilling-out-of-the-abdomen manner. 'Jambo!'

Brenda also believes in doing the hard work ahead of time, so she'd make the marathon calls while I hopped from one Web page to another, trying to find all the elements that would make this the trip of a lifetime. I spent plenty of time learning the basics of the various dialects so that, no matter what happened, I could be polite, and have a means of connection (*I'm no stranger, my friend . . . after all, we speak the same language . . .*), but Africa thwarted even this simple goal. All my hours of studying *Say It in Swahili* meant nothing to the Maasai (who speak Ma), the Ugandans (who have thirty-two different languages, but not Swahili), the Hadza (who speak a click-sound variant of Khoisan), or the Datoga (who also speak click, but not like the Hadza). By the time I'd gotten to the mainstream parts of Tanzania where Kiswahili is actually understood, all my vocabulary had long been forgotten.

Of course, it's fun to imagine ahead of time the scary encounters one is certain to have traveling to such a place. I'll be eaten by marauding lions. I'll be stampeded by enraged elephants. I'll be bitten by the highly toxic mamba, an almost certainly fatal encounter unless antivenin is administered instantly. I'll be swimming in the Congo and be struck by the electric catfish, which can easily throw off 350 volts. What no one mentions, however, is that in Nairobi we'd stay in a Holiday Inn with a cashier named 'Festus.'

I was sure we'd gotten an above-average airline for the New York–Nairobi leg, but was proved wrong immediately. KLM may try appearing as regal as possible, with crown logos and Queen Beatrice-blue uniforms everywhere you look, but the actual experience is, mostly, just like every other coach-class trip – a Calcutta bus. At least the giant microwaved Handi Wipes they pass out at the end of every meal are a nice touch. When the feature turned out to be the Robin Williams and Billy Crystal megaflop *Father's Day* (underlined with Dutch subtitles), and we got screwed with Brenda's requested vegetarian meal three times in a row, one Nederlander commented: 'You really got the Royal Dutch treatment!' (Still, I want to know: What kind of name is 'Crystal'? Were his parents a couple of strippers?) The best part of KLM, however, turned out just at the end, when we boarded our flight from Amsterdam to Nairobi, and the presumably non-English-speaking Dutch stews were perkily handing out complimentary copies of the *International Herald Tribune*. The newspaper's big headline right at the top said, 'Demonstrations in Kenya Turn Violent!'

A NATION OF IMANS

The first thing I noticed about Nairobi is that nobody there looks like anybody I know – I guess because the slaves sent to the Americas were the captives of West African kings, while the Easterners were sent to Arabia. Nairobians in fact look sort of like the model Iman, and about one third of everyone you see on the street is ready right there and then to pursue a career in modeling and spokespersoning. They are a drop-dead good-looking bunch of guys and gals, those Nairobians, which made it all the more annoying when I saw all the local Coke and Pepsi billboards teeming with white people. We drove down Uhuru Avenue (which I assumed was named by a *Star Trek* fan, until I learned it was Swahili for 'independence') to the African Heritage superstore, where we met a Kikuyu from Mombasa who called himself a gymnast, but in fact was the resident contortionist, with the stage name 'Plastic Boy' and a deep scar on his forehead from his tribe's painful wedding limbo ritual. He, too, looked like a model . . . and could put his hat on with his toes, which sure comes in handy.

The city is so dangerous that it's nicknamed 'Nairobbery,' and Benjamin, an Ohio botanist getting his master's, told us how he was once attacked by ten muggers who stole the pack right off his back. We'd all heard so many of these kinds of stories that every tourist in the Maasai market clutched their bags to their chests like refugees streaming off the boats.

I always make sure when traveling to visit a grocery, and Kenya's shelves were a bonanza, featuring Blue Omo Power Foam detergent, Vim cleanser, Frooto soft drink, Afrikoko chocolate-coconut liqueur, KCC Superfine ghee butter, Giv soap, Doom insecticide, and Konyagi banana liquor that comes in plastic shot TotaPaks, perfect for drinking and driving. The only sign we saw of those violent demonstrations, however, was the fact that the stoplights by Nairobi University were covered in cages so the protesting students couldn't keep breaking them. In fact, while we were in Kenya, the American nightly news reported that the Kalenjin (the tribe of current President Arap Moi) were fighting with the Kikuyu (the tribe of past President Kenyatta), and over a hundred people were killed in the Rift Valley, exactly where we were heading. Moi-haters were rampaging through Mombasa, with political factions cutting off each other's hands. A series of floods had destroyed highways and bridges, severely damaging the cash crops of tea and coffee, and creating epidemics of malaria and cholera. We saw none of this because, of course, we were in the travel bubble.

As we took off for the Mara, I turned to my South Indian neighbor, who was busily reading *Men Are from Mars, Women Are from Venus*. I pointed out the plane window at the round, tin-topped buildings we were now passing in Nairobi's outlying zones, and asked what they were. He peered at me over his glasses like I was an idiot and said, in that beautiful Queen's English that only Indians have, 'These we call *slums*.' A half-hour later, we passed over a vast grassland spotted with mud circles bordered by huts – the *kraals* of the Maasai. We were here.

ABOUT GNU

We scheduled this trip to the Mara at the end of the Long Rains since that is the start of the Great Migration, which is considered Great because it involves a million brindled gnu (and all the animals that eat them) running in a five-hundred-mile ellipse from Kenya's Mara down to Tanzania's Serengeti and back in a year-long search for better, thicker, greener grass. Brindled gnu faces look just like Moondaddy – a Grateful Dead wannabe in a Brünnhilde helmet – and they have big shoulders and little tiny butts and minuscule brains.

How stupid are they? Seeing a thunderstorm will make them stampede toward it (they know that rain equals grass), while high brush that could hide a cat will make them stampede away. 'God's cattle' (their Maasai name) become so hysterical to get to new grazing lands that they will commonly stampede too fast, trip and break their legs, and then be trampled to death by the other gnu coming after them. During these out-and-out runs, a large number of calves will get separated from their mothers, which then become even more hysterical and trample each other. No mother will then take care of a calf that's not her own, so almost every lost and unprotected baby gets eaten. Another common way gnu die is when a certain kind of fly larva burrows its hungry way up their noses and into their pea-brains and renders them insane. When you watch a herd of gnu, in fact, you can tell exactly what they're thinking: 'Mmm! Grass! Mmm! Grass! Mmm! Grass!' The grass is, I must admit, really beautiful, so brightly colored it looks lit from below, just the way an inventive Hollywood cinematographer would do it.

The Maasai Mara is an exciting place – very few Marans die of old age – and baby gnu have an especially hard time of it, since every carnivore considers them the ultimate delicacy. Hyenas are so taken with fresh baby gnu, in fact, that they track the Migration over vast distances, and frequently a little conclave of hyenas will follow a pregnant gnu, trying to induce labor, waiting for dinner to be served. The gnu answer is to give birth en masse, with over 500,000 born in the twenty-eight days of February, overwhelming the predators. Even with this trick, one of three baby gnu never reaches adulthood.

On our first day of safari, I learned that tracking animals involves sharp vision, the ability to scan vast distances and notice small matters, ferreting out the subtlest of clues: the black tips of a cheetah peeking out from the tall grass; the drape of the tail of a tree-sitting leopard; the slightly off-tone semicircle of a lion's mane. Or you can just look for where a bunch of the other Range Rovers have congregated and go see what they've found. This was usually my solution, since every time I was sure I'd spotted some significant charismatic megafauna, it turned out instead to be a stick or a rock.

After a spectacular morning of meandering around, watching the animals, we went to our Mara home, Camp Olonanna, named for its Maasai village neighbor, which immediately quashed all my fears of African campdom. Our tents were carpeted, the beds were extremely comfortable, the food was terrific, and the service was knock-your-socks-off. Every morning one of the Maasai would bring hot water in a sink for washing up, and any time you wanted a shower, you just said so, and someone would load up the shower bag with hot water from the kitchen. I soon learned that the ultimate goal of the African tourism industry is to bring you intimately close to nature, while always ensuring as many creature comforts as possible. This means tent 'lodges' that include electricity and plumbing; haute cuisine buffets; and unparalleled service that recalls the days when 'gentlemen' had 'boys.' For a democrat, this is often bizarre and disturbing . . . and when you are sipping espresso from a cliffside Craftsman-furnished patio while scanning the far horizon for elephant, it is love at first sight.

Another thing I learned about the African tourism industry is that they won't let you pick up bags or anything else that weighs over five pounds; they insist on lifting and carrying it themselves, even if you're a man and they're a woman. It turns out that they aren't acting servile from some history of colonialism; it's because they think white people are pathetic and too weak to lift or carry anything themselves. They are sincerely just trying to help.

Olonanna has two spectacular features: it's practically inside a tribal village, with Maasai running around all over the place, and its tents sit on a ridge overlooking a river filled with schools of hippopotami. I'd lie back on my canvas patio, watching these behemoth moms and kids floating in the water, and they'd watch me back. The hippos spend all day bobbing up and down, their noses snorting out exhale, their babies following every move, roaring like giant, insane bullfrogs.

Besides a Kill, it was here that I discovered another great African sight: the yawn. Hippos and cats have monumental yawns you just have to see to believe. Their mouths keep opening and opening, wider and wider, clearly demonstrating an entirely new concept of 'bite-sized.' As those jaws stretch further and further apart, you think, *they could fit an entire impala in there . . . no, a cheetah . . . maybe a zebra . . . a buffalo . . .* I wanted the hippos to come out of the water so I could get a really great picture, but at the same time I wasn't so sure it'd be a good idea having a three-thousand-pound hungry thing with huge canines nosing close by.

The gap between what Africans think about wildlife and what everyone else thinks is formidably wide. All non-Africans find hippos instantly adorable, with those beautiful cow eyes, those wagging, enormous eyelashes, and the same general body shape as Santa Claus . . . Brenda calls them 'three tons of fun!' It's especially charming to see hippos in the water with birds plopped on their heads, and I also like that they have two sets of vocal cords and ears (for communicating above and below the water), and that after a good meal, they hold perfectly still and leave their mouths open, so the fish can swim in and feast on the particles stuck in the gums, like living toothbrushes. Africans, however, do not find hippos one bit adorable.

Wouldn't you think that the continent's biggest dangers are its meat-eaters? Actually, every one of the three most lethal, the ones who, year in and year out, kill the most people, are:

3) the buffalo
2) the hippopotamus
1) the mosquito.

The first rule for traveling in African wildlife parks in fact is 'never get between a hippo and the water,' since, if they get nervous, hippo can stampede right over you without a second thought. They may spend most of their lives nibbling delicate water plants with their two-foot-wide lips, but they've also got canines that are twenty-four-inch spikes. One of the greatest wildlife filmmakers of our time, Kenyan Alan Root, was swimming at his regular water hole one afternoon when a bull attacked. It got his right calf in its jaws and shook him back and forth in the water, finally letting go after rendering his leg into a jelly and leaving a hole in the soft flesh of his calf the size of a Coke bottle. Gangrene set in, but after much antibiotic and drainage, the doctors of Nairobi Hospital were able to save his leg – though for a year afterward, the wound would throw off pieces of what the hippo had been eating before the attack. This is actually the big danger of being bitten by a wild animal – not what damage the teeth can inflict, but what sepsis the bacteria-filled carrion leftovers in their mouths can create once they get in your bloodstream. Even a brief mauling from claws unwashed since lunch can be fatal.

On game drives, our constant companions in the Mara were Isaac (a twenty-four-year-old Kalenjin) and Diana (a thirty-year-old Range Rover), the latter brought to Africa by a big-game hunter, with a bronze plaque in the dashboard to prove it. Diana was constantly pulling other, lesser vehicles out of trouble, and went through streams with such snap that Brenda would say, 'That Diana *loves* the water,' while every time we'd suddenly drop through a rut, Isaac would say, 'Oopsie!'

It was dark, time for my first night of African camping, and even though I was dead-tired from a day of travel and safari, a good night's sleep was not in the cards. First there was a tremendous noise coming down from the river, since hippos are not restful sleepers. All night long, they grunt, snort, groan, croak, ribbit and murmur . . . giants who snore. Just as I got used to all this, however, some big animal started nosing around just outside my tent, crashing through the bushes and making a ruckus. I thought I heard some giggling and assumed it was a hyena. It ran around, and then settled down for the night, just on the other side of a thin piece of canvas right next to me, and I got to spend a few hours convincing myself that it (whatever it was) wouldn't try to claw its way inside.

The next morning, we shared our dreams. Brenda and I had had various ridiculous nightmares featuring a murder cover-up, a car accident and Frank Sinatra, while Isaac dreamed he was being chased by hippos, and Peter dreamed a hyena was trying to pull the blankets off his bed. When Brenda mentioned she slept like a baby, Isaac said, 'Oh, did you wake up every hour and cry?'

American Boy Scouts sit around fires and tell stories, most of which they have to make up to make interesting. Not Africans: 'One time my friends and I went camping and they went off to get some firewood while I set up,' Isaac started. 'I heard a little "woof" behind my head and turned around to see a big buffalo staring right at me. He charged! I ran as hard as I could right up a tree and he stood down there, snorting, and finally sat down. Right at the base of the tree. And wouldn't leave! Then I heard some other snorts, and right in a line, eight more came over and stood right under the tree, watching me, and waiting. Two hours went by and I was stuck there, but finally my friends came back and scared them off.'

The incident only served to buoy Isaac's obsession with this noxious wild cow, and every one of our game drives included so much time spent with tedious herds of buffalo that Brenda finally whispered, 'You know, he could look at them *all day*.' We couldn't, since after one glimpse, they're about as thrilling as a pack of Holsteins. Every African from a cattle culture, however, is preoccupied with wild Cape buffalo and the possibility of ranching them, a possibility that has never been successfully effected, since, in a group, these formidable oxen with *That Girl* pigtails clearly enjoy chasing, trampling, goring and killing both lions and human beings. As they weigh two thousand pounds, move at thirty miles an hour, and have horns on top of their heads which they point directly at you while hurling their two-thousand-pound bodies at thirty miles an hour, this danger isn't academic. As you watch them in the field, the lead females always stare back at you, balefully considering a charge, with a look that anyone can understand: 'Don't even think of coming closer.' Perhaps they are eternally in a bad mood, since, if the buffalo birds riding their backs can't find any parasites to eat, they'll rip open a new cut to attract more.

'Another time we were camping,' Isaac continued, 'and a pride of nine lions showed up. Just like those buffalo, they hung around the site and wouldn't leave. They sat outside the kitchen, they could smell the food, and were willing to wait until they could get at it. The guy hiding in the cook tent got sick and tired of waiting, so he took a kitchen mallet and threw it right at the lead female, and she ran off and all the others followed. But the mallet had been used to make hamburger, and still had the smell of the meat on it, and a hyena, who I guess had been following the pride to see if they'd come up with anything, ran in, and grabbed it, and ran off. Very lumpy hamburgers the rest of the trip.'

Peter Gordon, Olonanna's manager, chimed in: 'One night, I

was out driving with a friend, and he had to take a leak, so we pulled over and he went out in the bush with no torch, did his business, and came back. After waiting so long I had to go, too, and I went over to exactly the spot where he'd been, but this time with a torch, and found seven lions sitting there. He'd peed right in the middle of them, not ever realizing it, and I guess they were too stupefied to jump him.'

Peter said that he gets plenty of excitement just working with tourists. 'I spent some time in a big posh place in South Africa. One morning at breakfast, this older French lady came up to me and, very hoity-toity, said, "There is a lee-zard in my room. Could you come and e-veect it?" This hotel's grounds were crawling with little geckos, and I told her that this lizard was actually a good thing to have around since it eats the mosquitoes, but she wouldn't hear of it, she just kept saying, "You must e-veect it! E-veect it!" So finally I went to the bungalow with her, really annoyed, and there, climbing the walls, was a huge monitor lizard, at least a five-footer. I'd never seen anything like it, and it took a goddamn hour to get the hissing thing out.'

Olonanna's gourmet cook was Jehosephat, but he'd never been taught the excellent *Superman* phrase *Jumping jehosephat!*, and we were proud to introduce him to it. Africa is overrun with Anglican and Cath- olic missionaries who are still converting tribal people and giving them these two-thousand-year-old baptismal names. I think the least they can do, for chrissake, is start using names from the *New* Testament.

We told everyone how honored we'd be to get a look at some pygmies (who have a dispossessed and brutalized history in Africa much like the American Indian), and Isaac told us how disappointed he was in seeing Zairian pygmies, supposedly the world's finest, since they just smoke pot and get stoned all day, and have so intermarried with other tribes that their distinctive features have all vanished. Now, they're just short.

DO YOU GROW
OR DO YOU GRAZE?

After being raised in a Texas suburb where next-door ranches were filled with idiotic, white-faced Herefords and flabby, loping

Brahmas, one of the most alien practices I've ever encountered traveling overseas is the worldwide practice of *cow worship*. I just don't get it, since even the dictionary considers 'bovine' to be 'sluggish, dull and stolid,' and besides, cows are cloven . . . two-toed . . . just like *Satan* . . . yet, the worship of cows is universal. Ancient Egypt bowed down to Hathor, the goddess who's half beef but all woman, and India still considers Brahma bulls holy, letting them wander and shit wherever they please, no matter what traffic snarls or public health menace this might entail. None of this can compare in the slightest, however, to the *Cow Cults of the Sub-Sahara*.

The Dark Continent is bloated with over 750 different tribes, tribes which have historically divvied up crops and herds. When agriculture is integrated, farmers will raise hay, alfalfa and oats to feed their sheep, goats or cattle, whose manure is in turn used to fertilize the fields and whose muscles are used to pull the plows. Almost nowhere in Africa, however, does this system prevail; either you grow (crops and settle), or you graze (herds and wander). The Bantu, who came out of Nigeria and Cameroon to sweep across the continent some two thousand years ago, were farmers who ended up making cities, kingdoms and nations out of jungles and deserts, driving out the pygmies, Bushmen and pastoralists before them; almost every urban African is Bantu. These, however, are not the people we've come to see . . . the people we've come to see are those bovine-loving nomads.

The Nuer, the Karamajong, the Ankole, the Turkana and the Maasai – to name just a few – all wander wherever there's good grass for their herds, and they all believe that God gave cattle as a special gift just for them. They also prefer male nudity, shaved-bald females, a one-legged 'heron' stance, extracting the two center bottom teeth, and ear piercings you can stick two fingers through. Nomad men in their early twenties are allowed to eat beef, since it's considered healthy for that age, but otherwise, unless an animal dies of its own, they don't eat their own meat. The cows are holy, giving milk, cheese, blood, tanned hides, dung for fuel and plaster, tails for fly swatters, and bones for jewelry, utensils, arrows and spear tips.

All the nomads are big milk drinkers, but what they really find delicious about a cow is its blood, and when one of their animals is dying, they've developed a slaughter method that conserves every drop. A group gets together and, as much as possible, immobilizes the animal while one spears it straight away into the cerebral cortex, bringing on death in seconds. Immediately a pouch is knifed out from the loose skin of the neck, and here the blood pools and is drunk immediately, hot and pungent.

In the Ma (Maasai) language, there are thirty words to describe cattle. The men sing lullabies to them, write poems about them, and give each one a name (though one Maasai family we met called all their cows 'Maria'). The more you own, the wealthier and more blessed you are. This cow belief is so powerful that any time a nomad sees cattle owned by someone not of their tribe, they believe it is their inalienable, God-given right to steal them. As you can guess, this makes for more than a little civil unrest, as everyone is out cattle-raiding against both their farming neighbors and each other. The Maasai were so fierce in their raids that they drove the Gallas, the Tatogs, the Datogas and the Dorobos away from almost all of Kenya and Tanzania, and they did a great job terrorizing both European colonizers and Muslim slave-traders. They volunteered to help fight against the Tanganyikan Germans in World War I but were turned down, since, for some reason, the British were reluctant to give the Maasai lots of guns.

Those that actually get to do the raiding are *morani*, or warriors, which is every Maasai male between the ages of seventeen and twenty-four. It used to be that *morani* had to prove their manhood by killing a lion, but that's been successfully halted, and now they can prove it by pulling a lion's tail. Brenda and I spent a great deal of time running around with the current Olonanna crop of six warriors, who always wanted to take our hands when walking, like shy young girls. We spent a morning marking their territory, watching twenty-two hippos having sex all on top of each other in a ravine, trying the local narcotic weed, and having a contest to see who could jump the highest while whooping. They sang us a war song, an a cappella number with a growling bass line knocking out the rhythm and a melody that shouts like hip-hop.

Morani stride across the grass in a confident, high-legged strut that is quick, but proud. They henna their hair, which is then tied back with beaded wire and mirrors, put quarter-sized plugs in their ears (resulting in many missing lobes) and scarify themselves with burning spear tips. They never leave the *kraal* without painting their biceps and forehead, sticking some feathers in their do, slipping on an assortment of multiple necklaces, bracelets and anklets, and wrapping the whole package up in Day-Glo-red tartan blankets. Hitchhiking *morani* will go wherever you're going, even if they started out in the opposite direction. They just want to *go*. Being a Maasai warrior is easily one of the best jobs anyone can ever hope to have: you get to run around and launch raids and steal cattle; you get to eat cow meat; you get to have sex with anyone who'll say yes; you look fabulous; and you have no responsibilities whatsoever. They are as vain and haughty and stylish as millionaire drag queens, and don't you forget it.

Given all that, it's not hard to see why plenty of adult Maasai aren't happy to be married and settled and no longer living the life of a *morani*, and one who was especially bitter about this was our guide, Olé Koyendo, who for tourists used his Dutch Catholic baptismal name 'Pierce,' though why anyone would give up 'Olé' I don't know. Olé explained many of his tribe's beliefs, such as that they don't think much of their Luo neighbors who are gentiles (uncircumcised) and unclean, and they don't go for 'the Christian story' either, since if God has a son, then why isn't he married?

Olé took us to see Olonanna village, which like all Maasai *kraals* is a big fence enclosing a series of huts, all slathered in dried-dun mud, with the holy cattle kept in a corral at the very center. The Maasai use wattle-and-daub (stick, twigs and dust) for the walls, and straw (waterproofed with cow-shit) for the roofs. As we arrived, one woman was in the middle of waterproofing her own roof, and Pierce offered to let Brenda join in the fun, but for some reason she declined.

We took a meeting with the females – shaved bald, and tough – in their group room, an open-air corral of stripped tree branches. One was blind in one eye, while another and her baby seemed barely awake, perhaps suffering from malaria or tsetse. They wanted to know many things, including the central topic of all Third World women: Do we have children? At first we say yes, we have over a hundred kids, and they ask, looking at our ages, are many twins and triplets? When we say we're joking and neither of us has any children, this causes great consternation. Finally, one of the women asks, 'But do you have pets?' *Yes*, we say, relieved, yes, we have pets. 'Then who,' she demands to know, 'is taking care of them while you are traveling?' Some friends, we say, and this appears to mollify their concerns. We then mentioned how Olé had thought Maasai were just like gazelles, with each male getting plenty of females, and was this true? They assured us that the opposite was in fact the case, that all Maasai women, especially the married ones, have lots and lots of gentlemen callers. This made Olé nervous.

Later that day we went back to the village and visited a Maasai woman in her house. She and her children lived in one room, while their young goats and calves lived in the other. After some tea and talks, we got up to leave, and Brenda said, 'I hope your life is good, and that your children are healthy and happy.' The woman thought for a while, and then replied, 'I hope your life is good, and that your *pets* are healthy and happy.'

We went to see the Maasai elders, who wanted to know all about our home, so we explained that New York City is eleven million people all trying to steal the same cattle on a massive pile of huge buildings with no farms. This also is cause for alarm, and one of the elders asks, 'With all those buildings, where do you raise the cattle? Where will the next generation live?' Of course we can't really explain this to their satisfaction. 'How we live is much better,' he says. 'We have beautiful land, and much room to grow, we have children, and we let our cattle roam.' Who could argue?

In fact, there is quite an argument going on throughout Africa over the way the nomads graze their herds. While zebra nibble the tops of grasses, gnu gnaw the middle, and gazelles daintily pluck close to the ground, cattle devour as much of a plant as they can fit in their mouths, chewing it all the way to the root. This keeps the grass from regenerating, and many now believe that where a steer goes, desert follows. Pastoralists cut down all the trees for firewood and, without wind breaks, violent rushes of air blow away the topsoil in the dry season and devastate crops in the wet. Twenty years ago, Nouakchott, the capital of Mauritania, was a three-day brisk walk from the Sahara. Now, it is *in* the Sahara, since the desert is growing by 250,000 acres a year.

'Listen: I'm both a doctor and a farmer, and I've kept my eyes open,' explained 'Flying Doctor' Anne Spoerry. 'Personally, I believe we need better farmers more than we need less reproduction. When I see the forests being burned to make way for unproductive farms, when I see ranches being carved up to be made into one-acre plots that will support no one, when I see the Tana River flowing chocolate-brown because farmers don't know how to stop erosion – that's when I really want to weep. The lifeblood of this country is in the earth, and right now it's all flowing into the sea.'

The desert isn't the only thing expanding by leaps and bounds; so are the people. Over the past twenty-one years, the populations of Kenya, Tanzania and Uganda have tripled. With so many new mouths to feed, one bit of cattle overgrazing combined with one extended drought is all it takes to produce mass famine like that seen in Ethiopia or Biafra.

One man thinks he has an answer that would solve both cattle and overpopulation. Dr. David Hopcraft is a third-generation Kenyan who grew up on a cattle ranch and who believes game ranching is the future. He conducted an experiment where he raised cattle and gazelle side by side, and he found that the Maasai open-land grazing method required one acre of land to produce one pound of meat, while modern steer ranching produced four pounds an acre, and gazelles could top fourteen pounds an acre. This success led Dr. Hopcraft to convert his entire ranch to gazelles, but it's expensive, requiring lots of acres and a vast perimeter fence to keep out predators and keep in wildlife – not exactly feasible for most of the continent's tiny farms. It's too bad; I'd love to run a gazelle ranch, going out to check on my herds of Tommies, fawn-sized antelope who stare directly into your face with tiny arching horns and erect black ears before running away with white flanks and wagging tails, like excited ponies.

Cattle competes with wildlife in every way, from the nomads driving off plains game to keep the pastures for themselves to the herds eating all the available food. There's one animal, however, who's fought back, one animal perhaps responsible for maintaining African wildlife on its present course. The trypanosome parasite carried by tsetse flies causes sleeping sickness in humans and nagana in livestock but is harmless to wildlife. Twenty thousand Africans die from it every year, and it keeps the nomads away from vast parts of the country. The major tsetse scientist is Dr. Glyn A. Vale, a Welshman who invented the perfect tsetse trap by breaking down the smell components – carbon dioxide, acetone and octenol – of oxen breath. Plenty of ecologists, however, hope Dr. Vale doesn't figure out how to eradicate tsetse, since they believe it's the one ingredient that keeps all of Africa from turning into a big dusty cattle ranch.

Enough of the bad news; enough of scientists desperately praying for tsetse. It is dusk, and growing chill, and the Maasai wrap themselves up in their signature orange-red tartan blankets, and they go off in the distance, wandering solo, red-shot lozenges against the rolling green hills.

RAGING BULL

The next morning was our last in the Mara, so we got up while it was still dark. Diana lurched through the muddy ruts along the Kechua Ridge as the sun inched up, muddy and gray. The broad sweep of the soft grasslands, dotted with spindly, flat-topped acacia trees, was as welcoming as ever, the perfect hide-and-go-seek landscape that murmured, 'Come closer, and see.' What we really wanted to find was the beast that looks so cute and adorable in zoos and circuses back home, but is really the one thing that can scare the bejesus out of you out here on the plains.

We drove along until we came to a thin strip of forest, and suddenly there they were, a whole family of the ones we've been looking for – *Loxodonta* – eight tons, thirteen feet high, with one-ton teeth and a nose of fifty thousand muscles, eating six hundred pounds of grass and leaves a day. They are the only Marans besides giraffe who commonly die of old age, except of course during the decades when Margaret Kenyatta, the then-president's daughter, was mayor of Nairobi, as she annually exported around 150 tons of ivory (meaning about 1,500 slaughtered elephants) to Hong Kong alone.

For many years, it was thought that elephants had some kind of extrasensory perception, since they can act in uncanny, supernatural ways, with a reputation among Africans of being evil. Trackers and poachers would quietly try to come up behind one, only to have it suddenly turn and kill them as if it had eyes in the back of its head. We've only recently learned that they can communicate across several miles through infrasound calls outside the range of human hearing, a sound also produced by blue whales, crocodiles and volcanoes. There's no question, however, that elephants are extremely intelligent and care for each other. In Tsavo, Kenya's most elephant-intensive park, one of the animals has figured out how to turn on the warden's water tap and get a drink, and another would smell ivory jewelry and try to pull it off the women's necks and out of their earlobes. When a young cow got her trunk caught in a poacher's snare and severed the muscular, handlike end, the other elephants fed her. They've been seen spending a week with a dead comrade, trying to nudge and lift the still-warm body, repeatedly sniffing the flesh (perhaps to determine the cause of death), and passing around the tusks to every member of the herd.

We sat in the field, watching our own herd pass by. Female elephants stay with their mothers their entire life, and their leader is always the oldest cow, who's related to every other member, a matriarch who protects her family with an astonishing display of cunning, analysis and courage. These matriarchs do not merely cry out or call if they want you to leave, they SCREAM. At one point, the herd wanted to cross the path in front of us, so the matriarch walked right up to the front of the car, huffing and shaking her head, making herself a distraction, and forming a protective block between us and the babies scurrying behind her across the road.

To our right, a beautiful and immense old bull elephant, with big, arching tusks and half an ear missing, was nodding his head back and forth while strolling through a sea of wheaty grass . . . an astonishing, perfect moment. Quite deliberately and from a vast distance, he strode across the plain, coming closer and closer. In an exact motion, he turned, facing us, and started walking directly at us, quiet, intent and serious, planning a charge. He was saying, in no uncertain terms, 'It's time for you to go,' so we did.

I came to Africa with visions of *Tarzan* and *National Geographic* and the nightly news and Sally Struthers lodged in my head, expecting great famine, gut-wrenching poverty, 'jaws and claws,' snarling cats and stampeding herds. Though the Dark Continent does have all these things, what I instead found was the Peaceable Kingdom, with mothers caring for their babies amid flocks of everything browsing in a golden sun.

It is a landscape of pasture so beautiful, and so immense, and so blossoming with life, that it forced me, overpowered, to believe that such a vast harmony must mean something, that it just can't be the random, haphazard result of an oblivious, unknowing universe. The power of life in Africa is so strong and so stirring and so overwhelming, that it made me believe, all over again, in the power of God.

P.S.: Two months after coming back to the U.S., we saw our Maasai *morani* once again. They were on television, starring in a Visa commercial.

WHEN WE WERE PREY

On a stark outcrop of gneiss in the middle of the Rift Valley is a string of tents, permanently sited, each with plumbing, carpets and electricity, arrayed against a centerpiece of towering thatch that is lobby, restaurant, pool and piazza. We'd lie back on our patio recliners, Tusker beer in one mitt, binoculars in the other, and gaze out at an endless prairie marked with baobab, euphorbia and sansevieria, set against a gently curving river with banks of sand. Far from Kansas, this is a prairie of fish eagles, fiscal shrikes, fire finches, sunbirds and bee-eaters; of hoopoes, boubous, bulbuls and oxpeckers; of hamerkop, nightjar, avocet and jacana; of widow-birds, chats, stilt and wigeon; of gnu, zebra, elephant, leopard and lion. It is, as Carl Jung would have it, 'the stillness of the eternal beginning, the world as it has always been.'

Our view is of one of Tanzania's main parks, Tarangire, and one day at noon the vast herds were immobilized, stockstill and gazing fixedly at a point on the river's bank, various zebra honking and barking in their hiccupy, donkeys-with-emphysema fashion. We're told that Africans have succeeded in domesticating gazelle and eland, but not zebra, but how can this be, since don't you remember chimp Cheeta riding a zebra in *Tarzan's Greatest Adventure*?

Our waiter, Desderus the Pogono, then told us that all these grazers were frozen since they wanted to go to the river, but they could see a lioness there, waiting for prey. Time stopped, as did the honking, into a moment of dead silence. There was a signal hidden from us, perhaps given by the subsonic elephants, and the herds now made their way to the river in an *en masse* choreography, while a half-dozen buzzards winged the updrafts just above the spot where the animals had been staring. Lunch had been served.

If you've ever been made uncomfortable being treated as a sex object, just wait till you go to Africa and have the sensation of being treated as a *food* object. You know the feeling you get, deep down inside, when you're in the middle of eating and a cockroach scurries across the table? That's exactly the attitude man-eaters have toward prey. When they spot you, their eyes fill with loathing and disgust. During that afternoon's drive, there was this leafless, dead tree, and sitting at the very top was a big brown martial eagle, scanning for food. As Brenda and I passed directly under, reclining on the back bench and looking up at him through the roof ports, he scanned to determine if *we* might be tasty, and that yellow-eyed, predator gaze of pure hate was so direct and unsparing that, even though we were completely protected, we felt the harsh chill of fear that only prey can have.

Later, a lioness decided to sit by the toasty asphalt road, and her mate followed. She snoozed, perfectly carefree; he glared at every car going by with such hate and ferocity that we thought he'd attack at any minute. When you see a Kill, there's always this moment when the food candidates seem like they could easily fight back, but instead they just give up and give in to the inevitable. You can't understand why until you are yourself the object of a lion's overpowering stare, a look hypnotic with raw hate and the power of will. It made us want to give up and give in, and we were inside an ATV.

That night, one of the lions killed something, so all the other lions started screaming. The donkeys, the elephants, the buffalo, the birds, the monkeys and the baboons, hearing this, all started screaming, too. I had imagined that being out in the savanna wilderness would be peaceful, but guess again. The animals roared, and barked, and screamed and hollered, and they were so loud it sounded like they were right outside the lightly zippered door of my thin canvas tent. I could only guess what the four young French children staying next door were thinking, as their walls fluttered in the breeze. It's the pit of the night, and the lions' roar, directly outside, grows louder, and louder, and louder . . .

THE WORLD WITHIN
YOUR HANDS

When you were a child, did you have your own bowl of goldfish, or a terrarium of lizards, or, at least, a pot of *Sea Monkeys*? Do you remember the engrossing sense of comfort and joy you had in holding that entire world of living things in the palm of your hands? One thing you must see before dropping dead is the African version of this self-contained world, a mesmerizing place that began when a raging volcano blew itself into collapse, its peak falling into a soft crater. Inside, the eruptive spew settled to a ground of perfect fertility, and the earth's convulsions formed, at different spots, a grassy plain, a wood, a soda lake and a series of muddy pools, swamps and streams, which in turn attracted every animal in the neighborhood, from termites to rhinoceros – all of Africa in the palms of your hands (if your hands happen to be carrying binoculars, which they will). The crater's two-thousand-foot-high ridge throws the same beauty that hits you when you're on a tropical island with palm trees in the foreground and a stark rock mountain in the back, for there, in one view, are two opposing landscapes that seem to offer the whole world, yours for the taking.

Ngorongoro's caldera walls are dried dun brown, with a rim of evergreen forest whose condensation creates a permanent halo of clouds encircling the ridge. Off-center is a soda lake of salt-white, with a continuous ashy vapor rising to the sky. There's one grove of flat-topped acacias, another of strangler figs, and a third marked by the jaundice-yellow bark of the fever tree. This is another kind of Eden, far different from the golf-course lawns and amber waves of the Mara. It is a landscape that is stark, lunar, spectral, and exactly how I imagined the earth looked at the dawn of the hominid. It is the First Days.

In the opening twenty minutes of driving through this ex-volcano, we saw a pair of jackals, eight ostriches, two bat-eared fox couples (who can hear the footsteps of insects), a hyena mom with four cubs, two forest elephants, and countless, vast herds of gazelle, buffalo, gnu and impala. With wildlife so luxe, Ngorongoro crater has become such a draw that in one corner of the park, there's always a dozen Rovers and minivans staring fixedly at a barely visible leopard sleeping off lunch in the limbs of a flamboyant tree. We ate our own meal while black kites, a kind of small falcon, swooped and attacked like Hitchcock's *Birds*.

The oval scar of ash at the crater's center is the fishless Lake Makat, which come spring will bloom into a spinach-soup green as a dense mass of algae chokes its way across the waters. As the algae become visible, a pink, waving stripe descends across the sky – 100,000 flamingos, with blood-red eyes and legs, black beaks and pink-peach feathers, arriving from across the Rift to feed on their only meal – the spirulina blue-green algae. Since there are no fish in Lake Makat, all the Ngoro fish eagles have switched to flamingo meat, and as the pink clouds descend, these raptors gather to patiently watch from the shoreline.

Soda lakes are oozing with natron, a substance refined to make glass and detergents (and, at one time, Egyptian mummy preservative). These lakes are saltier than the ocean, and the reduced rainfall over the past thousands of years has concentrated their minerals into a corrosive alkaline broth: stinging, soapy, bitter, hot and caustic. One biologist working in nearby Lake Natron got soda crust inside his boot by accident. By the time he made it back to shore and took off his shoes, he'd nearly lost both feet from chemical burns, and couldn't work for a month.

Half the world's six million flamingos live in the Rift Valley, and on the ground, they look just like a huge flock of big pink gawky chickens who spend all day running back and forth between the algae moldering in burning lakes, and the fresh springs on land; between lakes filled with food, and water fit to drink. Flamingos feed with a jaw of colanders where their beaks ought to be, and the chicks can develop soda rings around their legs which, if not regularly washed off in spring waters, will grow larger and larger until they cripple. Ornithologists call these 'the anklets of death.' Waiting offshore for the chicks to fail are those eagles, as well as patient, dour marabou storks (the undertakers of the avian world), and the most mythical animal in all of Africa, an animal P.J. O'Rourke described as 'nonchalant but shifty, in little groups meandering not quite aimlessly . . . [with] circular eyes set on the front of their faces like people. They look at you like people do. Not good people.'

BLOOD FEUD

These animals are to Africa what black cats and bats were once to the U.S., the premier supernatural beasts, mysterious, incomprehensible and a little frightening. Certain Africans believe that witches milk them, and that it's dangerous to kill one, since its witch owner may find out and retaliate. They melt perfectly into their background, as the fur is the exact color of the dusty brown hills, but close up their mottled pelt looks like it's afflicted with mange. With that loping gait (from the front legs being one third longer than the hind), that prominently long and fat neck, those lunatic giggles of joy, and those disturbing meal habits (such as eating dead people), they really do make you think of Cerberus, the hound of hell . . . and every African we met had more than a few great stories about them:

One village was having a lot of trouble with a hyena that kept breaking into the houses and the stables and eating the calves and chickens. But no matter what they did, they couldn't catch it. He was so fast! Finally, someone got a bucket, and filled it with gravel, and then filled it with blood. Even though it was in the middle of the village, the hyena came that night and ate it. You see, this animal is never afraid, and once it's decided it wants something, it will persevere against all odds. So this hyena ate the tub of bloody gravel, and then it couldn't run so fast, and that's how they caught and killed it.

If you're out in the bush and someone gives you trouble and you have an enemy, there's a simple answer. You just get a bone from the kitchen and tie it with a rope to his tent while he's sleeping. The hyenas will come that night and run off with the bone, taking the tent with them.

I knew that hyenas were the stupidest animals of them all when I saw one in a feeding frenzy start to eat itself. He was in the middle of a bunch of them, all eating a zebra, and this one got some of the zebra blood on its stomach, so it started eating that spot where the blood was, and it chewed on its own belly until it killed itself! Well, when the other hyenas finished the zebra and saw he died, they ate him, too.

Off in the distant grasslands we saw a den of cubs, their puppy faces suddenly appearing on the horizon as they reared up to take a peek, too cute by half to be related to the mangy-looking, feral creature that in fact was their mother. Hyenas may look like dogs, but are genetically related to cats, and one field scientist has claimed that the female purrs while suckling. If one of its cubs dies, a hyena mother will delicately remove it from the nest and, a few hours later, eat it. Their immensely strong jaws can support their body weight – they can hang by their jaws from prey trying to escape – and those same jaws can crush and chew up bone, which hyena stomach acids can digest. Perhaps their most interesting, peculiar and alarming quality is that female spotted hyena have giant, elongated, erectile clitorises, and sacks of tissue that look just like a set of testicles. Just as dogs sniff each other's butts, hyenas sniff each other's genitals in a 'hello, who are you?' ritual. It meant, however, that Brenda and I were dying to ask our guides the ultimate African question, the question for which we never got up enough nerve: 'Excuse me sir, but please could you tell us all about the renowned pseudopenis of the female spotted hyena?'

It's ironic that humans today have such a low opinion of scavengers, carrion-eaters and parasites, since in the First Days, when we were all weapon-free hominids, this would've been our own position in life. We'd be right in there with the buzzards, the marabou storks and the jackals, all patiently waiting for a lion or hyena to have enough of feeding so we could rush in and fight for leftovers. In Africa, half the battle is in the killing and half is in the keeping, with plenty of carnivores spending most of their time looking for other predators in the middle of dinner so they can try to take the meal away from them. We may think of hyenas as shifty thieves, but in fact it's the male lion who spends more of his time stealing kills from hyenas than in doing his own hunting. The two species hate each other so much that one biologist characterized it as a 'blood feud.' Lions will chase and kill hyenas for no reason, while hyenas will keep chasing a lion long after its kill has been claimed.

The Ngoro lions have been so extensively studied that every individual is known personally. We met two sisters, Wedge and Bounce, daughters of Hook and Ahab, who hid their cubs in the tall reeds next to a hippo pool. Girl lions are sleek and muscular, while the males are tubby; as a couple, it's Demi Moore meets John Goodman. Wedge and Bounce had brought down a Cape buffalo; the riskiest and most dangerous thing for a lion to try to eat because those pigtail horns can tear open a stomach just like that. When we found their prize, they had dragged it into a tree-shaded stream to keep the meat from spoiling and away from the other kleptoparasites. We could easily see, in the shade of the clearing, the eaten-away ribs and the head lying in the water, a still life certainly unique to this continent.

All of the buffalo above the waterline had been eaten, and now it was time to bring the carcass ashore and get at the rest. While one of the lionesses pulled with all her might to drag the thing up, a young male, whose mane was just coming in, decided that now was just the right time to plunk down on top of the buffalo's neck. She pulled; he sat with his hiney in the water, looking around; finally she yanked, he fell off, and she landed supper, which he was only too happy to run over and eat. Soon enough, the whole pride was inside the carcass, five big lions crowded together, gnawing at whatever leftovers still clung to the bones, and snarling at each other's poor table manners.

There's nothing like seeing a lion sleeping off a big meal – its belly matted with blood and its face covered in flies – to understand what 'king of the jungle' really means. On a ridge above this gory sitcom, two just-born cubs were nursing, their tiny kitten faces popping above their recumbent mother from time to time to catch a look at the puny humans below. Not one single beast, even the kittens, seemed to care that a line of Rovers (whose accelerators sound just like a predator's growl) was sitting and watching them gnaw and suckle.

In the 1960s, a sudden population boom of blood-sucking tsetse flies decimated the Ngoro lions, killing off 85 percent of them. Now the fly population is back to normal, and the various Ngoro prides number about a hundred. It's always the little things that'll get you.

They got us. Tanzania, besides all its other troubles, is filled with big, black, biting flies who swarm over any carbon dioxide exhale. They infiltrated our Rover, giving us a whole new respect for Maasai giraffe-tail fly swatters and big cans of *Off!* As followers of Shirley MacLaine know only too well, flies were once human beings who made many bad choices in life, and as a result were reincarnated as dreadful flies, flies who deliberately try to annoy you so that you will kill them, releasing them from this mortal coil and giving them the chance to be reincarnated as something better . . . perhaps worms.

We were only too glad to help.

Our guide in Tanzania was a Meru named Billdad, who had one of the oddest personalities to ever become a hospitality industry employee. Billdad was incredibly well educated, and knew the answer to almost every question about African history, nature and culture that we could come up with, but getting him to talk was torture. He was shy about his English, and so was perfectly happy just driving from one great spot to the next, never saying a word.

Billdad did enjoy discussing his thoughts about the various nationalities he'd encountered. In order, Tanzanian guides' favorite tourists are Americans, Japanese, Spaniards and Germans, with the English and the French in a dead heat for last. In New York City, where we come from, the British tourist is quite famous – famous for trying to move into your apartment, eat all your food, drink all your liquor, take all your drugs, and get as many of his friends in on the act as he possibly can. It turns out the English have exactly the same reputation in Tanzania, where the guides' nickname for them is Mompari, a tribe so notoriously cheap that when they eat the Tanzanian national meal, they don't cook it with fish . . . they just have a picture of the fish sitting at the table. Billdad also told us that Australians call English tourists 'whinging poms,' because they complain all the time that nothing's ever good enough for them.

JAMBO-HO!

The most popular Swahili phrase of tourist-infected Africa used to be 'Jambo!' (*hello!*), from the popular children's television program of the same name featuring a grown-up Dennis the Menace accompanied by a trick-wielding elephant. It has since been joined by 'Hakuna Mattata' (*What? Me worry?*) from the immensely popular children's movie *The Lion King*. Today, every Tanzanian working the tourist trade approaches you with downcast, sorry eyes and dour lips to say, 'Jambo . . . hakuna mattata.'

Now I don't know about you, but in certain situations I can only think, 'What would Hayley Mills do?' Though the star of any number of memorable motion pictures, Hayley's most profound role was when she portrayed a winsome and mischievous nun trainee, a genre Sally Field would later attempt to perfect. Brenda and I were in a Hayley mood when we decided that these sad African 'hellos' and 'hakunas' just weren't doing the trick, so we went up to all the Africans we met and said, 'Do you know the new, fun way to say hello? It's Jambo-ho!' And they would say, 'Jambo,' and we'd say, 'No, it's the new, fun way to say hello. Jambo-ho!' and they would say, 'Jambo,' and we'd say, 'Jambo-ho!' and finally they'd concede with a 'Jambo . . . ho . . .' Sure do hope *The Trouble with Angels* gets picked up for African broadcast real soon.

We were hurtling along the main savanna road in the late afternoon, noticing one particular love-drunk purple ostrich, who'd started running an hour ago and was still at it, when Billdad mentioned we probably wouldn't be seeing any rhino. Ngorongoro had one hundred of them in 1965, but only thirteen are left today, and they like to hide (no wonder). Just as the words left his mouth, we saw two couples, most likely mothers and daughters, trundling through the grass exactly like squint-eyed dinosaur tanks. They've been here on earth looking just like this for fifty-five million years, and they can be frightened by the sound of a camera click. If you're ever walking around Africa and that little click causes your own rhino to charge, remember to wait until almost the very last second and then step aside. The rampaging beast is so blind, it'll just keep going and going and going.

In 1900, one million black rhino ran through Africa; today there are twenty-four hundred left. The Chinese think crushed horn can cure fever and skin disorders, Indians think it fixes impotence, while baby rhino urine is drunk in Rangoon to alleviate sore throats (a practice that brings $750 a year to the Calcutta Zoo rhino urine export business). The biggest rhino poaching, however, took place during the 1970s, when half of Africa's population was slaughtered to satisfy an OPEC-fueled Yemeni shopping craze. Yemeni men, it turns out, have a craving to own a traditional *jambiyya* dagger, the handle of which is made from a rhino horn. When their oil reserves created a new class of local millionaires, everyone could now afford to get these spiffy knives. Thankfully, the country placed a ban on importing the horn and the OPEC economy faltered enough to stop this peculiar shopping spree.

In April of 1997, the chief of Ngoro's anti-poaching division had ordered his team away from the park for a night, and the next morning one of the crater's rhino was found dead, its horn missing. The warden has been charged and will likely lose his job, but a local (who wanted to be anonymous) thought little else would happen to him: 'Maybe he gets a fine, maybe jail, one month. But then he goes home, rich man.' On the black market, a rhino horn is currently worth $10,000, making it exactly twice as good as gold.

Our only disappointment in Africa was never seeing a cheetah, or an aardvark, or my favorite of them all, the bushbaby, an insect-eating, tree-living, branch-jumping nocturnal creature, six inches high. Part-monkey, part-cat and part-mouse, the bushbaby has big, round, amber eyes and a haunting, ghastly cry. I'm keen to see cheetahs, and soon, because they saunter around like skinny rich girls, bark like dogs, will kill for fun, and their population has so diminished that now, all the cheetahs in the world are directly related to each other and completely in-bred. Just think – within a few generations, we'll get to see three-eyed cheetahs, and six-legged cheetahs, and two-headed cheetahs . . .

BUMPS AHEAD

At the very heart of the Rift Valley is the town of Arusha, the terminus of the Tanzanian tourist industry, which turned out to be a big slum filled with fly-by-night travel agents and energetic touts. Don't do what we did and get conned into visiting Cultural Heritage, the world's most egregious and overpriced tourist trap. Instead, you should tour the world-class auto shop *Dimple Motors* (where you can get great deals on fully stocked Dimples), as well as the local nightspot, Friends' Intensive Care Bar & Butchery, an operation that reminded me of one of my college friends' failed franchise ventures: Joe's Bar, Grill and Vasectomy Clinic. Just down the road is the wonderful town of Keratu, on whose highway you'll find serious-faced ten-year-olds, performing the boogie-woogie for your pleasure and your tips, along with a flautist in a devil's mask prancing across the meridian, and little girls making the 'check, please!' symbol in the air so you'll throw them a pen.

You may be a tolerant person who doesn't mind the many ups and downs of Third World travel, but even you won't be so forgiving when you drive from Arusha to Ngorongoro or Serengeti on Tanzania's key highway for both its tourists (who bring in $100 million a year in park fees alone) and the vast number of businesses depending on them. This 'road' is an unpaved avenue of rocks in such terrible condition that any knowledgeable driver uses the parallel, unpaved Maasai cattle track instead. The world's fastest speed-demon can't top ten miles an hour and so the thirty-mile trip to Ngoro takes three solid hours. Pitched about like a Vegas roll of dice, we couldn't read, we couldn't write, we couldn't eat, we couldn't drink, we couldn't even think; we could only look out the window, hang on for dear life, and endure. After the first two hours passed, there was one thought that kept going through my head over and over again, and it was the question of whether or not it is medically possible to be *bounced to death*. After three hours of this nauseating endurance test, we saw the greatest road sign in all of Africa: BUMPS AHEAD.

Before getting there, I imagined that Tanzania, built in independence on the merger of Tanganyika and Zanzibar, would be a world of exotic lushness. With its British and German past, it's a nation where zebra rhymes with Debra and hyena rhymes with sienna. There's Lake Tanganyika, which features swimming cobras, rock-licking chimps looking for a mineral supplement, and a thriving tropical fish export business. There's Zanzibar, land of clove plantations, where it's easy to get hungry, since, as old Africa hand Denis Boyles observed, the air is filled with the odor of just-baked hams. Next door is perhaps the most exotic island of them all, Madagascar, home of our evolutionary forebears, the nervous, hopping lemurs, with their mix of cat, raccoon and chimpanzee personae, and where I would wander, hand in hand with you, through the steamy mists of the vanilla farms, watching young boys hand-pollinate their shy orchid blooms.

We saw none of this, as Zanzibar was in the middle of a cholera epidemic and vacations in Madagascar were priced for indolent spendthrifts. What we saw instead was how two countries in almost identical economic straits at the end of colonialism in the 1960s – Kenya and Tanzania – could, in a mere four decades, evolve in exactly opposite directions. While Kenya is so developed it's practically no longer of the Third World, Tanzania has pretty much become an economic black hole. Of the three countries making up East Africa's Rift Valley, even Uganda (which spent decades in civil turmoil while its president ate its citizens) is doing far better than Tanzania, which consistently rates as one of the five poorest countries in the world. Sad little Haiti is 80 percent wealthier than Tanzania, and Stone Age Papua New Guinea is almost ten times as rich. On average, Tanzanians earn thirty-five cents a day.

From the statistics, it's baffling. The country has plenty of food, diamonds, tin, phosphates, coal, gold, natural gas, gypsum, cobalt, nickel and gemstones. African scholar Sanford Ungar calls it 'the most aided country in all of Africa,' with Scandinavians alone providing $320 million a year. In the thirty-five years since independence, $37 billion has been loaned or given outright to a country of twenty-nine million people.

History, though, has the answer. In the 1960s, when Africans started demanding their independence, the European colonial powers basically responded with 'enough of this,' and ran back home. Even considering their dreadful expatriate crimes, the way in which

Europeans turned over the reins and evacuated the continent may in fact be the most seriously heinous act in European-African history – the equivalent of throwing your six-year-old daughter out on the street in her underpants – and the resulting power vacuum was filled by local horrors and incompetents of every type. When the Brits pulled out of Tanzania, the entire country had a total of thirteen college graduates, one of whom, Julius Nyerere, became president. Nyerere was one of the few African leaders to try to solve one of the continent's key social ills, tribalism (the thinking that you're a Maasai first and a Kenyan second), and he was the only African head of state to stand up to Uganda's Idi Amin. Nyerere is a great man, admired and respected all over the world . . . but not for his understanding of economics.

In 1967, the president collectivized the farms, with around 65 percent of the rural population herded into eight thousand preplanned cooperative villages. It was a catastrophe. At a mere one acre, the redistributed farms were too small to support their owners, much less evolve into agribusiness. He then nationalized over 330 companies, which was just as disastrous; half of them went bankrupt. Today, Dar es Salaam, the capital, is plagued by blackouts, and practically every office comes equipped with kerosene lamps or candles to make do with the daily power cuts. The few Darians who've succeeded in spite of all this are so rare they have their own nickname – *waBenzi* – the people of the expensive German cars. Prostitution is on the upswing; meet the right pimp in Dar and beautiful, dusty whores will knock at your hotel room all night long, saying, 'I am your friend. Please let me come in. I will be good to you.' A hippo appeared in a Dar suburb during a drought and no one, not even the police, had ever seen such a thing before, so they ate it.

These are Tanzania's unique problems, but the overriding reason for Africa's endless, insurmountable continental traumas is that all these nations are so very young. Kenya, pretty much the oldest independent, is just about to turn forty, the equivalent of the United States at around 1816 – not a great time to be living there, either.

When you are traveling through Africa, however, hardly any of this strikes you personally. You, after all, are in the travel bubble.

You are there, and you watch the equatorial night falling with immense haste to reveal all the stars in the sky. You are there, and you are forced to ask yourself all the important questions, such as: Is there anything more romantic than the shadow of a trotting giraffe couple set against the orange-purple sunset of the plains? Will anything in our lives beat just watching a line of baby elephants following their mothers through a waving field of tall grass? Can you believe how so many of these animals have no fear whatsoever; how as you're sightseeing them, they come right over and sightsee you? And, is there anything as disturbing as an elephant with a full erection?

At dusk one evening in Tarangire, we stood on the back seat and held on to the rails as the Cruiser raced across the plains, the rut road bouncing us to a horse's gallop, the dry wind in our hair, a breathtaking red/blue/purple sunset (that Turner only wishes he could have been able to paint) floating in the sky. Animals from elephant to gnu ran pace with us, and it was one of those exhilarating moments you can never forget; one perfect hour of magic and beauty. It was also the moment all who come here hope to find; the moment when we could feel the continent personally, just for ourselves; the moment that we knew damn well (regardless of whatever the paleontologists may ultimately claim) that in the middle of this mad bounty of life, Africa is our Motherland. Africa is where our ancestors came from; Africa is our first home.

P.S.: Three months after getting back to the States, I got some letters. On our last day in Tanzania, the car's axle had thrown a bolt, and there was nothing to do but wait out the fix over coffee in the Keratu #1 Restaurant. We introduced the staff to the idea of business cards, and they used these to write their first overseas letter to us. At the top of these letters, it said:

JAMBO-HO!

THE LAST OF THE BUSHMEN

'I knew him for a Dorobo, one of that race of hunters living in the forest on game they trapped or shot with poisoned arrows. They did not cultivate, they existed on meat and roots and wild honey, and were the relics of an old, old people who had once had sole possession of all these lands – the true aborigines . . . They knew all the ways of the forest animals, even of the bongo, the shyest and the most beautiful, and their greatest delight was to feast for three days upon a raw elephant.'

—ELSPETH HUXLEY

Most Third World people see American movies and TV shows and are completely inspired. They just can't wait to get California ranch homes and Aprica baby-strollers and Star-Tac cell phones and unlimited Internet access. There are a few left in the world, however, who live as they've always lived, maintaining their traditions against all odds, fighting for the life they prefer against whatever schemes their government or Red Cross or U.N. may hatch to drag them into modern times. These are people who want nothing to do with the twentieth century . . . in fact, most of them want nothing to do with the nineteenth, fifteenth, eleventh or fifth centuries, either. You can think they are traditionalists, maintaining their ancient culture in the face of global homogenization, or you can think they are anachronisms, refusing to accept modern benefits, from housing to nutrition to medicine. Whatever your opinion, these compelling and remarkable beings from another time are now quickly vanishing from the earth.

Whenever I get the chance, I like to go look at them.

BY THE SHORES OF LAKE EYASI

If you took the vast, bleak asphalt of a derelict parking lot covered it with six inches of black and gray dust and grime, littered it up with trash and garbage, and then constructed a series of feces-colored wattle-and-daub huts with hammered tin roofs, you'd have a fairly accurate model of the village Ongden, Tanzania, a free-for-all eco-horror. One of the Third World's greatest problems is overgrazing, which ultimately leads to barren, aseptic deserts, and here you can see it in action. Nothing grows in Ongden besides half-dead, dust-choked bits of scraggle weed, dead-white bramble bush and leafless thorn trees with two-inch spikes. Overgrazing and desertification also produces a gritty dust that gets in every crack of your body, as well as a roaring wind, unstopped by any leafy trees, that continuously throws grime into your face. If there ever was a landscape that was godforsaken, this was it . . . but Brenda and I had to come here, since Ongden is the nearest village to where we could search for the last of the Bushmen.

Originally called Hottentots, the nomads here are now known as the Hadza, relatives of the Kalahari's San Bushmen, whom you may remember as the stars of that international sensation *The Gods Must Be Crazy!* As Africa booms and ceaselessly overpopulates, people like these, who refuse to join mainstream society and settle into farming or ranching communities, get pushed deeper and deeper into the back bush, into places where no one else wants to go . . . to the continent's no-man's-lands. In the mountains of north Uganda live the Ik, and in the Ituri forests of Congo live the Twa, and in the Kalahari Desert live the San, and in each case, these were the first people living in their territories, pushed aside by emigrant Africans into the outlands. Ongden, near the shores of Lake Eyasi, is right at the nether-point of Turkana, Laetoli and Olduvai, the greatest of the archaeological hominid finds. This is where the Hadza have ended up in Tanzania, at both the very beginnings and the farthest ends of the earth.

Our guide to nowhere turned out to be the young, vivacious, baseball-cap-loving Momoya. While his mother, siblings and friends live just down the road exactly as their tribe, the Datoga, have lived for thousands of years, Momoya is completely a man of the twentieth century, one extraordinarily busy entrepreneur running his own convenience store, farm and travel business. He's Ongden's version of a movie star. As we pass the ripe and welcoming gaze of a beautiful woman carrying a huge jug on her head, Momoya returns her look, and then admits that he, like all the area's males, is very attracted to a strong-necked woman . . . which is something we hope makes it onto Dylan's next album.

As he goes about his business, Momoya turns his entire life into mini-rap ditties that he sings unselfconsciously and continuously:

> Now Momoya is driving
> Driving into the desert
> He turns the wheel
> And the car turns too fast
> Slow down, Momoya!

As we're walking through Ongden, a voice calls out from the town's biggest house; it's another Momoya admirer, the daughter of the Onion King, the area's richest man, just back from Arusha with some mail:

> Momoya has some letters
> Here's one from his sister
> She's having a baby
> And he'll be Uncle Momoya!

After seeing the look in the eyes of the Onion Princess, we tell Momoya that he should pursue this girl and combine forces with

219

her father to take over Ongden and rename it Momoyaville, but he laughs this off. Later, watching him do all his various business dealings, however, we realized that maybe he doesn't need an alliance with the Onion King to take over . . .

Our first stop on the Momoya tour is to see his mother, Melongsin, who lives just outside of town in a wattle-and-daub, thatch-roofed cabin with chickens and kittens and a magnificent Datoga wardrobe. She shows us her various outfits: black cloaks ringed in ostrich feathers . . . a tanned leather robe completely embroidered in beads . . . and just like a Maasai woman, she shaves her head, pierces her ears, and wears spectacular amounts of gold, brass and beaded necklaces, earrings, bracelets and anklets. It's hard in most cases to distinguish a Maasai from a Datoga, but they are mortal enemies; the Maasai drove the Datoga out of the rest of Kenya and Tanzania to live in this bushland, and the Datoga, in turn, drove the Hadza Bushmen deeper into the desert.

We ourselves drove deeper to meet a very traditional band of Datoga, one extended family living alone on the edges of the wilderness. The men were out hunting and driving the herds, so we hung out with the women: Ooshoka (who looks just like a happy Janet Jackson) and Udamaip (a thin Aretha Franklin) are both married to Gidobat, while Gidobat's sons are married to Udamashagah (a Grace Jones look-alike) and Utehambi (a hatless Erykah Badu). I'm not making this up; these women could easily pass as celebrity impersonators save for the fact that they wear embroidered leather robes and huge amounts of brass jewelry (Udamashagah also wraps a red-tartan blanket around her head, just like a stylish Arabian princess), and for the fact that they've scarified themselves. They've all used razors to prick a series of knicks in the pattern of interlocking sideways crazy-eights around their eyes, and then rubbed an ash paste from the fire into the cuts to make permanent, raised dots.

There's a problem when we first arrive, however, because these women don't care for my looks: 'Your blue eyes are bad! They're the same as a leopard in the moonlight.' So I took them at their word and growled like a leopard, and hooted like a monkey, and lowed like a cow, and meowed and hissed and made sci-fi-effect sounds and carried on like an idiot . . . and soon enough, we had a language-free 'who can sound the most like an animal?' contest going, and they loved it.

It turned out that their primary experience with Anglos has been with scientists (who are distant and watching and take notes and then leave) and doctors (who come on relief missions to vaccinate the women and babies with hypodermic needles). Brenda and I, however, were their first clown act.

The four women seemed like the best of friends, and after getting over my leopard eyes and realizing we weren't here to coldly study or poke them with needles, they started playing around with us, a troupe of high school girls . . . trying on our sunglasses, looking through our cameras, trading back and forth my business cards, and teaching us Datoga dancing, which features an awful lot of hopping up and down.

Like the Hadza and the San, the Datoga speak a click language, which is hard to translate. One word is what we do with the tongue in the front of the mouth to make 'tsk, tsk.' Another is the 'hey baby!' or 'giddyap horse!' ticking noise from putting your tongue on the side of your teeth, and clicking. Another is half click, half pop, when you put your tongue at the front of the palate and let it flop. Another is the smoochy kiss you use with cats and babies. I tried getting them to teach me these things, but I was such a bad student they quickly gave up, obviously thinking I must be retarded.

Much of their day was spent walking miles to the nearest river, filling up huge plastic tanks with water, and then walking back home, so we gave them a lift; their first time in a car. They screamed, laughed and clicked the whole way, but sadly, Utehambi got too excited and turned carsick and puked all over the back seat. They laughed till they thought they would die at this, with even poor Utehambi giggling and puking simultaneously. After dropping them off and cleaning out the vomit, we set off for the middle of nowhere.

HOW TO RUN AWAY FROM HOME

If Ongden looks like hell, then the desert where the Hadza have been run off to scratch out a living is hell's deepest pit, a remarkably

221

ugly, ravaged and desolate place. The soil is black-gray dust and gravel; the only plants are nightmarish thorn trees, baobabs that look dead, prickly pear cactus groves, and straggler bushes grasping at the poor soils. The heat is relentless . . . literally breathtaking. We gasped and tottered, praying for shade.

We arrived to find a very happy bunch of Hadza with two stewpots going at once. In one pot boiled the meat of an impala, while its head hung from the branches of a nearby thorn tree – food for the wife and kids. The other pot, with a meal destined for the chief and his four brothers, was stewing the flesh of a baboon, which is easily the Hadza's all-time favorite food. The baboon's and antelope's pelts had been smoked and were drying, stretched out and pegged, in the sun. The chief had celebrated this wonderfully successful hunt by skinning the baboon's head and wearing it as a fur cap, prompting Brenda to note:

> *Yesterday: Baboon.*
> *Today: Baboon hat.*

After baboon, impala and other wild meats, the Hadza's favorite foods are honeycomb, figs, dates, tamarinds, seeds, mushrooms, tubers, roots and berries. They find bees' nests by always listening for the loud, insistent call of the honeyguide, a black-throated bird with a piercing trill that leads badgers and humans to honey and then feeds after these others have opened up the nest. If no honey is left for this bird, Africans believe, the animal will lead the next man who follows its call to a hidden lion, or perhaps a snake. If the Hadza kill something really big, like a buffalo, the entire band goes and lives by the carcass until it's fully digested.

The Bushmen look like people who get by on very little in the middle of nowhere; they are short, sinewy, dusty and snaggle-toothed. The chief has one eye that runs wild, and with the ears sticking up on his fuzzy baboon hat, he resembles a Lost Boy from *Peter Pan*. At first the children looked on us with terror, probably assuming we were about to inject them with hypodermic needles, but their mother clicked-sang until they calmed down.

The Hadza used to wear grass skirts and sandals made from animal pelts; now they wear Goodwill donations too tatty to suit the tastes of other Tanzanians. Their clothes, their land, everything, is a hand-me-down from the rest of the country, but if you dream of leading a lifestyle of simple abundance, here are your ultimate role models. All they own are shorts, shoes, shirts, bows, arrows, knives, cooking pots, pipes and a few pieces of handmade jewelry. For dancing music, they turn a hunting bow into a twangy, one-string fiddle.

The tribe offered me a lunch of baboon and Brenda some fresh impala, but in an amazing coincidence, we'd just eaten and had to pass. Then to celebrate their good baboon luck, just like the Twa and the Ik, everybody must get stoned. When Peter Matthiessen, watching exactly the same event thirty years ago, commented that 'both men and women smoke the stone pipe with gusty sucks accompanied by harsh ritual coughing, which is followed in turn by a soft ecstatic sigh,' he doesn't mention that they're smoking hash, and that he could've just as easily been describing my dorm room in college.

After the chief had celebrated enough, he and two brothers invited us on a hunt, and even though I'm too clumsy to silently stalk anything, we accepted. As we walked, they explained how much they loved living here, since just a quick jaunt away, in the shadow of Lake Eyasi, are acres of desert rose, the source of the poison for their arrows and spears. We followed them, in that unbelievable heat, under trees of thorns that stuck into your back, and through bushes of spikes that stuck into your legs and arms, and the dust kept blowing right up your nose. It was hell on earth. The Hadza were having the time of their lives.

In 1924, a Tanganyikan district officer came across a tribe of Bushmen, and his description remains just as accurate today: 'He is a creature of the bush and as far as I can see he is incapable of becoming anything else. Certainly he does not desire to become anything else, for nothing will tempt him to leave his wilderness or abandon his mode of living. He asks nothing from the rest of us but to be left alone . . . He worries little about the future and not at all about the past; he is happy and envies no man.' In 1972, Tanzanian President Nyerere had a housing complex built and forced the Hadza to move there. They lasted four days before running back into the bush.

The Hadza's nearest relatives, the San of the Kalahari, have been decimated to a population of around fifty thousand, with half of those still living as neolithic hunter-gatherers. The other half were moved by the Namibia government into a territory called 'Bushmanland,' which looks as charming as any American Indian reservation . . . but without the casinos. The San people living here still speak in clicks, but now they hunt with horses and guns, are driving the local wildlife to extinction, and are allowing their land to be overgrazed by neighboring cattlemen. The *New York Times* described a recent San encounter:

> Xaixae is supposed to be overseeing a 'self-help project,' a tourist campsite under a huge baobab near his village, but rabbits have shredded its water pipe, the outhouse is tipping into its pit, and Mr. Xaixae has the disconcerting habit of appearing at 7 A.M. to stare at visitors' breakfasts, hinting in Afrikaans, 'We're very hungry.' He also cadges cigarettes and sweets, and spends much of his day like the rest of the twenty people in his village, lying around in broken-down huts doing not much of anything.

When the Hadza were first discovered in Central and Eastern Africa, they seemed to spend a lot of time ritually dancing, but no one could understand their language and so couldn't understand the meaning of the dance. A South African expert on the Hottentots was brought north to try to translate and, after some time, this linguist was able to make out what the Hadza were singing over and over again as they danced in a circle together:

> *Hamana nale kui,*
> *Nale kui . . .*
> *Hamana nale kui,*
> *Nale kui . . .*

Which means:

> *Here we go round,*
> *Go round . . .*
> *Here we go round,*
> *Go round . . .*

A GORILLA
NAMED 'BOB'

HEART OF DARKNESS II

If you were going on a big safari to Africa, wouldn't you want to see the great apes? We sure did, but the question was: *How?* Those Dian Fossey *Gorillas in the Mist* live on a range of near-extinct volcanoes at the intersection of Congo, Rwanda and Uganda . . . about the worst piece of real estate on the planet. All the nightly news horror stories you've heard about Africa over the past decade? They've all happened right here.

No pack of historic archenemies can compare with the vicious, ten-year blood feud going on between the Hutus and the Tutsis of Central Africa. What happened is that a thousand years ago, the Hutus (who are short and squat – they resemble Mike Tyson) showed up and settled down into farming communities, followed by the cowherd-grazing Tutsis (who are tall, lean and graceful: think Michael Jordan). The Hutus took one look at the Tutsis' sacred cattle and decided they just had to have cows of their own, and the Tutsis were able to leverage this desire into political control, setting up a feudal system where a small band of Tutsis controlled a great number of Hutus, a system lasting over five hundred years . . . until the Europeans moved in, took over, and then abruptly pulled out, leaving behind a power vacuum that needed to be filled.

Control of the region seesawed until 1994, when the plane carrying the Hutu presidents of Rwanda and Burundi was shot down out of the sky, killing everyone on board. In the six weeks that followed, Hutus slaughtered more than a million Tutsis, and in response, Tutsi rebels overthrew Rwanda, took back control, and went on killing sprees of their own. Over a million Rwandan Hutus fled into refugee camps in the eastern states of Zaire, leading to civil unrest and another Tutsi rebellion, which caused 700,000 Hutus to flee back to Rwanda. That rebellion, led by Laurent Kabila, would become the Alliance of Democratic Forces for the Liberation of Congo, which would eventually take over the whole country. Their symbol? Disney's cartoon *Lion King*.

All this fighting and fleeing, all this genocide and civil war, took place right around those *Gorillas in the Mist* volcanoes. After learning all this, Brenda and I decided that perhaps Rwanda and Zaire/Congo (normally the key destinations for gorilla-watching) might not be the very best vacation picks. If we wanted to see mountain gorillas, Uganda was where we'd have to go . . . a country with a tourism business that began, from scratch, one year before:

Travel Warnings and Consular Information Sheets, Democratic Republic of Uganda, U.S. State Department:

- Because of rebel and bandit activity and fighting in the area along the Sudanese border, travel in the northern part of Uganda is dangerous. The inability of the Ugandan government to ensure the safety of visitors makes any travel in the area unwise. Vehicles have been stopped and destroyed; passengers have been robbed and/or killed.
- Travel to Murchison Falls National Park is unsafe. Three Americans were robbed in a violent attack by armed men in March 1997 near the southern entrance to the park.
- Travel to western Uganda is unsafe. The Ugandan military is pursuing rebel groups in the Rowenzori Mountains and Queen Elizabeth National Park.
- Travel to the southwestern corner of Uganda near the Zaire

and Rwanda borders can also be risky. There have been attacks by bands of armed men in and near Mgahinga Gorilla National Park.

INTO THE LAND OF IDI AMIN

We arrived in Entebbe to be met by a beautiful woman named Prossie, a well-padded Land Cruiser and Gabriel Ochieng, forty-two years old, with coal-blue skin and bloodshot eyes. We'd soon learn that this was one of the three unique African eye styles, the bloodshot caused by urban pollution, dusty roads and growing up with smoky home fires. The other distinctive looks are the liquid bedroom (probably a sign of malaria or tsetse) and the zombie, which occurs when the pupil and iris are both the same obsidian-black color, and the owner looks like he's staring, unblinkingly, at you.

We drove up to the Victoria Hotel, located right alongside Lake Victoria, to discover that this once luxurious resort has now become subject to huge swarms of gnat-like lake flies. They'd installed the largest bug zapper I'd ever seen right next to the pool and it was going day and night, with electrical crackles and an ozone smell just like Frankenstein's lab. Besides that and a family of terrapins trawling through a center courtyard, Victoria is one of those nice but generic places that have pizza, burgers and no sense of where you are in the universe. Of course, we wanted to get out of there immediately, so Brenda turned to the Ugandans and asked, 'How do we get to the Entebbe Zoo and Botanical Gardens from here?'

'Oh . . .' Prossie said, disconcerted, 'I am quite sure they are closed. And if they are open, it is much too dangerous for you to go there.'

'Well then, where would be a good restaurant to have dinner?'

'There are no good restaurants anywhere nearby. You will be very happy with the food in the hotel.'

'What about visiting the Sese Islands?'

'That would not be possible.'

'What else can you recommend we do tonight while we're in Entebbe?'

'The hotel is very nice! I think you should just stay *right here*.'

This line of conversation went on for some time, but Prossie wouldn't be dissuaded. She was one of those wildly protective agents whose main goal in life is to make sure her charges don't get robbed, raped and killed, and she interpreted anything we wanted to do as an opportunity for mayhem. This was how Brenda came up with the nickname Bossy Prossie, whom we ignored completely, running off to the zoo (closed) and the gardens, which turned out to be like any city's park, with trails leading through parkland bordering Lake Victoria, but with some serious differences. We'd heard about the tree-living tribes of colobus living there and had to see them, which we did, lying on our backs in the grass, while big black monkeys with fluffy white-fringed tails and beards leaped through the branches above our heads. Floating down the walkways were huge swarms of lake flies, and caught in the slanted rays of the setting sun, they looked like waving clouds of protoplasm . . . a horror movie's lovely special effect.

The next day, Gabriel picked us up at the crack of dawn and we set off (with no Prossie). To see gorillas in Uganda, we had to drive across the whole country, which meant a lot of car time, but also the chance to really catch the action. Like post-Franco Spain, the Ugandans have finally recovered from Amin, and are ready to take over the world. They are proud and sexy and doing big business, with a real *we're back!* in the air. Out of all of Africa, this is the intelligent American's favorite foreign investment since, for the past five years, it's been the world's fastest-growing economy. Much of the countryside is lush and tropical, like Costa Rica, and a local joke is that if you move into a new house there and throw a few seeds out your front window and spit, next month you'll have a farm.

Driving along, your eye gets caught by the many buildings shellacked in the mega-saturated colours of the local *Cock Paint: the Paints with a Difference*! Here, roofs aren't pink, but baby-doll pink, and doors aren't blue, but glow-in-the-dark blue, while the red-clay roads are crammed with neon-eggplant-colored trucks, and the shoulders are lined with big women wearing big dresses and carrying big baskets on their heads. This is the national outfit, the *goma*, a blouse and skirt combo in light-colored patterns with a scoop neck, shoulders gathered and peaked, sleeves to the elbows, and a waist tie. If you're a big, curvy woman, you look really good in it; I wanted to get one to send to Aretha Franklin, but I lost her address. Another eye-popping accessory is the ubiquitous giant plastic screaming-yellow can of mass-produced banana liquor, which I was keen to sample, and which turned out to be just as delicious as it sounds.

There's one view out the car window in Africa that is not to be seen anywhere else. You're in the middle of a big, desolate landscape and there, off on the horizon, is one solitary creature, and that creature is running. It's a big open prairie, and you're always seeing a very young kid running down the road as fast as his legs can pump, or an ostrich running through the fields as fast as he's physically able, and then you won't see any other people or ostriches for miles and miles and miles.

At home in Manhattan, we have shopping districts – a flower section, a diamond neighborhood, a fur district, a meat-packing purlieu and a highly esteemed *schmatte* center. Ugandan towns have similar specialties: there's a metal-gate village, a floormat district, a loofah-sponge and papyrus-paper *arrondissement*, and the most successful of them all (from war and AIDS), an Entebbe suburb that produces elaborate carved-and-painted coffins. You can choose to be interred in a wooden Cadillac, or in a giant bald eagle, or you can even bring in a picture and they'll make a life-sized pine caricature to bury you inside of you, like a Russian nesting doll. Just outside one village there were dozens and dozens of roadside malls selling hand drums, used for both communicating between villages and for big-time dancing. On every full moon, the widows of the Buganda kings, living on the property of the ancestral tombs, gather together and drum the night away.

The first thing we wanted to know about our guide, Gabriel, was the first question everyone asks in Africa, which was his tribe, but oddly, Mr Ochieng wasn't forthcoming with this information. He finally admitted to being Karamajong (*care-a-ma-chong*), people who, just like Maasai, roam the fields naked with cattle that are only butchered for religious ceremonies (mostly funerals). The Karamajong teach their cows to come like dogs when called, and they sing them lullabies at night to guarantee pleasant cow dreams (which you can be sure are all about grass). They fight continuously with their cow-owning neighbors, the Turkana, each believing that all cattle belongs to them alone, and this used to be primarily ritual warfare. Today however, the Karamajong and the Turkana have AK-47s and Kalashnikovs left behind by Idi Amin Dada's army, so the northern Ugandan hills are filled with naked men running around with machine guns.

In Uganda, the Karamajong are ranked with the British in local esteem, since it's said that if you become friends with a Karamajong and invite him for dinner, two will show up to eat, and the next night four will show up, and then six, and on and on until your house is filled with them. Because of this, many Ugandans do not wish to become friends with the Karamajong. Gabriel told us how his tribe celebrated a success in battle by carving a fresh mark into the skin. He showed us two raggedy scars on his forearm, and said that this proved he was a failure, since he only killed two men, and then he said he was joking, but who knows? He was a Ugandan Karamajong during some of the country's worst years, and even though he was by far the best guide we could ever hope to have and we loved him completely, it wasn't hard to imagine the quiet of the evening, dinner finished, the radio broadcasting a mournful wail of song and Gabriel, thinking of the inevitable, patiently oiling and loading up his Kalashnikovs.

He called smoking 'making clouds,' and warned us to stomp around before using the toilets in game parks because 'something may be resting in there.' Many Ugandans have this delicate, sweet way of talking in euphemism; they call AIDS 'Slim,' and since 40 percent of the patients in Kampala's Mulago Hospital tested positive for HIV, the government has launched a campaign against promiscuity with the slogan 'Zero Grazing.' 'You see,' said one official, 'a man has a wife, and a woman has a husband. But they also have many, many good friends.' Ugandans think it's rude to point with a finger . . . so they use their lips.

That these people were so extremely sensitive was lovely, and baffling. A restaurant waiter would bring us the wrong thing, and if we mentioned it without using the greatest delicacy, he'd be crushed and humiliated. When something like this would happen, it'd make me think about Uganda's history, since trying to put together the very tender people I was meeting with the bloody and disturbing past that I'd read about was just completely impossible.

The first Ugandan president after that country got its independence was Apollo Milton Obote, who started out being a fine leader, modernizing the medical facilities and promoting education. Then he went power-mad, got the army on his side, suspended the constitution, and gave himself absolute control. In 1971, when Milton (only Africa could have a dictator named Milton) was out of town, Commander Idi Amin Dada Oumée took over in a military coup, declared himself president, dissolved parliament, and created a new constitution that gave *him* absolute control. After Milton's excesses, Ugandans were thrilled with this news, since Dada seemed like such a down-to-earth, regular kind of guy, with a good military record and announcements that his would only be a caretaker government. In person, he was terrifically likable, the type who jumped into the pool at parties wearing his full uniform, and caromed around town in a big red sports car.

What happened soon enough instead was that the country's chief justice was dragged from his courthouse in broad daylight by Dada troops and never seen again, which also happened to the army chief of staff, the national university's vice chancellor, and Dada's personal physician. Every other minister under the regime ended up either fleeing the country or being executed. The president-for-life's first wife was found murdered and dismembered, while his foreign minister was found floating in the Nile, missing a liver; many Ugandans assumed their president cut out the organ himself and ate it. It was also rumored that, after he'd executed all the army chiefs who hadn't supported his political ambitions, he'd have dinner with their heads sitting on the placemats, scolding them for being disloyal.

In the eight years of his reign, Dada had at least 300,000 Ugandans killed by the 'Public Safety Unit,' had himself declared national heavyweight boxing champion, banned tourism, engineered the slaughter of over a million wild animals, and took accordion lessons. Being a loyal Muslim, he supported the 1976 Popular Front for the Liberation of Palestine when they hijacked an Air France plane to Entebbe. Israeli commandos landed and released the hostages after a bloody gun battle that killed all the hijackers, some passengers, and forty Ugandan soldiers. Today, the jet still sits on the outskirts of the capital, with plans to turn it into a disco.

Dada took away all foreign-owned businesses and gave them to his cronies, causing Uganda to immediately go bankrupt. He then launched a *Wag the Dog* diversionary war against Tanzania, which fought back, and won. The president-for-life fled to exile in Saudi Arabia, having completely destroyed the economy of one of the continent's few modern success stories; Winston Churchill himself, after all, had called Uganda 'the pearl of Africa.' Post-Dada, it was common to hear shouts of 'You still exist!' on the streets of the capital as old friends, long assumed dead, bumped into each other.

During the next year, Uganda would have four different leaders until fixed elections brought Milton back to power. Having learned a lesson from Dada, he exiled the Red Cross and Western journalists, reinstated the State Research Bureau, and slaughtered around 600,000 people. After fighting an on- and off-again civil war with rebels seeking to oust him, Milton was removed by military coup, and fled to exile in Zambia. The army negotiated a cease-fire with the rebel forces and made their leader, Yoweri Museveni, Uganda's new president. He won a second term with a landslide 74 percent of the vote and a female vice president; *The New Yorker* has called him 'the *éminence grise* of the new leadership in central Africa,' and he's so popular that, everywhere you look, Ugandan men have copied Museveni's haircut, which is to shave your head just this side of bald.

COW CULTS OF THE SUB-SAHARA II

We knew we'd reached the town of Mbarara when we saw Uganda's largest billboard:

MY CATTLE ♥ STELADONE!

followed by a big statue of a demanding cow straddling the middle of the highway. This is another nest of bovinophiles, home to the Ankole tribe, known for cattle whose horns rise in perfect, graceful upturned parentheses. The cows are carefully, genetically bred, not to engineer the finest meat or the richest milk, but to get the most beautiful, the most geometric, the most perfect pair of horns. That shape seemed familiar, but it was months later that I remembered where I'd seen it before: carved into the five-thousand-year-old walls of ancient Egyptian temples. Ugandan President Museveni himself is Ankole, and he's built the district a dam and a weaving mill, not just as local pork, but so they'd stop being nomads, settle down, and stop killing the Karamajong and Turkana. As we pulled into town, his motorcade was pulling out, a black limo beeline headed straight for Kampala.

The nicest hotel in Mbarara is also the world's best restaurant for Ankole steak, which is tender but extremely rich in flavor, with a feral top note of buffalo. Next to our table sat a coterie of young Greek Orthodox missionaries, who'd just come back from building a school in Tanzania. They were dressed in identical neon-pink knit shirts and khaki pants, and looked like an itinerant band of nomadic cheerleaders. While eating, we all gazed at the man-made lake, where dozens upon dozens of the local marabou stork (which eat only meat and ants), come to bathe the blood from their feathers. Big animals, with naked, hairy faces, woolly necks, red cheeks, black, mournful bodies and the deliberate, stalking gait of hungry predators, marabous are like turkey vultures, but far more sinister, the Grim Reapers of the avian world. They follow up their baths by drying their feathers with those huge black wings arched and spread, heads bent in unison, a corps of huddling morticians on the freshly mown lawn. This disturbing sight is not exactly the view a deluxe hotel prefers for the diners of its world-class restaurant, and so the staff keeps trying to scare the birds off . . . but those storks keep coming back, back to the lake of Mbarara.

BABETTE, THE HARVARD CHIMP GIRL

Down the road a bit is Queen Elizabeth Park, which used to be flooded with wildlife, but no more. It was a preserve for so many decades that packs of hippo, elephant, waterbuck and warthog, all demi-tame, would walk right up to the veranda of Mweya Lodge at dusk and watch the guests. There's even a sign recommending you 'Do Not Feed the Hyena Sitting on the Lawn. *He Is Not Tame!*' During his reign, President-for-Life Amin would sit on that porch, sipping whiskey, barking out orders, and shooting everything in sight, while Ugandan National Radio would announce the results of his spectacularly successful hunting expeditions. During that era, the park's elephant population went from four thousand to four hundred.

Even post-slaughter, however, we found that the central gardens behind our rooms were a hotbed of demi-tame, feeding warthog, who would get down on bended knee to sup at the tree blossoms littering the grounds. So ugly they're cute, these wild pigs have protruding jaws, a swaggering walk, and they'll suddenly decide to run away from you with their thin, arched tails wiggling in the air. The babies look exactly like legged kiwi fruits.

We watched a ritual battle, which the males do just to reiterate who's the boss around these parts; when there's serious warthog trouble, they hide themselves in aardvark burrows, tusks facing out. If a lion decides to take on a warthog, even field scientists have a tough time watching; between the ivory pig's tough skin, tight, muscular body and tusks, it is a prolonged, endless kill filled with ear-piercing screams. That fight does show, however, why warthogs are on nobody's endangered species list.

Queen Elizabeth's Mweya Lodge is quite beautiful, with an immense patio shaded by jacaranda and bougainvillea, facing a vast lawn on a promontory overlooking Lakes Edward and Albert and the Rowenzoris . . . the Mountains of the Moon. There aren't many guests today at Mweya, but there are plenty of field biologists who sleep elsewhere (in a campsite visited each and every night by inquisitive hippos) and who come here to drink and dine, grad students off on a great adventure before settling down to lives of labwork and tenure tracks. The first of these we met was Babette, a woman studying chimpanzees with the Goodall Institute next door in Kibale. When I asked another scientist about Babette and mentioned I thought she was snotty, he responded with, 'So what'd you expect? After all, she's a *Harvard chimp girl.*'

One night we got extremely drunk at a going-away party for Michael, who'd just finished up his two-year tour of duty studying the local mongoose, and who spent the evening worrying over what the conservative Ugandan customs authorities might think about his vast library of urine samples. Michael was returning to Oxford with the discovery that, even though all the mongeese would have sex on different days, the entire troop would bear young on the same day, perhaps the same safety mechanism used by gnu. He also found that the mongoose's preferred food was the scarab beetle, and that in order to break open the insect's tough carapace, the mongoose would face away from a good-sized rock, grab the beetle, and toss it under its arms, like a football snap (these beetles have a better sense of smell than any other creature, all of which goes to ferreting out dung, which they roll into balls across the plains to the waiting, egg-bearing arms of their beloveds). Tossed by a mongoose, the insect would hit the rock, squeal like a miniature E.T., and crack open, ready to be served. Mongeese were all over the place, running around in giant packs, and they're sort of cute, if you like that rat-sized, weasely look. The dwarf species is something like a carnivorous chipmunk, with beady, flat-green eyes, while the bandeds are like ferrets. Both communicate with squeaking rackets that sound just like those plastic hammers swung by toddlers everywhere.

Michael was assisted in his research by the charming, brave pygmoid Francis, who followed his quarry on a massive fifty-pound Chinese bicycle. At one point in our alcoholic dinner, Frances apologized profusely to Michael for not coming back with certain crucial data. He said it was hard to get near the mongeese and record the information, as they were so terrified by the leopard who'd spent the afternoon stalking him.

We were particularly interested in the work of one scientist, John

MacLachlan, who was also with Goodall working on chimps, but a very unusual set of chimps. The Ugandan government had discovered that the heads of the Wildlife Commission had embezzled $1.2 million, and in prosecuting them, had uncovered a corrupt parks official who'd kidnapped nine orphan chimps and sold them to a Russian circus. Through great effort, all of the chimps had been returned, and were now living on their own island in the middle of Lake Albert. John and his Ugandan co-workers aren't trying to rehabilitate the chimps back into the wild, which would be impossible; they just want to see if they can give them a better home than a zoo cage. Babette the Harvard Chimp Girl thought John's work was disgusting, and not real research, and invalid as science, and that we were wasting our time going there, when we could be seeing her chimps, who were *actually wild!* They were also two hours away and not easy for people with limited time to see.

Baroness Jane van Lawick-Goodall said: 'When I first started at Gombe, I thought the chimps were nicer than we are. But time has revealed that they are not. They can be just as awful.' No kidding; over the past thirty-seven years, her Tanzanian research has uncovered that chimp life features cannibalism, war, deception, scheming, tool-making, teaching, meat-eating, planning, coalition-forming, adoption and the use of plants as medicine. One time, a band of chimps was seen going into new territory, where they discovered their first waterfall. Their reaction was to suddenly and spontaneously dance around in a theatrical manner that looked almost choreographed. Goodall believes that this is the thinking animal's version of awe, and similar to the emotions that led early man to spiritual beliefs and religion.

Who were the chimps of your childhood? Mine was New Jersey's world-famous Mr. Jiggs, a female who's been entertaining audiences for twenty-six years and was raised by her owner, Ron Winters, to be as human as possible: 'I used child psychology. Lots of love and discipline.' He also used a radio-controlled unit Jiggs wears around her neck that gives electric shocks when she doesn't do what Mr. Winters says, and had her front teeth pulled out to inhibit biting the audience. Adult chimps, after all, can yank your arm out of your shoulder if they think it'd be a fun thing to do.

The great apes have so much in common with humans that many

of them even like to paint. During a 1950s craze, monkey canvases were included in the collections of Picasso, Miró and the British royal family. One of the most fervid ape artists is a sign-language-speaking chimp named Washoe, and when her handler asked, 'Do you prefer to paint or to eat?' Washoe replied, 'Eat, paint, eat, paint, painting good!' Roger Fouts, a psychology professor, claims that 'it is part of ape nature to paint.' The chimpanzees he's studied prefer finger paints, pencils and crayons. Fouts does admit, however, that 'they also like to eat them.'

We took a launch out with John while he explained his own situation. The Ugandan orphans were very different from wild chimps, in that they were completely used to being around human beings, they loved playing in the water (most chimps are afraid of water), and they were currently in the process of trying to train the island's local warthog. Though it's unclear what they were trying to train him to do, it is clear that this training was not going well. The warthog's constant squeals of irritation upset Megan, one of the chimps who seemed to have arrived mentally damaged. You could watch her up in a tree, obviously nervous and agitated, wondering when all this will end and worrying about what good can come of it.

All that human beings love about chimps we saw immediately visiting this island sanctuary. Their coarse, graphite hair . . . their naked faces, palms and soles . . . the way they gaze directly back at humans, with wondering, inquisitive eyes . . . the way they can stand upright, and use their hands just like we do . . . all this makes us think they're the adorable, teddy-bear baby version of us. In the wild, however, you can also see how much they *aren't* like us – that they are, in essence, muscular three-year-olds who can literally climb walls.

When the orphans heard the boat pull up and saw the mangoes and bananas thrown ashore, they screamed in hysterical, nervous-breakdown huffs and hoots, grabbed up their booty, and headed for the trees. One finished her meal and ran to the water, splashing in glee; another tried to make her tree-sitting friend fall into the lake by hitting her with branches. Plenty of the females were in heat, which upped the hysteria level of the bunch considerably.

We motored away, and at first we couldn't believe it since it seemed like a dream, or a mirage, but there, pulling on a tree in the middle of nowhere, on an island all by himself, was an elephant. John explained that at first there were two elephants on that island, but that one died, and he doesn't know (and no one else seems to know) how they got there in the first place. Now the other elephant is left behind, completely alone, on an island in the middle of Lake Albert . . . but at least he isn't running.

John seemed completely devoted to his animals and to finding ways of making them as happy as he could. It wasn't until later (when everyone was smashed) that we found out he was so dismayed by the difficulties of working with Ugandan park management that he actually wanted to go back to doing research in Burundi . . . even though his site was in the middle of a Hutu-Tutsi war zone.

Queen Elizabeth game drives aren't what they used to be, between the animals getting massacred and our infernally noisy Land Cruiser. Our only hope, Brenda pointed out, would be a deaf leopard. There is one truly spectacular drive here, however, a bird-watcher's dream come true, and it is the Kazinga Channel, a body of water connecting lakes Edward and Albert which had been set aside as a wildlife preserve. We sat on a bench in a roofed boat quite a bit like the Disney Adventureland ride, floating by acres and acres of wading hippo . . . vast flocks of diving black cormorant . . . hordes of white-bodied and black-headed sacred ibis . . . vast, magisterial families of yellow, pink, peach and white pelicans . . . alert white-headed fish eagles (looking much like the balds) . . . ugly buffalo soaking in the water with birds on their heads . . . Egyptian ducks ashore and drying their feathers . . . baby hippo grazing across the lawns (and pigtrotting when alarmed) . . . sunning crocs . . . stalking marabou storks . . . and even the enormous Goliath heron, the skin of their necks flapping in the breeze. At one point, our boat's steering mechanism broke down and we were set adrift, but the whole place was so magnificent I could only think: Who the hell cares?

From this boat, in fact, is where one of the guides, a teenage girl, suddenly began yelling her head off, and we looked to where she was pointing and shaking and saw a big spotted blur falling behind a ridge. It was our Kill: a leopard attacking a kob (a local kind of antelope). We couldn't see anything much of the cat, now holding the antelope's neck in its jaws, hidden behind a sandy ridge. We could only watch, for some time, as the four spindly, upside-down kob legs kicked pathetically in the air, while all the other herbivores present – more kob, and buffalo – ran over to watch.

It turns out that while predators track prey, the vice versa is also true, and all the animals were running over to see how long the cat would be busy and not worth worrying about. Still, from our vantage point it looked exactly like what would happen with rubberneckers at a highway car wreck. The kob squealed and kicked, those skinny little legs twitching and shaking, while the rest of the herds made a direct beeline to catch all the action.

IN THE SHADOW OF WAR

It turned out that the national highway from the savanna of Ishasha to the impenetrable forests of Bwindi was so rutted and pockmarked that we spent as much time jolting up and down and being thrown around in the seats as we did moving forward. Gabriel called it 'dancing,' and explained that this used to be a fine road, but it'd been severely damaged by massive U.N. trucks carrying supplies to the Hutu refugees in Zaire. Our only fellow road warriors were Overlanders, groups of young Limeys, Ozzies and Kiwis running around in cheap tents and packed willy-nilly into the backs of open cattle vans; Brenda called them 'Club Med in a truck.'

At various points, when the road would rise and clear, Gabriel pointed out where we could see Rwanda here, and Zaire/Congo there, and it was in the middle of the battles and the fleeing refugees, but we were in the travel bubble and all of that was completely invisible. The only sign we got of the massive horrors going on right across those fields was that plenty of the small Ugandan border villages were doing big business. They had the goods that their slaughtering refugee neighbors couldn't get through the normal distribution channels, and so every Congan and Rwandan with a car was here, stocking up on plastic cans and metal tools and crates of chickens.

Just outside Kihihi, we bought a beautiful set of African Art

Deco baskets from a weaver, and asked to take her picture. She felt this should require an additional fee, but I told her that we paid a good price for the baskets and that, even though I support the redistribution of capital to enact a fair and just society, I'm not going to pay for pictures. She still wanted the money and refused, so I explained that if she didn't want Americans to know who made these terrific baskets, I'd just take someone else's picture and say they did it. This worked.

The stretch from Kihihi to Buhoma was a dramatic pass through one third red-rock Grand Canyon, one third golf-course farm Bali, and one third blue-hazed Smoky Mountains. It was also dramatic because every few minutes, very young children ran at our car from out of nowhere to scream, '*Abazungu! Abazungu!*' ('Whites!'). In the town of Rafifi where we stopped for Cokes, there was a beautiful young girl, perhaps around ten, who was so shy that she never made one sound. Dressed in a bleached-white, lacy confirmation dress, she followed our every step with her warm, tender eyes as her delicate hands fluttered about, not knowing where to land or what to do. As we were leaving, she drew herself up until she was tall as she could be, and she said her only words to us, in a harsh, demanding voice: 'GIVE ME MONEY!'

We were now in gorilla territory, an alpine set of low, rolling green mountains, the lower slopes quilt-patched by leafy banana fields and dark green tea plantations, striped with bronze-henna clay roads and dotted with thatched huts and the local version of bird-of-paradise blooms. The high slopes were crowns of forests as green and lush as any wood can be, and at least 25,000 years old ... Pleistocene forest. Here and there, the gray smoke of cooking fires rose up, and young men with chickens, banana carts and drifting, parentheses-horned cow herds moseyed on by, along with schoolgirls in turquoise uniforms making their way through emerald fields.

Just as at the Mara's Olonanna, Brenda and I were the only guests at Camp Mantana, with a staff of twelve. No Four Seasons can match the luxury of having so many people working just for you; every time we came home to camp, we were met with fresh-squeezed juice and warm, wet wash-cloths, extraordinary service that rivaled the original great safaris of years past. To be in the middle of the jungle and eat a gourmet dinner of lightly pan-fried Nile perch and cauliflower in white sauce, to have someone bring coffee and cookies to your tent, turn down your bed, and constantly inquire after your well-being and be at your beck and call, is indescribably comforting, and the ultimate in superfluity. Sometimes it even went over the top; pitchers of Ugandan coffee and milk, for example, were always served boiling hot, but I'm way too much an addict to be patient enough to let them cool, so I'd always immediately take off their covers. Inevitably, a Ugandan would just as immediately run over and put the lids back on.

All this attention made us feel just like a big Bwana and Bwaness, but we also felt a little uncomfortable having all these people constantly attending to our every need and whim. The answer came from *Say It in Swahili*, where I put together 'Thank you so much, boss!' with '*Ahsante Sana Bwana!*' . . . which wasn't exactly the right language for this neighborhood, but they liked it anyway.

The camp manager was Hussein Kivumbi, a Muslim Muganda with a coppery undertone to his skin and liquid, bedroom eyes. In the flesh, African tone ranges from espresso grounds to *café con leche* underlined with an indigo or cinnamon tint that is warm and glowing. You want to touch it. At every meal, Hussein would appear before us and describe in extravagant detail, inch by inch, everything we'd be eating, so that by the time he finished, we were ravenous, even though of course we'd been stuffing ourselves like pigs the whole time already.

Our waiters and all-around good guys were three Bachiga gentlemen, Noah, Stanley and Gordon, and at the end of our first meal I insisted they bring out the cook so we could worship him like a god. That night it was a full moon, huge and white over the pitch-black forests, and Stanley showed us how the Anglicans taught him to see Mother Mary and the Baby Jesus where we see the man. I couldn't believe it but, once you look at it the right way, there is in fact a lunar *Pietà*. With coaching from Stanley, I told Gordon in Bachiga, 'You are as cute as two shoes,' and he giggled and ran off, but came back a few moments later, with extra cake.

The guy looking after me in particular was Andrew, a twenty-eight-year-old Muganda who grew up in Entebbe. To earn money, he, like many other Ugandan boys in the wake of Amin, raised a specially bred large rat to sell for food. Through reproduction, he soon had his own herd, feeding them yam leaves and selling them for five dollars each. One day when he was away from home, a pack of wild dogs broke into the house and ate his entire business.

Besides the hyena, there's another animal that troubles Africans because it is so smart and aggressive, and because it groups into packs and behaves just like a gang of juvenile delinquents. At some camps, you have to hire men to sit around guarding your tents because wily baboons have learned how to unzip the doors, get inside and cause endless mayhem. At one point in our travels, a troop of many hundreds crossed the road right in front of us, each in its age-set, each according to its status, the infants riding their mothers bareback, nestled in the crook while leaning against the firm, upright tail, or hanging on underneath and suckling for dear life. It was a remarkable sight, perfectly ordered and choreographed, and it was frightening, since a troop of that size and that discipline could do just about anything it wanted.

One night at dinner, Noah told us: 'You know, baboons are very wise. The first one comes and climbs the tree and looks everywhere, and then it barks for everyone else to come into the farm and eat. They must bring him part of the food they get and, if he does a bad job looking out, they will punish him. In 1982, I went to see my mother's maize fields. I was still schooling. A troop of baboon came in and began to eat there. I threw a rock at the leader to scare them. Instead of killing the big one, it touched the baby. So . . . the baby died. The baboons started fighting to find out what had happened, and I hid myself in a tree. I knew they could kill me if they wanted. They looked all over, but I kept very still, and finally they left.'

East African baboons are termed olive, with pelts exactly the color of martini fruit, doggy-dog noses and sizable canine teeth. Like chimps, they are wildly political creatures, establishing diplomatic tit-for-tats, favor-trading, and manipulating foes against each other to gain the maximum benefit. Males under attack will even grab babies or females and use them as living shields. They are packs of hostile, muscular Nixons; Andrew said: 'If the baboons see you are out, and you are having a picnic, they have a plan. They will send one over, and he will run across the table screaming, and when everyone at the picnic is upset, the rest of the troop will come, to steal all the food. Also, a friend told me that his neighbor saw baboons always eating his crops. So he borrowed a gun and waited for them, and he shot at them and killed their leader. That night, while he slept, they came into his house, and bit him until he died.'

Before coming to Camp Mantana, Gordon had worked as a porter in the preserve, and he'd been warned that, if a gorilla charged, he shouldn't run; he should hold his ground, and nothing bad would happen. A gorilla did charge, and the petite Gordon did hold his ground. The gorilla picked him up by the shoulders and threw him down the trail.

INTO THE MIST

We'd now spent a week in Uganda and really did love being there, but it was time for the real test, the whole reason for this difficult, complicated trip, as that morning we set off to Bwindi Impenetrable Forest, just outside the village of Buhoma. The name comes from the Luganda word *mubwindi*, meaning, dark, damp, mysterious, and is it ever. Mornings are chilly from the elevation and from the constant, rising mist, the result of packed vegetation exhaling more oxygen and sweating more liquids than the air can handle. It's thought that half the world's remaining mountain gorillas live here, separated from the other half by fifteen miles of cultivated farmland, all in that range of not-quite-extinct volcanoes, the Virungas, made famous by Dian Fossey.

This is where the Belgians created Africa's first national park in 1925, when they found fifty of their gorillas slaughtered. Even with worldwide attention and a Hollywood blockbuster, there are still lunatics desperate to get a baby mountain gorilla of their own; as late as 1995, four of Bwindi's habituated apes were killed while they tried to keep one of their infants from being kidnapped by idiots. No one has successfully been able to keep a mountain gorilla in captivity past a few years, but they keep on trying.

It took a very long time to get the local Ugandan farmers thinking that live gorillas were better than dead ones, since their primary experience with these creatures is when rogue males rampage through the banana fields, eating up profit margins and attacking anyone who gets in their way. Like elephants and lions, teen male gorillas are driven away from their mother's group and then either form coalitions with other males or wander solo. 'They are big and black and very powerful,' said one Buhoma farmer. 'They're very attractive. You feel like you want to go look at them. We are very much for the protection of the gorilla, but also what we are asking for is protection for our crops.'

We arrived in the middle of one escapade, with a solitary male, Katome, having injured four people in Buhoma over the past week. Now, if you saw a gorilla attacking your father and a gun was right there, what would you do? Because of the extraordinary accomplishment of the Ugandan wildlife effort, miraculously, nobody had shot the marauder; instead, a park vet was tracking him with a tranquilizer gun. The next day, Katome would be found, subdued and helicoptered back into the wilderness, far from banana plantations and people.

While much of the rest of Africa cordons off its wildlife refuges and only allows political cronies and kickbacking corporations to benefit from the tourist dollar, what Uganda has done instead is to directly engage the Buhomans into the business of eco-tourism. Ten percent of the park entry fees is paid directly to the community, and the town additionally owns and operates the campground and restaurant at the park's headquarters. In return, the locals don't hunt, or honey-gather, or use traps and snares in the park, and if they see anything suspicious, they tell the rangers immediately; it's clearly meant that the park is theirs. We wanted to know how the town spent its income, and Enos Komunda, chairman of the Buhoma Community Campground Development Association, said, 'Our priorities are education, health and maintenance of facilities and roads, in that order.' All those young girls in turquoise uniforms we saw every morning were marching to the brand-new primary school, right next door. Three times, we were told exactly word for word the same thing by Buhomans: 'Now we know the gorillas' value.'

This raging eco success story is more or less the case for the entire range and the entire species. There are isolated incidents of would-be poachers, but in the past decade, as two million people were killed and another two million turned into starving, homeless refugees, as two thirds of the Rwandan Parc des Volcans gorilla preserve staff were either murdered or exiled, as 750,000 Hutus were living in camps at the base of the volcanoes, as the entire human world around them swirled in chaos, only six mountain gorillas died because of human beings, and only one of those was directly affected by the war. He stepped on a landmine.

Fidele Nshogoza worked at Fossey's camp for twenty years, starting as dishwasher: 'When I was a boy, I heard that gorillas were men who were very bad and who went to live in the forest. But the gorillas are better than us. They are peaceful. They have no tribes. When they fight, it is for a good reason. We cut one another with machetes for zero.' José Kalpers, Fossey's successor, had to be evacuated during the uprising: 'When I first came back in August, I found my best friend in the office, a Tutsi biologist who'd survived. He had just come back from Burundi, and he was putting some order in the mess. His family was put on line at a barricade, and militiamen came and said, 'You and you and you.' He and his son lived, and his wife and the other children were hacked to death. He doesn't know why he was spared.' Until the Hutu-Tutsi devastation, gorilla tourism was neck and neck with coffee and tea export for being Rwanda's number one income generator, bringing in $9 million annually, and the animal has become the national symbol for the people of Zaire/Congo. The eco-tourism that has accomplished nothing for the cheetah, nothing for the tiger, and very little for the rhino or the leopard, has accomplished something truly spectacular here. It has saved these animals.

AN APPENDIX IN THE NAME OF SCIENCE

Dian Fossey loathed the tourists who showed up to see her, ranking them as being about as beneficial for her animals as the Batwa pygmy poachers who killed six of her gorilla family and kept stealing her dog. After she became worldwide famous, tourists overran her camp, and Fossey watched as local people made money by taking groups in to see the animals she'd habituated, helping them pick up babies (which frequently precipitated a silverback charge), and getting them so close that it was dangerous for both species. Because they are so genetically similar to us, gorillas can easily catch human diseases, and because (like the Inca and Aztec), they don't have a history with these bugs and haven't built up antibodies, one bad pneumonia microbe launched by an aggressive sneeze could wipe them all out. Fossey would never let anyone touch her animals when she was there, but after she found out they loved being tickled, she touched them plenty if no one else was looking.

When Richard Leakey first approached Fossey about becoming his 'gorilla girl,' he told her that appendicitis is a terrible danger in the Central African highlands, and that she'd have to have her appendix removed if she wanted to go. She did so immediately, and Leakey then told her it wasn't necessary; he just wanted to see if she was determined enough for the job. 'Determined' was exactly the word; studying gorillas in the mountains of Africa for fifteen years may sound idyllic, but in fact it turned out to be hard and long and difficult, and included learning a great deal about spoor. When Fossey wanted to see if gorillas were cannibalistic like chimps, she went through their dung looking for clues, and when Pablo, one of the youngest, stole her notebook and ate it, she went through his feces, trying to resurrect the pages.

One day when she first started out, Fossey was following a group who vanished into thick foliage. She decided she might get a good view from a nearby tree, but couldn't climb it solo, and finally had to get a push up into the branches from a helper. She turned around to see where the gorillas had gone and found all sixteen of them sitting in a line, watching this strange, dopey white gorilla who couldn't even climb a tree. Their intense curiosity about humans helped her in developing her study techniques, a way of getting a band of gorillas used to humans so they could be observed . . . and wouldn't attack.

It took many years of watching to perfect, but by learning what the gorilla sounds and gestures meant, Fossey could get herself accepted. She'd keep her arms folded, which in gorilla means, 'I'm no threat.' She'd keep low to the ground, and never look directly at the eyes, even wrapping her binoculars in vines to keep them from looking like a stare. She learned how to say, 'Hello! I'm not here to kill baby gorillas so you don't have to be afraid,' in gorilla, which is to pretend like you're going to growl, but instead make two puffs like you're blowing out a candle. She learned how to mimic the frightening purr noise gorillas make to each other when they're happy, a growl of *naoum* that essentially means, 'I'm over here, you okay?' 'Yeah I'm fine, how about Gladys?' She learned to smile without showing teeth, which also might be interpreted as an aggressive act, requiring a four-hundred-pound mammal with huge canines to attack. Finally, she tried 'monkey see, monkey do,' imitating whatever they were doing down to the smallest degree: scratching, yawning, stretching, feeding, napping. It would take two years of almost daily contact (and to make gorillas safe for human study and tourists, it still does), but then a magical thing would happen. *They* would start imitating *her*, and that's when Fossey knew she was accepted and the habituation was accomplished. Sometimes it was too accomplished; sometimes when she tried to study gorillas from the trees, various members would climb up to sit with her and ruin the observations.

THE IMPENETRABLE FOREST

At Bwindi headquarters, there was an assortment of carved branches for us to use as walking sticks leaning against the cabin's wall, and I was sure that this would just be a nuisance, but took one anyway. Bwindi's main guide, Phenny Gongo, told us the rules: we could not touch the gorillas; we could not get closer than fifteen feet; we had to turn our heads away if we sneezed; we couldn't stare directly at them; we couldn't smile and show our teeth; we couldn't point; we couldn't talk above a whisper; and if we must defecate, we'd be given a machete to dig a hole since there might be health problems if the gorillas are exposed to human feces. If we get charged, no matter what, we must not run away, because the gorillas would interpret that as a sign that we were the enemy – but what about Gordon? If we felt at all sick, we must be honest with ourselves and cancel now, and the $160 fee would be refunded. Then, just as we were setting off, the cool of the morning evaporated, the heat began to rise precipitously, and one of the group mentioned how her friends spent seven hours tracking the previous day . . . and never saw a thing. She did, however, get back the $160.

We were led by Tracker George, who swung a machete to clear a path wide enough for a Ugandan (if not for me), and a guide named Levi – Brenda told him that he and she must be from the same tribe – as well as the young kid porters, Ebo, Caleb, Ephraim and Fulgence. Passing the last outpost of civilization, a thatch hut covered in blacklight-indigo morning glories, Levi found a tiny hand and arm – perhaps from a gorilla fetus. George took us to where the apes were last seen, and then followed their trail of scat, nests, broken tree branches, bent vegetation, knuckleprints, bitten leaves and peeled fruit.

As we walked, Tracker George and Levi told us as much as they could. The apes we were looking for had been habituated by George himself, and they knew his face as a friend. Levi said that the baby apes love to make themselves dizzy, while the adults love to carry their children on their shoulders. They eat bark, nettles, vines, thistles, insects, snails and slugs, but their favorite food of all is hearts of palm. Every night, they make nests just like a bird's, and with newborns, frequently dad will sleep at the base of a tree while mother and child sleep up in the branches. George said that they actually aren't fat, but like pandas, the barrel vault of the stomach is a digestion pit for massive quantities of vegetation, and that they lived to around the age of fifty (which is older than the average Tanzanian).

I asked if it was likely to find them today, and they said absolutely . . . but you never know. At one point, a family of gorillas had become so habituated that they were hanging out beside the road, but the European tourists complained that this was too much like a zoo, so they moved the gorillas farther back into the forest. Then the Europeans complained that this trek was *way* too much effort, so what can you do? Some tourists showed up one time without gorilla permits and didn't make it into one of the groups, and so they just went for a walk in the forest – only to bump into gorillas. At another time, tracking commonly took seven hours, and the tourists would have to be carried back home in blanket stretchers.

Levi and George said they'd never heard of the West's most famous living gorilla, so I told them all about primatologist Penny Patterson and her 230-pound lowland, Koko, who knows a thousand American sign language gestures, has an addiction to ViewMaster, and loves to browse through *The Three Little Kittens* and *Puss in Boots*. One day, Koko said she wanted a cat of her very own (using a pull of two fingers against the cheeks, like whiskers), and when Penny gave her a toy cat, Koko pouted. When a litter of three orphaned kittens was found nearby, they were shown to Koko, who replied, 'Love that.' She examined them, finally choosing a tailless one, and called him 'All Ball.' The gorilla would make cat clothes out of folded napkins and make All Ball wear them, which commonly led to the cat biting her gorilla mom. Koko would then sign 'Obnoxious,' but usually her comments were, 'Soft good cat cat' (when she gets really mad at her playmate, she calls him 'Bad, bad toilet'). All of this sounded perfectly reasonable to Levi and George.

I learned soon enough how Bwindi got the name 'Impenetrable,' since the minute our feet left the trail, they never again made contact with the earth. The ground is a giant mass of vines, leaves, branches, sticks, twigs, mulch, moss, thatch, thorns and bark, all soaking wet, and if you didn't have a good stick to use as a third leg, you'd be really sorry. Often enough, I'd take a step, climbing sideways up or down the mountain, only to find my five-foot walking stick sinking three feet into this groundcover and there I'd be, doing a Charlie Chaplin slapstick against my will. Stinging nettles and thorny vines tore at our clothes, arms, legs and faces; slogging through mud, we were attacked by swarms of buzzing flies and a mob of aggressive, biting black safari ants the size of a little finger, who climbed up inside our clothes to pursue their main diet: skin.

After two hours of seriously climbing around in this stuff at high elevation, of suffering through pure endurance with a sweat rag so drenched I could wring it out, I realized: *I could do this for hours.* No matter how many creature comforts you try to ensure on these trips, sooner or later, you're always running up against some *Outward Bound*-type experience . . . an experience completely against my 'are you *sure* smoking is bad for you?' natural state of being. In *Outward Bound*, you climb a mountain and look around; here, you climb a mountain and look at gorillas. *Maybe*. But it seemed like this mood was affecting everyone, that we were all now getting used to the physical demands and discomforts, as the six of us were chatting and moaning and cracking jokes and laughing, and just as I'm having this extremely mild epiphany, Tracker George told us all to shut the hell up.

There, in complete silence, in the middle of the jungle, completely sheltered by vegetation, he'd found them.

No TV special or *National Geographic* or Sigourney Weaver blockbuster comes close to capturing how extraordinarily beautiful and peaceful-as-Eden these enormous, potato-shaped vegetarians are in real life. Their pelts are indigo-black, thick and rich as any mink's, and they spend most of their time lolling in the shade, framed by their jungle's lush greenery. The overgrowth here was so extensive that it completely covered them, not allowing one speck of sunlight to reach the ground. There's an incredibly human expression in their shining, pitch-black eyes, and an extremely human manner in the way they use their hands. They smell half like well-made wine-oil-and-vinegar dressing, and half like a skunk.

This was the Mubale group, eighteen in all, surrounding their lead silverback, Rohundaza ('he who sleeps'), who was sleeping on his stomach and showing us his silverback. Well, not sound asleep; Rohundaza's intermittent growl was deep and resonant and alarming, but this was the only thing about them that was a little scary. The other adults all lay on their backs, eyes open, faces lost in thought, while the young'uns rolled around in the grass, gawky, awkward, stumbly and squirming, just like human toddlers.

Of all the excruciatingly adorable baby animals running through Africa, these are the most adorable by far, much more attractive than a mere human baby could ever hope to be. If there ever was an animal you wanted to pick up and coo over, it's the baby mountain gorilla. The Mubale's group youngster was named Bob, who kept crawling toward us, or swinging in a tree while watching us. Lying on her back, his mom kept a gimlet eye on these proceedings, and every time she felt Bob was getting a little too close for comfort, she'd reach out a hand and idly, as if as an afterthought, pull him back to her.

Since in gorilla society child-rearing is shared by all, not letting us ugly white gorillas touch her Bob was a little offensive, so mom tried to do it as subtly as possible so we wouldn't know that she thinks we are too creepy to be trusted with her son, which is exactly what she thinks. Finally she picked up Bob and carried him off, so they were lying on the other side of Rohundaza from us. There, just like any human mother, she rolled with the baby in the grass, played with it, and then picked it up and held it inches from her face, the two gazing at each other with maternal love and the making of goo-goo eyes.

While an older female, perhaps the grandma of everyone, groomed the mother, the baby looked on, watching and learning for a moment, but then got bored and wanted to try some grooming himself. Apparently Bob wasn't accomplished at this yet, since grandma immediately picked him up and flipped him over on his back to show him how it was done. Brenda whispered, 'I want to see one climb a tree,' and a minute later, two did.

After exactly one hour, the total amount of time we were allowed, there was a signal hidden from us, and all eighteen of the tribe crawled out of the clearing and slid away, one by one, into the brush. Just as they left, we heard the leader . . . beating his chest . . .

The experience left us breathless, just glowing inside, and we made it back to camp for juice, washcloths and fresh, hot showers. That evening, all forty members of the Buhoma Women's Development Club came to the camp to perform traditional Kiganda dances. It started with quite an entrance: the sound of a goatskin drum and forty delicate voices chanting, 'We are coming . . . we are coming . . . we are coming . . .' and there they were, in kinte cloth skirts and T-shirts of every stripe, 'Detroit Institute of the Arts' and 'I Am a Share Holder in My Tea Factory Company' being the standouts. The music was a call-and-response series of chanting choruses, a rap-and-rhythm version of gospel, and one song claimed that 'In Museveni's regime, it is time for all women to come forward.' The women danced, barefoot, on top of sharp-edged rocks, and each time I looked down and saw this I had such empathy twinges of pain running up and down my spine I couldn't look anymore. One of the grandmothers had her cap set for camp manager Hussein, and she kept dancing closer, and closer, and closer . . .

After dinner, we turned on the boom box and danced ourselves, joined by the staff guys, who had tapes of Zairian music with lyrics none of us could understand. Gordon turned to me and said, 'I'll not forget you . . . you are a very special man,' but I couldn't accept this compliment, since of course, only the opposite was true.

P.S.: Dian Fossey, murdered in 1985, now shares a private Rwandan cemetery with seventeen of her beloved apes, a dog and a monkey.

At the time of her death, there were 239 mountain gorillas in the world.

Today, there are over 650.

THE SOUTH PACIFIC

PUTTING YOUR FATHER ON A SLOW BOAT TO TONGA

When he turned seventy-three, my father ran away from home again, and I went along for the ride. Dad always had two big loves in his life, riding horses and sailing boats, and a few months back, he called me up from Texas and said, 'I'm thinking about a sailing trip through the Caribbean. If I put it together, would you come with me?' Since he's almost hit the three-quarters-of-a-century mark, I couldn't say no – after all, how many more big trips could there be?

For years and years in my childish mind, my parents were eternally middle-aged, stuck like magic in a warp. They'd always be in their thirties, their forties, their fifties, so of course, they'd never die. Then I myself turned forty and went home for a visit. Now they were so frail it felt like, at any minute, I might have to catch them. Now they'd make jokes about nursing homes and Depends adult undergarments. I can't make these jokes.

I started thinking how, in fact, if Dad wanted to go on a big trip, he should make it *really* big, the trip of a lifetime, and he should do it right away while he could still physically get away with it. So I called back: 'Why stop there? If you want to go on a voyage, why don't you think about what your dream sail would really be?'

I could hear dead silence, and I knew what this meant; he was thinking, 'I couldn't do *that*,' and then he was thinking, 'maybe I could . . .' So I sent him some travel agency background, and he jumped into an epic round of research on every sailing trip in the world, finally settling on his dream: He, my brother and I would crew for three weeks and a thousand miles on a restored nineteenth-century brigantine, the *Søren Larsen* (a square-rigger with two masts and eleven sails – the pirate look), plying the trade winds of the South Pacific from Tonga to Fiji. Since my great-grandfathers were named Lars Christian Nielsen and Ingerbret Thorson, sailing on something called *Søren Larsen* seemed like coming home. The route (Tongatapu–Vava'u–Ovalau–Kandavu–Beqa–Suva) sure sounded exotic enough, as it would traverse the cusp, skinwise, of the black and the brown. It also seemed to fulfill exactly my kind of vacation agenda, since it would feature ethnic conflict, humpback whales, a narcotic drink religion, a history of cannibalism, the home of *tabu* (forbidden) and *tatu* (puncture), as well as many opportunities for major snorkeling. Finally, it was a strategic choice on Dad's part; my mom and his friends couldn't scare him off with paranoid ideas about going to Tonga, since they didn't know, exactly, where Tonga was.

One afternoon I was out on the town, and ran into a friend who'd just become publisher of Ballantine Books. I said, 'I'm thinking of going sailing with my dad to Tonga,' and she said, 'Really? My father went to school with the king of Tonga,' and I could only think: *It is your destiny.* Growing up, my family always owned sailboats, eighteen- and twenty-five-footers for swooping around on bays and lakes, and we even spent one summer touring fiberglass factories, looking at custom jobs. I thought we were all ready to sloop through the waters of the Southern Hemisphere, that this trip would be exactly like the sails I remembered. Sometimes, I'm just an idiot.

My father prepped like he was training for the Olympics. He learned that while we were there, the moon would be waxing, and he found out the exact night it'd be full. He memorized bits of Tongan and Fijian, as well as the entire vocabulary of the vessel. He researched sea chanteys (the songs you sing when your team's pulling rope and chain together), and got our neighbors to pick them out on a piano. He even read up on *Condé Nast Traveler's Dos and Don'ts* to find out that in Tonga, flowers are not considered proper gifts. He called every week with new discoveries, new information and plenty of questions.

One night, he and my brother Kurt rang up, and Dad said, 'You know, it'll be winter when we're there, so you better bring plenty of warm clothes.'

'It's the tropics,' I said, 'it's right next to the equator.'

'It's not *right next* to the equator,' Kurt said.

'Okay,' I reasoned. 'Do you have a map there?'

'Yes.'

'Look at how far Fiji and Tonga are from the equator, and then look at the same distance in North America, and where are you?'

'Okay . . . Miami.'

'It'll be as cold as winter in Miami.'

Whether or not this was truly our destiny and we'd actually set sail, however, was a looming question, since all four elements of this dream suffer from profound medical handicaps. I have herniated spinal discs, and my father (whose original name was 'Verne,' but he had it legally changed to 'Bill') has blood pressure problems. My mother (whose original name was 'Arlene,' but goes by 'Tomi') had a couple of minor strokes – if there is such a thing as a minor stroke – and my brother 'Kurt' (oddly, he still uses that name), at fifty, just had a heart valve replaced.

A jolt in any of these conditions, of course, would instantly derail the trip. My mother wasn't coming (since she doesn't think spending three weeks on a rocking boat to be any dream come true), but Dad certainly wasn't going to leave her home alone, paralyzed, if she had any further cranial misadventures. In fact, there seemed to be so much cancel potential that I couldn't really believe we were actually going anywhere. The months of planning and making arrangements for the trip had an undertone of tension and suspense, but a tedious, expecting-the-worst kind of tension and suspense, as if all this work would be for nothing.

If in fact we did go, what a trip it'd be, sailing through the settings of both *Mutiny on the Bounty* and *Moby-Dick*, on the ship used by *The French Lieutenant's Woman* and a wildly popular British soap *The Onedin Line*. If you threw a handful of sand over your shoulder and turned around, there'd be a map of the South Pacific, a four-thousand-by-four-thousand-mile sprinkle of thousands and thousands of islands running from New Zealand to Hawaii and from Easter Island to Tonga, most of them uninhabited (with Fiji alone having over two hundred empty paradise worlds). We'd start out at Polynesian Tonga, whose capital city is Nuku'alofa (*nuke-a-loaf-a*), 'The House of Love.' This particular house of love, however, is filled with ardent Methodists who'll have you arrested if you go fishing on a Sunday. Tongans feel sad for people who don't live in Tonga, and to them, being fat is a sign of power and luxury. The king, Taufa'ahau Tupou IV, tends to be an immense tower of flesh.

In the 1960s, the king weighed in at 460 pounds, so he went to see an American doctor who told him to go on a diet immediately, especially one cutting back on starches like bread, rice and potatoes. 'What about our vegetable, taro?' asked the king, and the doctor, who never heard of taro, said, 'You can eat as many vegetables as you want.' Taro is a yam, just as caloric as any starch, and on the American doctor's diet, the king gained fifty pounds. His subjects admired him greatly for it. During courtship, in fact, one of the most popular Tongan sayings of devotion is *Foi'atelolo, ta o mu'a mata mahina hopo*, which means, 'Oh, fat liver full of oil, let's go watch the moon rise!'

We'd end up in Melanesian Fiji, home to giant bats, sandalwood forests, an underwater visibility of 150 feet, necklaces of smoked sperm-whale tooth, giant Afro hairdos, the ability to sing sea turtles to shore for supper, and elaborate carved forks used for chowing down at 'long pig,' since the Fijians think that eating human flesh with your bare hands is bad manners. Ra Udreudre, their most famous chief, ate 872 people in his lifetime, and one retired people-eater commented, 'What part did I like best? Oh, I don't know; when we took a town, we clubbed everyone, and they all went into the ovens together. I learned to tell by the aroma when warriors were being cooked though, because they always rubbed themselves with scented coconut oil before battle.'

The minute the Europeans arrived, all the Tongans and Fijians gave up cannibalism and their native religion and culture, and converted. 'We Fijians are logical people. The English showed us their knives. They were much better than ours. If the English knives were better, it followed that the English god had to be better,' the same ex-cannibal remembered. The ultimate insult in Fiji is still, however, *kaisi mbokola* – 'low-class human meat' – and the island empire is now home to an endless conflict between native Fijians and the Indians who were imported a hundred years ago as indentured servants. Plenty of Indians stayed, swelling to over half the population, and they've taken over much of the local economy. Since, as I'd discover, the Indians are personality-wise something like native New Yorkers while the Fijians are more like Southern belles, you can just imagine how well they get along. Native Fijian politicians are busily passing laws to tamp down the Indians' political and financial power, while the Indians, in turn, vote with their wallets to retain the status quo. 'Just because we're not as intelligent as Indians,' Fiji military coup leader Steve 'Rambo' Rabuka declared, 'doesn't mean the Indians can take advantage of us.'

We'd be sailing through Oceania, from Polynesia to Melanesia, just next to the International Date Line, a part of the earth that is unbearably beautiful. We'd drop anchor at cream-beached atolls, ringed by cobalt waters, and topped by a canopy of slick green rain forest. Our boat would frequently be accompanied by leaping dolphins and surfacing humpback whales, and we'd be asked in for *kava* ceremonies at various ports of call. It'd be a major family reunion, and the first time, together, we'd ever done anything like this. Of course, at any moment, something could go terribly wrong . . .

THE SCREAMING BABY SYNDROME

No one medically collapsed, and we met up at LAX for the Air Pacific flight to Fiji, which would take eleven hours. We tried getting comfy, but my father immediately started squirming and fussing in his seat, and wouldn't share the armrests. He'd start off trying to share, but the minute he nodded off, his arms would inch apart in bigger and bigger arcs, and soon enough, he'd cornered the armrest market.

Going to this part of the world would be something of a homecoming for him, since he was stationed in the South Pacific as an air force sergeant during World War II. He spent two years in New Guinea, moving from Nadzab to Finchaven to Biak, suffering from jungle rot and having to drive on the left side of the road. He always wanted to be a pilot, but got turned down since he was color-blind, and served instead at Pacific command, helping set up the details for squadrons to reclaim Oceania and, ultimately, conquer Japan.

Just as I was about to fall asleep with no armrests, three infants started shrieking their heads off, and this reminded me of something that I'd been thinking about lately: the Screaming Baby Syndrome. Every international flight today includes at least one (and usually between two and four) Screaming Babies, and this just can't be a coincidence. I believe that the airlines always keep at least one Screaming Baby standing by, just in case the reserved Screaming Baby doesn't show up for its flight, and they even put their Screaming Baby on board if it looks like the paying one might not have the power to wail and shriek continuously, nonstop, for the entire flight. My brother explained that the eustachian tubes in young kids haven't developed enough to easily handle the change in air pressure on a flight and, without something to suck, chew and swallow, they are in real pain. Still, I want to know: What is this new trend of parents forcing their very young kids on extremely long flights? When I was a Screaming Baby, I never got taken anywhere, especially not to Tonga.

When Dad finally woke up and gave back the armrest, I asked if it was frightening being so young and away from home in the middle of nowhere during the war, but he said, 'Well, the bases were just like being in a camp in the U.S., there wasn't that much contact with the rest of the country. The New Guineans we did meet filed their teeth into points and chewed betel nut until their mouths were stained blood-red. Three moments, though, I really remember. One was when we first left, and shipped out on a boat from New Orleans, and had to dodge German subs in the Gulf of Mexico. Then in Biak, our airstrip was bombed by three Japanese fighters, and a lot of men were coming out of a movie the time they struck. Plenty of the squadron were injured, and some died. After the war ended, I went to Japan for four weeks, which after what we'd been through, was a vacation. I went into one place to get a trim and a shave, and there I was, looking in the mirror, as the Japanese barber used a big, shiny, straight-edged razor right across my neck. I couldn't help but get the willies.'

My brother Kurt is a lawyer for the insurers of everyone from plumbers to neurosurgeons, and he has the mind to prove it. He and I are like some kind of genetic experiment, since he got my father's hair, lips and chin, and my mother's eyes and nose, while I got the exact obverse. In fact, when the *Søren* hosted a 'Come as Your Opposite' party, we dressed up as each other, and everybody got the joke.

In Fiji, we transferred to a local flight, and I should report there is a real feeling of suspense as you board Royal Tongan Airlines, since it's very likely you will find yourself sitting between two people weighing in at, oh, four hundred pounds each, their ample flesh cascading over into your seat and pressing against you, firm and insistent. As we touched down, Kurt led us in a round of Melanesian airplane calisthenics he found in the in-flight magazine. On the next page was the announcement: 'Get a Real Taste of the Tropics with Fiji Meat!'

A SEVERE DISINTEREST
IN MAINTENANCE

We landed at Tonga's capital, Nuku'alofa, against a giant clear-blue lake dotted with soft hills of casuarina, sandalwood and coconut palm, which really do sway. Outside, glowing Polynesian couples slurped at lurid pink ice cream cones, and lots of fullback-sized men wandered around wearing skirts, which only made their butts seem bigger than they were already. The snappiest of these dirndls, scalloped in white linen (like a big festive napkin), were reserved for the cops and the army, and resembled something Betty Rubble might wear. They are easily the least threatening police uniforms you will ever see. Skirts are so common on men, in fact, that the international symbols used for rest rooms don't work, so the Kingdom of Tonga has invented its own ladies sign, a female body in the shape of a Taco Bell . . . which we were soon to learn was anatomically correct. At the Tongan Centenary Chapel, in fact, the toilets were mysteriously labeled 'Men' and 'Others.'

Our hotel, the Pacific Royale, was acclaimed as the country's second best, so I was surprised to find chips and stains all over the place, rooms with ants, flies and no-see-ums, forgotten laundry abandoned in the hallways, and a patio garden littered in trash and condoms (unused). It was as if the Tongans believed doing a little plaster and paint work, and tidying up here and there, would be an overwhelming chore. Perhaps this is a sign of the region's famed torpor: 'Polynesian Paralysis.' A popular T-shirt even says, *Do It the Tongan Way – Tomorrow!* Or perhaps 'they suffer from a lack of dreams,' as Sebastian Junger gently put it in *A Perfect Storm*. Whatever the cause, the Pacific Royale down-at-the-heels style is true for all of Nuku'alofa, a faded, devil-may-care, trailer park kind of burg, warm and pleasant, but also seedy and tatty. It was a Sunday, and the Pacific Royale's public address system was broadcasting the local radio station, which, as it does on every Sunday, played nothing all day but eighteenth-century Protestant hymns.

Now I don't know about you, but when I think *South Pacific*, the next thing I think is: *The Musical!* (Well, maybe first I think: *Mutiny on the Bounty*.) So I assumed South Pacific islands would be filled with lei-drenched, long-haired topless girls in canoes, and bare-chested, tattooed men in grass skirts, everybody carrying torches and doing the hula. Instead, it's a hotbed of Protestant religious fanatics, almost all of whom, strangely enough, also have that easy-in-the-islands, *Do It Tomorrow!* attitude. In the mind of religious maniacs, Pacific islanders are not lovely innocents living a life of *au naturel* splendor, but heathens needing to be saved from a guaranteed one-way ticket to Hades, and missionaries have run through Oceania on a conversion rampage. Plenty of South Pacific church services even feature a man wandering the aisles, finding snoozers and smacking them awake with a big pole, a technique straight out of seventeenth-century Salem.

How did this happen? As far as I can tell, when the European explorers and missionaries ran all over the world telling South Americans and Africans and Asians and Oceanians that 'We're the civilized ones! Our culture and our religion are *so* much better than yours,' the South Pacific islanders were the only ones who said, 'You know what? You're absolutely right.' Many Polynesians we met, in fact, couldn't understand why we wanted to sail the South Pacific, and seemed to think we must be poor or deranged that we wouldn't instead want to motor around in a luxury power cruiser. When our translator in Lautoka, Joseva, questioned this, I brought up his great ancestors, who traveled thousands of miles in double-hulled outrigger canoes pulled by huge, ovoid sails. Joseva shrugged and said, 'That was them.'

The missionary movements in both Tonga and Fiji were remarkably powerful and generous, handing over schools, food, equipment and English lessons. It makes perfect sense that they'd throw such an effort this way, since both countries were once the major stomping grounds of bloodthirsty cannibals. In the minds of the missionaries, there is no greater achievement than dragging heathen savage people-eaters into the arms of Jesus.

In the peculiar case of Tonga, when the Reverend Shirley Baker, a Wesleyan missionary from Australia, arrived on a conversion spree in the mid-1800s, he became best friends with the king (who'd recently been baptized under the name 'George'). King George and Reverend Shirley got together and designed the national flag, wrote the national anthem, created the national seal, and drafted a constitution that includes, 'The Sabbath Day shall be sacred in Tonga forever and it shall not be lawful to work, artifice, or play games, or trade on the Sabbath.' Nuku'alofa on a Sunday during daylight hours is a ghost town, but sundown, we'd find out, would change everything.

Besides all the damn hymns, the hotel's radio broadcast did offer an especially memorable public service announcement: 'Now, if you've been drinking all week for the festivities, maybe it's time to cool. We don't want any road accidents, any drownings, anyone lost at sea. You're listening to Radio Tonga, broadcasting from the royal city of Nuku'alofa, in the heart of the kingdom!' These festivities were Heilala, July 4, the king's birthday, and Tonga's national party of the year. We'd arrived in time for his eightieth, and many Nuku'alofan businesses had gone all out to celebrate, erecting giant, colorful woven archways over the roads screaming 'Happy Birthday King Tupou!' with paintings that made the monarch look like a cartoon orangutan. It would've been nice if they'd spent a little less money on archways, and a little more on picking up the trash.

The Tongan severe disinterest in maintenance was painfully obvious even at the Free Wesleyan Centenary Church, which the king attends each Sunday, and where we went to watch him give the sermon on his birthday. The royal church's ceiling was cracked and peeling away, with mynahs (the pigeons of the South Pacific) nesting in the eaves, while the fluorescent lamps right over our heads kept winking on and off, and buzzing ominously. Two chairs had been decked out with bark cloth and beadwork as thrones for His Majesty and Her Highness, while ushers prowled about in starched white suits with plaited grass skirts, like organic car floormats worn as belts. I guess these would protect the magnificent Tongan tummies in case they had to prostrate themselves in the presence of the nobles. We didn't, unfortunately, get to see any of them hit a snoozer in the head with a pole, since apparently nobody naps when the king's watching.

A uniformed choir, backed by a chamber orchestra, made up about two thirds of the congregation, and they sang as well as any Mormon Tabernacle operation, with three-part harmonies and a big, booming, bust-out-the-door power. Two of the royal accompaniment looked just like Tonton Macoutes, with shaved heads, sneers, permanently crossed arms and vigilante sunglasses, and it was especially odd to see people looking like this in church.

We couldn't keep our eyes off the eighty-year-old king, sitting at the top of the altar, five rows away, neither tattooed nor circumcised. He'd spent ten years dieting, and now weighed a mere three hundred pounds. In repose, His Royal Highness appeared foreboding, judgmental, and barely paying attention, with genial, froggy features, like a Polynesian Jimmy Cagney. When it was time to speak, however, Taufa'ahau Tupou IV rose to address his people, and though his voice was halting and breathless, there was a twinkle in his eyes and a faint smile around his lips, and he transformed into a South Pacific Santa (who looked a lot like Jimmy Cagney). He told the many foreign guests that they should sit next to a Tongan, all of whom were encouraged to translate, and his sermon was brief, culminating with: 'I believe that each of us must have both of the sacraments, both baptism, and communion, just like a kangaroo needs two legs to fight.' He was hard not to like.

A UNIQUE FEATURE OF TONGA IS THE FREEDOM OF PIGS TO ROAM

Back at the hotel we met Charles and Mary, New Yorkers who'd be joining us on the ship, and Mary had just uncovered the most remarkable postcard ever created in our time. Why did someone come up with this? Who (but Mary and me) would ever buy it? Lettered KINGDOM OF TONGA, the front was an atmospheric shot of a gorgeous beach, filled with the dying rays of sunset. Enjoying this beautiful view, and basking in the golden light, were three trotting piglets. The back caption explained everything:

A unique feature of Tonga is
the freedom of pigs to roam.

And roam they did. As we drove around the main island of Tongatapu, black, hairy pigs were everywhere, running out onto the highway, usually followed by troops of crazy-eyed dogs. So many idiotic dogs galloped right in front of our car, in fact, that Dad finally said, 'You don't see many dead ones on the shoulders. It's surprising, isn't it?'

267

Kurt saw a golden opportunity, and asked our guide, Davita Paea (who looked just like an American Indian), 'What happens when a driver kills a pig? Does he have to pay the farmer?'

'No,' said Davita, firmly. 'It's thought to be the fault of the farmer.'

'But what if the pig damages the car? Does the farmer pay the driver?'

'No. It's just a part of life.'

Kurt smiled. 'You people need lawyers.'

Dad was interested in practical matters. 'What does the king do all day?'

'He waits in his office for people who like to see him.'

'What about education? Social services?'

'We educate our children so they get their living from their mind . . . You have money for people who don't work, yes? It's good we don't have it in Tonga. Then, nobody would do a thing.' We ended up meeting many Oceanians who believed exactly this: unemployment benefits were sure to trigger an epidemic of *Pacific Paralysis*.

Seemingly for no reason, just outside the village of Kolovai, Davita suddenly pulled over to the side of the road and made us get out. He pointed up at big, wriggling black cocoons, hanging in a grove of casuarina. It was a vast troop of flying foxes, leathery, monkey-faced creatures that squirmed and giggled like naughty, black-winged children.

'We like our bats,' said Davita, without mentioning that plenty of Tongans like them enough to include them at meals, but aren't allowed to eat one particular group: *the sacred fruit bats*. 'They are harmless. There are no poisonous things on Tonga. Nothing evil.'

The road swerved past fences covered in poinsettia, yards of blooming yellow mango trees, plots of butternut squash pumpkin (a prized Japanese export), trees heavy with pendulous green breadfruit, and a major Tongan highlight: cemeteries. The Wesleyans may be in charge now, but everywhere you look there's plenty of evidence that the first Tongan religion, ancestor worship, is still mighty popular. Graves are hung with strings of Christmas ornaments, bordered by clumps of plastic flowers, and meandering lines of beer bottles shoved into the ground. Tied wooden frames hold giant sheets of dazzling embroidered geometric patterns waving in the breeze, and tombs are festooned in needlepoint-it-yourself *Last Suppers* and *Jesus Tending the Lambs.*

Tonga's main island, Tongatapu, is run amok in tiny farms, their ground so fertile that plowed, it looks just like manure. 'Every Tongan gets a plot of land for growing,' said Davita. It's a birthright written into the constitution by King George and Reverend Shirley, with results about as successful as Africa's. The farms are too small to make economic sense, and every year they get smaller as Tonga runs out of room. We stopped off for a look at the main grocery store, stocked with the latest stamp set, *Two Hundred Years of Christianity in Tonga!*, giant tins of Nestlé Milo Boisson Energetique! (a depressing instant chocolate malt mix) and enormous cans of New Zealand's contribution to South Pacific culture: Corned Meat. This much-loved import could (and did) include everything from mutton by-products to withers to tallow, and even hippo fat. Paul Theroux found that all the ex-cannibals and dog eaters he met in Oceania loved the taste of tinned, salty, porky-flavored beef, especially *Spam*. One man even joked with us that, 'It was good for our older people when the Europeans arrived. Black meat is so salty!' Another, seeing his first hot dog, said, 'That's the one part of the dog we don't eat.' From the looks of the grocery store, they sure do love their Corned Meat in Tonga.

We went to Davita's house for a lavish, traditional lunch of octopus in lime, raw fish in coconut, fried snapper and various forms of yam, all made by his wife, Lucia. There we met the afternoon crew, Tupou and Akuila, young kids just learning the guide business. They were very earnest, and wanted to discuss many things. A favorite travel moment of mine is when you get a guide or a translator with such a thick accent that you can hardly understand a word he says and inevitably, no matter how much effort you put into trying to clear things up, the conversation just gets murkier and more confusing. This can add an element of drama and excitement to any trip.

'I was working in Chellen, but it made me *sick*,' Tupou declared. He drove the van with the same look in his eyes that Dennis Hopper had in *Blue Velvet*. 'So I came back to Tonga. But now, I'd like to go to Mazeppa, maybe . . . On the right, you can see the mystery of hafee. The verns mystery of hafee.'

'This is a Mormon school,' Akuila proudly pointed out.

'Are they popular today?' I asked.

'Yes. There are many benefits.' Including, I found out later, the chance to go to school in Utah or Hawaii.

'I was in Hawaii on contract for attacking canoe weddings,' said Akuila.

'Canoe weddings?' I asked.

'Yes!' he said.

'What are canoe weddings?'

'CA . . . NOE . . . WED . . . DINGS!'

We talked all afternoon like this, but there was one issue no Tongan would seriously discuss: the succession. Crown Prince Tupuo'toa is a fifty-year-old playboy who's never been married, who once starred in a jazz combo, the Straight Bananas, and who just quit his various government posts in order to concentrate on his various private businesses, which have made him a multimillionaire. We drove past his house, which looked like it'd been designed by a French Donald Trump. Not surprisingly, Tupuo'toa is wildly unpopular with both the church authorities and the thirty-three archconservative Nobles of the Realm (inherited positions like Britain's Lords), and very unlikely to take the throne. The second in line, Prince 'Ulukalala Lavaka Ata, unfortunately fell in love with and married a Samoan commoner, so he isn't eligible. No one we met would talk about all this (beyond making mild jokes and quickly changing the subject), and they were just as evasive when I tried discussing the passport scandal.

A dozen years ago, there was a huge outcry when it was discovered that government ministers were selling Tongan passports for $20,000 to fleeing Hong Kong Chinese and even Imelda Marcos, passports declaring them 'Tongan Protected Persons,' but not allowing them to live in Tonga. When asked where all the money from selling these passports went, the ministers didn't have much of an answer, and Tongans (who are extremely proud to be Tongan) were none too happy that their birthright was being auctioned off for private gain. In practically the first sign of anti-royal politics, ordinary folk took to the streets and published mimeographed newsletters denouncing these TPPs, and the Tongan High Court ruled them unconstitutional in 1990. Immediately, the Tongan parliament (starring these same ministers) held a special session, revised the constitution, and started selling passports that did indeed allow the holder to live in Tonga . . . for $50,000.

We spent over six hours driving around the tiny island of Tongatapu, but because it was a Sunday, we hardly saw a single living Tongan. That night, after dinner, we decided to go for a stroll around town. The sun had set, and everything had changed. Now, mobs of young men and women ebbed and flowed along the main drag, slowly taking in the night air, and each other. Unlike everywhere else I've traveled (where in such a crowd a tourist is guaranteed to be hawked by touts and yanked by kids and beseeched by layabouts), the Tongans ignored us completely. We were old *palangi* (whites, or 'sky-breakers'), and to them, we might as well have been invisible. They, on the other hand, were young, hunky, good-looking Tongans. The men were big and brawny, and plenty of the women did indeed look just like Taco Bells.

Though every Nuku'alofan may be spending their Sunday morning hours solemnly attending to religious duty, the minute the sun sets, the 'house of love' opens wide its doors. There are no Tongan social restrictions on premarital sex, and here, in the evenings, you can meet practically every unmarried Nuku'alofan between the ages of fifteen and forty, thronging the streets, not-so-shyly eyeing each other, and moving in their great, majestic Tongan manner, as slow as the turning of the world.

LEARNING THE ROPES

The next morning, we piled into taxis and headed for Queen Salote Container Pier, and there she was: 320 tons, white oaken hull, double masts, and a bowsprit soaring twenty feet into the air. Originally built as a Danish cargo vessel, the *Søren Larsen* first sailed between Scandinavia and Northern Europe until 1972, when she was restored to nineteenth-century grandeur, circumnavigated the globe, and moved to a new home port of Auckland, New Zealand.

This ship is truly the end of the line, not only because the *Søren* was the last vessel engineered by its builder and namesake before he went out of business, but also because she's the ultimate in three hundred years of sailing technology, as sophisticated with rope, pulleys and sailcloth as any computer is with bits and bytes. We looked in awe at the dizzying miles and miles of line running into the sky, a furiously complicated set of controls for eleven big sheets to catch and carry the wind. Besides the GPS, radar and an ionizer that converts seawater to fresh, we'd be plying the trade winds in the exact same conditions as anyone from the nineteenth century.

Our trip included thirteen crew and nineteen 'voyage crew,' which meant that we paying passengers were supposed to work. From reading the promotional brochure, I assumed this would mean that, every so often, someone would say, 'Could you hand me that rope?' and I'd say, 'Sure!' I also thought that sailing the South Pacific would be like sailing the Caribbean, skimming across a muscular lake . . . it's *pacific*, after all. As I've said, sometimes I'm just an idiot.

The 'real' crew included chief engineer Gavin, whose favorite thing to wear was a big black apron and no shirt, which made him look just like a classic English village smithy. Jennifer, the purser, was beautiful and reserved, but we'd find out later that she really knew how to cut a rug. Annette, the cook, would incorporate leftovers from one meal into something else entirely, such as a teatime's chocolate cake made moist and rich from that morning's oatmeal. Bilge puppy Basil and crew-candidate Ben were both on probation, trying out for permanent jobs, with Ben the most enthusiastic seaman you could ever hope to meet, even though he'd spent much of his adult life seeing the worst parts of the world, working on a container ship. He could swim like a dolphin and climb rigging like a Sherpa; it was like having Tarzan Jr on board. At first, the other, younger crew tried competing with him, but eventually they gave up and would stand by, watching him with looks of sullen defeat.

Originally from the Isle of Man (where the cats have no tails), the captain was James Cottier, who looked exactly like the perfect Hollywood casting of a seaman, lean and no-nonsense, with snowy white hair and beard, marble-blue eyes, one gold earring, and just those wrinkles you get around the eyes from a lifetime of squinting. The second mate (who'd be spending lots of time ordering us around) was Jenna, a robust Dutch blonde with a great husky accent. Having her on board was like going to sea with Marlene Dietrich in her *Blonde Venus* top-hat-and-tails prime. Every emotion Jenna had would appear on her face and the crew would tease her, just so they could get a look. Her last job was working as a cook on an African safari, where she had a chameleon as a pet. When the Namibians saw it changing colors, they thought she was a witch.

Besides the Dutch first and second mates, our cast and crew included a sprinkling of Brits, a smattering of Americans, a dash of Australians, and a vast majority of Kiwis from New Zealand, which they call 'NZ' and pronounce 'En Zed.' Enzedders are like a cross between Britons and Americans from the Midwest, and since my ancestors spent their immigrant purgatory in Wisconsin, I fell immediately in love with them. The passenger list included John, who looked just like a young Michael Caine, and Ozzie George, who could pass for Norman Mailer, and Jo and her daughter Natalie, the spitting images of Ali MacGraw and Minnie Driver. There was a retired customs inspector, Phil, taking his third *Søren* voyage, who tragically didn't look like anybody famous, and who'd had a lot of trouble with nuns trying to slip into Auckland with undeclared, dangerous fruit. 'I'm a religious woman!' one screamed when he confiscated her bag. There was Willie, a very successful Scottish carpenter with big forearms and calves, extremely friendly and hardworking, always offering to help with any chore. None of us, however, could understand a word he said. When we first met, Willie turned to me and asked, 'Off by gibbon, wanker bulton top?' I smiled and nodded agreeably, and he waited. I was supposed to say something back. What could it be?

We were all standing around, doing nothing, and then suddenly, we weren't. 'I need some roughtie-toughtie men!' said Jenna, who put six voyage crew on one side of the boat and six on the other, while I was sent to crawl out on the bowsprit, standing barefoot on ropes swinging high above the sea, to help Ben unfurl the jibs.

The *Søren*'s bow has a giant spar sticking out, the jibboom, which serves as a base for three triangular jib sails that run up to the foremast. Hanging from that foremast are four immense square sails (actually, rhomboid), and behind that, three triangular staysails (or stays'ls) run up to the mainmast, just like the jibs run to the fore. The mainmast hoists the giant mainsail itself, a gaff design, like a triangle with its tip removed at an angle, and all over the sides of the boat, controlling all these things, was a staggering series of ropes. There were halyards to raise and lower the squares, braces to swing the squares to catch the wind, bunts and clews to gather up parts of the squares, sheets to control the fill and shape of the jibs and stays'ls, reefs to accordion-up the mains'l and change its size, peak and throat to change the two-point height of the main, and preventers to keep the boom from swinging around too much and knocking people in the head. Now, in our first moments of 'learning the ropes,' we were taught *all* of them, and immediately had to brace the yards, trim the sheets, and clew to the course. We learned about the binnacle (which holds the compass), the foc's'l (which holds the crew), the baggywrinkles (that keep the sails from chafing against the ropes) and the windlass (that winches up the anchor chain). We set up 'flying nuns' (tubes of canvas) to air out the hold, got our drinks from a 'chilly bin,' tried not to get 'pooped' (which on a ship means a rogue wave sweeping you off the poop deck), and learned to talk like this:

> 'Ready on the peak?
> 'Haul away peak.'
> 'Steady on the peak.'
> 'Ease to the pin.'

We were divvied up into watch slots: 8–12, 12–4 and 4–8, all A.M. and P.M. You wouldn't think that in a million years anyone would pay to work these kinds of hours on a vacation, but in fact the more involved we got, the more fun we had. We helmed and bow-watched, swabbed decks and *Brassoed* fixtures, teaming up to pull rope, adjust sheet and make that baby fly. Whenever we did everything exactly right, Jenna would yell out: 'Beauty!'

It was thrilling work, the ultimate in techno-lust. Just like with a computer, where a few fingertaps can send you spinning around the globe, on the *Larsen*, the pull of a few ropes would make a three-hundred-ton beast plow through the seas. Soon enough, our watch turned into a happy, loyal chain gang, becoming so close that, late at night, in the black, misty dark, we could recognize each other by silhouette. Dad, Kurt and I worked together, and it made me remember how many who write about family reunions complain that their relatives force them to revert back to childhood. Instead, I've already thought of it as: *Opportunity knocks.* In normal adult life, I never would feel free to whine, as I did now:

'Daa-aad! Kurt won't let me helm!'

'Daa-aad! Kurt won't clean up his room!'

'Daa-aad! Kurt's bringing dishonor on our family!'

One unique member of our watch was Catherine, who appeared every morning to perform her own disturbing interpretation of tai chi, and who regaled us for hours with her mastery of the slide whistle. She was really smart, but in that harsh, abusive way of the kid who raises her hand to answer every single question in class. No matter what you said, she had a competing opinion, which she was always willing to share. Just as we'd get fed up and were ready to throttle her, though, some sixth sense would kick in, and she'd do something incredibly kind, thoughtful and generous.

We first met Catherine as the captain was explaining the difference between true north (what the charts read) and magnetic north (where the compass pointed). Jim said that the difference in our case, because of where we were in the South Pacific, would be fourteen degrees.

'I don't believe that's true,' Catherine declared.

'Well, it's not *exactly* true,' Captain Jim admitted, 'but it's close enough for our purposes.'

'I think you could be more accurate,' she insisted.

'There wouldn't be any point to it,' he said, not so calmly.

'I don't see why not,' she continued. He changed the subject.

Jenna came over to ask me, Charlie and Catherine to hoist the mast, and as Charlie and I went over to our ropes, Catherine stayed behind, saying, 'Just a minute, I have to put on my gloves.' Instead of helping to yank (which involves hanging from the line with your whole body, like Quasimodo), she shouted at us from the side, 'Pull up! Heave to in unison!' Dad, watching this, said, 'Catherine, you're not exactly *participating*,' and she replied, 'But I'm giving good advice!'

CALLING FOR HERB

The next day was our first on the open sea, and it was just like being a child whose daddy thinks you should learn how to swim by throwing you into the deep end of the pool. There was a tropical depression swirling a few miles off, a storm a bit smaller than an all-out hurricane, and boy did we know all about it. We woke to find the sky and ocean both a dank, gunmetal gray, at times so perfectly matching in color that the horizon line vanished. Gusts of wind, spray and sea-water rose over the boat and smacked us around right in the face, and we really learned just what *sailing, sailing over the bounding main!* is all about. Bow watches even had to sit on top of the deckhouse, since waves were crashing over where they'd normally be. 'Bluewater' turned into 'whitewater,' and the world's best log-flume roller coaster couldn't come close to matching this ride. We rocked and rolled in every direction, tossed to port, to aft, to fore and to starboard by wind, current and wave, and learned an important lesson: *the Pacific isn't pacific enough.*

My father was in ecstasy. I've never before seen him spending so much time with his mouth dropped open, looking at everything in awe. I asked if he thought he'd picked the right trip, and he looked at me, in silence, and pinched the skin on his arm, to make sure he wasn't dreaming. The rocking got so hard that we even tried on our life vests, which featured a whistle you could blow in case of emergency. I tried it out, only to get a feeble little 'whiss,' and decided that, if something happened, I'd just scream bloody murder.

At one point, I was crossing the deck when the boat suddenly pitched all the way left and then all the way right, each time just near perpendicular to the surf. In the middle of the pitch, a big wave appeared, crashing over the sides, rolling across the planks and knocking me on my butt. It swept me across the decks and right through the scuppers (the vents that let the water out), and if it hadn't been for the iron bars installed just for this purpose, more than just my bottom would've gone through the vents, and I would've been thrown into ten-foot swells. I got up shaking, steadied myself on a lifeline, and turned around, only to find

Charlie, sitting and drinking coffee. He looked at me and said, 'That was really exciting!'

The ocean was so rough that Jenna finally announced, 'We use *heave up* to mean two things. Raising the anchor, and curing sea-sickness. If you must personally heave up, please do so downwind, which is *that* side of the boat.' Thank God I was wearing *Transderm Scop*, a miraculous skin patch guaranteed to keep me from getting nauseous.

I was really loving every minute of this when one of the crew asked me to do an errand. I ran downstairs, but the minute I got below, everything changed. The walls tilted all the way to the left and all the way to the right, the air was hot, moist and fetid, and that was it. The patch stopped working. It hadn't worked for my brother, it hadn't worked for Paul Theroux, it hadn't worked for Dan Conner (who wrote *My Old Man and the Sea*), and now it wasn't working for me.

Being seasick is exactly like being really sick-drunk. One minute, you're having the time of your life and you just can't imagine being any happier than you are right now. Then a biochemical switch flips and suddenly, all you can think is: *HOW DO I MAKE THIS STOP?* Back up on deck, Martin (a British chemical engineer) sat next to me, gray as dead fish, trying to imagine a steady horizon line instead of the continuous forty-five-degree freefall we were looking at. He said, 'At least with a roller coaster, sooner or later, you know the ride is going to end.' Young Natalie had told us that 'I'm a sailor from way back. Nothing makes me sick.' This did. The ship pitched very far left and very far front and very far back and very far right, and you never knew which was coming next. I was cold, soaking wet, but afraid to go downstairs where a bed and warm, dry clothes were waiting, since being in the hold would only make me want to heave up even more than I did already.

Just after lunch (no thanks), Kurt was sitting quietly in the kitchen drinking tea, when he suddenly lurched up and out and onto the deck and ran to the rails and began puking (downwind, thank God, or there would've been hell to pay from Jenna). It was a call to arms, and a half-dozen of us ran to the rails and started heaving up right along with him. Ozzie Jim came over to explain that in Australia it was named 'calling for Herb,' as everyone was groaning, '*Herb!*' '*Herb!*' '*Herb!*'

It turns out that being seasick and sick-drunk have more than just the sensation in common; in both cases, if you vomit till you can't anymore, you almost always feel fine again, and this turned out to be true in my case. I was cured.

Feeling better, I went downstairs to clean up and change clothes. We were still twisting and turning, and I had to use both hands and both feet to brace myself to keep from being thrown off the toilet. Then to flush, I had to pump a handle, flip a lever, pump another handle, flip the lever back, pump the first handle, flip the lever, pump the second handle, and flip the lever to stop. It reminded me of something, but I couldn't think what, and then I remembered: it was just like being an astronaut in zero-gravity outer space. All we needed was *Tang*.

That night, the waves kept tossing us around, and the wooden hull echoed a deafening '*Creak creak! Groan! Whack Whack Whack!*' With the tossing came the feeling that any moment I'd be thrown out of bed. As a longtime professional insomniac, I now got to find out just how innately cruel my brother could be. He was lying in the downstairs bunk, and he turned off his reading light, put down his book and glasses, and within seconds, began snoring. I just couldn't believe it. The waves kept knocking me around in my berth, and I was sure that this roll, and then that one, would wake him up, and I turned to listen, only to hear those goddamn snores. I wanted to strangle him.

Enraged, I didn't sleep more than a couple of hours, and the next day, it happened all over again. I was feeling just great, went down to the hold, felt horrible again, finally convinced myself to throw up, and felt all right. But I couldn't eat or sleep for forty-eight hours, and at the darkest moment I wondered: *If I pretend to vomit blood, would they medevac me off this thing?* Kurt gave me a hard time about being sick and missing night watch, which makes perfect sense. I'd much rather spend my evenings dry-heaving instead of pulling a rope, wouldn't you?

I'm not the kind of guy who relishes serious physical discomfort, unless there's a big payoff. There was: I woke up the next day to find everything had changed. I'd finally gotten my sea legs (as well as Dramamine), I felt just great, I was hungry, the seas were calmer, and I'd even discovered the canvas sheet folded under the berth that you tie to the ceiling to keep from being rolled out of bed. The weather was magnificent, and the ship flew through the water with the winds at our back. At one point, we were even joined by a group of leaping dolphins, tandem duskies keeping pace with our bow spray.

That night, a big animal splashed around on both sides of the boat, but we were always too late to catch it with our flashlights, and could never figure out what it was. I lay on my back out on the bow, watching the towering foremast and acres of sail bob around an ocean of stars. There wasn't a speck of cloud, the air was as clear as I've ever seen in my life, and the longer I looked, the more stars I saw, until each celestial body's pinprick merged with its neighbors into a shining, clotted bowl of milky white.

A CASE OF CONSTIPATION LIKE YOU WOULDN'T BELIEVE

The scenery we watched as the ship rolled, danced and swooned across the Pacific the next day was just movie-magic perfect. I've always found that, when nature is at its zenith, it always looks fake, as if a vast team of Disney Imagineers had shown up and tinted, manicured and staged the landscape. I thought this every minute in the South Seas, where sunny days turned the ocean *Windex* blue, the same color used by any kid with a good set of crayons. The islands we passed ranged from soft mounds to volcanic peaks, every single one sprouting in lawn-green vegetation and waving palms, and then boundaried in white-coral swathes of beach. Almost all were surrounded by barrier reefs forming shallow lagoons, a ring of celadon aqua, edged in relief by the white lines of foaming breakers. It was completely picture-postcard hokey, ridiculous and absurd, and I couldn't get enough of it. At dusk, I even watched the post-sunset we usually ignore, not when it's really beautiful, but when the ground turns black and, in the air, color dies.

Willie the Scotsman came by and said, 'You stall wedding?'

It turned out he wasn't the only one whose English was hard to understand. As we docked at the island of Nomuka, the captain told me, 'You know, there's a whale on that island.'

'Really?'

'Yes, and the villagers get fresh water out of it.'

We ran ashore, I couldn't wait to see this whale, but it turned out to be instead a big muddy well. A Nuku'alofan had told me that Nomukans were snotty and aloof, so I was on my guard when we met the town's policeman, barefoot and shirtless with multiple kids, looking like the perfect South Seas islander living the good life in the middle of nowhere. Then, in perfect Queen's English, he told us all about what a great time he had in San Francisco last month.

On the other side of the reef from Nomuka was the absolutely perfect desert isle, with the happy name of a'a. The next day we anchored there for a snorkel, one of the greatest things human beings get to do while living on planet earth. Nats wouldn't go; she claimed, 'I've snorkeled more often than I've had hot meals,' but the rest of us worried on our gear and jumped into water as clear as a swimming pool, bobbing like quiet helicopters above an endless coral forest of elkhorn, staghorn, honeycomb, mushroom, table and brain, swooping through a secret continent of cobalt starfish, mouthy giant clams, schools of neon tetra, fatty, polka-dotted sea slugs, wriggling black-and-white-striped wormy sea snakes, clownfish swimming in the lee of fish-eating anemone tentacles, absurdly colored damselfish, big, fat green parrotfish, and even a few small, gape-mouthed sharks. If you've ever enjoyed solitude, this is its absolute depth, the only sounds your breath and the nibblings of tiny fish lips.

The most exciting part of South Pacific diving is right at the intersection of the reef, the lagoon and the open sea, and at a'a, there was a wall of coral dropping a hundred feet into the blue. This spot was also, I found out, not exactly safe. I'd been skimming over some very shallow waters, maybe three feet deep (meaning, with my girth, a few inches of clearance), when all of a sudden I was pulled into a tight shallow. I paddled and kicked as hard as I could, but I was angled perfectly against the undertow, and couldn't move a centimeter. If I didn't keep trying, though, I'd be swept out to sea. Finally there was a slight let-up, and I was able to get away from the shallows, out of the current and back into the boat, exhausted.

Ben had heard that we'd spotted a few sharks in the water, and he refused to go in. I explained that they were little, like the ones you see in a rich doctor's aquarium, that they obviously didn't eat people, and that even if they did, they certainly wouldn't be interested in a skinny guy like him. I tried everything, but still he refused, and this made the crew feel better. He wasn't so perfect after all.

Dad was running around the ship like a little boy on his first trip to Disney World. He was so excited, he stumbled over everything, and I watched him, just as decades ago he must've watched me do just exactly the same thing, tripping with happiness. He slid across the dinghy and smashed his hand, slipped on the stairs and cracked his head, didn't nail down a door and watched it slam shut on his wrist. Huge, mysterious new bruises appeared all over him every morning, and I knew I'd be in big trouble with Mom if we didn't get him healed up before going back home. Was he pushing himself too hard, trying to keep up with everybody else, or was he just giddy with excitement? Whatever the reason, the force of his absolute joy at being here and doing this made everyone on board fall in love with him. The captain created a certificate proclaiming him 'Voyage Crew Extraordinaire,' and Ben whispered to me: 'Your dad is so cool!' I said, 'I know.'

I've traveled plenty in the Third World, while my father hasn't, and I constantly found myself watching him exactly the way you eagle-eye a toddler stumbling into traffic. He'd tramp barefoot through a village and all I could think was: *hookworm*. He'd drink and eat just about anything, anywhere, and all I could think was: *cholera*. In the end, except for those stumbles, nothing ever happened to him, but all that worrying gave me a case of constipation like you wouldn't believe.

We Sorenians came from different Commonwealthy cultures, and this was especially clear at breakfast. You could always get normal things like cereal, toast, fruit, coffee, tea and milk, and you could have your pick of such oddities as Seventh Day Adventist-manufactured *Sanitarium* brand peanut butter (preferred, I'm sure, by nine out of ten NZ serial killers), along with generous helpings of Marmite, Promite and Vegemite (which taste like jam made from dehydrated beer). The ship's newsletter beseeched arriving Britons to bring extra cases of beer jam so the crew wouldn't riot, and it was so popular that on some mornings, I had to butt in: 'Okay you guys, stop fighting over that yeast!'

Every breakfast would also have a hot dish, usually delicious things like soft-boiled eggs, or thin, crepey pancakes. One morning, though, the cook yelled out, 'Get your beans on toast!' I thought this was kitchen slang, like 'Adam and Eve on a raft,' and asked Gavin what it meant. 'Do you know what canned beans are?' he said. 'Do you know what toast is?'

The next day the cook announced, 'Spaghetti on toast!' and this was the last straw. I asked the Enzedders if they'd ever heard the following in restaurants:

'I'll have the fettuccine Alfredo . . . on toast, please.'

'Yes, I'd like the deep-fried chicken dumplings. Do you serve them on toast?'

'And I'll have the baked potato . . . on toast, thank you.'

Customs inspector Phil brought me up short by saying that it was the U.S. who brought all these canned goods to the South Pacific in the first place, during World War II. 'Well, yes,' I agreed, 'but we didn't make you eat them all for *breakfast*.'

Willie finished his coffee and said, 'Canker soft, often, yeh?'

Jenna went by, growling.

We had another highlight of British cuisine for lunch that afternoon: the pastie (which doesn't rhyme with 'tasty'). Pasties are turnovers filled with potato, onion and cheese that sound really delicious. When properly made in the British fashion, however, they contain no potato, onion, cheese or pastry flavor. In fact, they have no flavor whatsoever. If someone blindfolded you and made you eat one, you'd know it was a carbohydrate item, but you'd have no idea which carbohydrate item it might be. Really, when you think about it, it's sort of magical. How do they do it?

THE ROAD OF THE DOVES

The most beautiful part of Tonga is the northernmost group of islands called Vava'u (which rhymes, sort of, with 'the towel'), a collection of thousands of soft green hills meandering in and out of the water, threading against each other. You can sail through these islets for days, watching the *Rinso* water hit the vertiginous limestone cliffs of one little world, and lap softly against the bone-white beach of the next.

We went to one Vava'u island, Pongaimotu, for a dance/feast combo, and met John, the chief, who wore a sweatshirt that said *California: Where the Fun Begins!* Overseas, sometimes I think American culture is like a virus. By the time you realize you have it, it's too late for the cure, and I thought this all over again when I found out that the most popular television show in the South Pacific today is *Friends*. I tried imagining what the Pongaimotuans thought about a recent *Friends* subplot, where one of the stars was surrogate-bearing the triplet fetuses of her long-lost half-brother, but I just couldn't do it.

Every Oceanian has a nickname they tell Anglos and a real name that is much better, and chief John's turned out to be the excellent 'Sione.' His village was overrun with feral-looking dogs with pinprick, predator eyes, and a submissive look that seemed to whine, 'Please don't beat me.' I eventually noticed that *all* South Pacific dogs have this look, so maybe it really means, 'Please don't *eat* me.'

Tongan dancing (women moving very, very slightly, while telling a story with their hands) is, like almost all South Pacific culture, now kept going only for tourists. The Pongaimotuans oiled up their bodies so the appreciative audience could stick paper money on their skin, and the oiliest of them all was an adorable little girl, just learning the ropes. Everyone wanted to encourage her, so we all gave her money, but it kept falling off, and to make it stay we had to stick it into her clothes, which started feeling like something you did with a stripper, and it gave me the creeps.

The women had set up an alley of sheets where they could sell handicrafts, and like everywhere else we looked in the South Pacific, these souvenir offerings were pretty sad, and I tried to figure out why. I remembered when I worked with Andy Warhol, and he and I were at a millionaire's California compound, where every room had a staggering view of stark cliffs falling into the Pacific. We were looking at a dazzling sunset, the water chromium blue, the clouds cotton-candy pink, when Andy said, 'Why should anyone bother with art if they're always looking at something like this?' No matter how far out of the way we roamed in the South Pacific, we never saw any handicrafts that were distinctive and original, and I could only think that, living in such a beautiful place, maybe the reason is: *Why bother?*

Our feast that night included the big Tongan delicacy, raw fish marinated in citrus, which I was always afraid to eat (especially here), along with sumptuous plates of big, purple yams. One of the essential mysteries of history is the fact that every Oceanian society has been raising these taste-free South American yams for over four hundred years, and no one knows how they got there. The Trobiands even have a big Yam Festival where everybody has sex with anyone they want for two months, and an Easter Island proverb goes: 'We are born. We eat yams. Then, we die.' The mystery of the yams is in fact what inspired Thor Heyerdahl to sail his balsa raft, *Kon-Tiki*, from South America to Tahiti, to show that Oceanians were originally from the Western Hemisphere. Unfortunately for Thor, DNA has now proven that the Polynesians sailed out originally from the East Indies and the Philippines, but this new evidence still doesn't answer the extraordinary question: *What about those yams?*

Of course, I couldn't mention South American agricultural mysteries without including my all-time favorite: that no one, to date, has been able to track down a single plant of wild corn. We know of thousands of domestic varieties, but the original grass where they all came from has never been found. Spooky!

Back on Pongaimotu, we took Sione's wife, Ginger, to Neiafu town for fun. Ginger was originally from the big city of Nuku'alofa, and had moved here when she married Sione, so I said, 'You must be very happy to be living in beautiful Vava'u,' and Ginger said, 'Ahh . . . maybe . . .'

Neiafu was where we'd go snorkeling with humpback and sperm whales, which to me would be this trip's highlight. We ran down the boat company that makes all the arrangements, but they refused to take us out, since the near-hurricane that made me dry-heave for forty-eight hours was now making it too choppy to swim with leviathans. Inside I collapsed, thinking: *Nature here is, mostly, not your friend*, and we went to the local yachties' hangout to recover.

The Bounty Bar is perched high up a hill with views of Neiafu's startling-blue harbor, and we gazed out at an extravagant panorama of ships, winding roads and gingerbread churches while listening to Jimmy Buffett, drinking bitters, and eating Bounty Burgers (which included fried egg and banana and were delicious, believe it or not). On this trip, it was always completely terrific to be ashore and look back at our beautiful, elegant *Søren*, as abstractly compelling as any Calder mobile. Behind us, a tableful of Tongans belted back Foster's and chain-smoked; one wore an earring he'd made from a match-box. After the sparse life of ocean-going, this was paradise, even though they didn't serve the french fries on toast.

Willie came over and said, 'Didn't all turn the best carver?'

Up the street, we found a Neiafuan with a car, asked if he could drive us around, and he said, 'Sure!' Tino was a cop who liked wearing cable-knit sweaters (it was maybe eighty degrees, just like winter in Miami), and he jacked up the radio so we could enjoy Tonga's three favorite kinds of music: reggae, disco and eighteenth-century English hymns. We went by the prison farm and waved hello to all his friends, and Tino explained that, 'The biggest crimes here are assault, improper assault and swearing in public.' By 'improper assault,' he meant rape.

Tino drove us down the island's main paved road, which turned into the Road of the Doves (built by women convicted of adultery), which turned into a dirt road, which turned into no road at all. On a barely cleared path, he crushed over saplings and under tree limbs that should've made us turn back, but he kept going, and I just couldn't believe it. How would we get out of here? How would we even turn around? He kept going and going, and finally we stopped, and got out, and walked up a little hill to see, on the far north of the island, naked black cliffs plunging hundreds of feet straight into the sea.

MANUFACTURER'S ERROR

The next morning we had to climb the riggings to unfurl the sails, and this was not my shining moment. I think all human beings should come to grips with knowing their personal foibles and fears, and one of my many personal foibles is that I am physically retarded. I drop things left and right, am a fire hazard in a kitchen, and can get all messed up just trying to put on a windbreaker. Climbing the masts is a job for small, trim, agile people, and I am none of these.

Riggings are tied pieces of rope that swing in the smallest breeze, and since I was the first up, I had to go all the way out onto the end of the main spar. I couldn't balance well enough to see where to put my feet or where to hold on, and the length of the footrope was set so that the beam hit right against my crotch. I was supposed to bend over the spar and adjust the sails, but I knew if I did that, I'd be swinging upside down from the safety harness in a matter of seconds. Between the wind and the fact that everyone else was crawling around on the mast, fussing with ropes, I was getting bounced around as sharply as a pogo stick, and as I moved across the beam, ropes would catch my jacket and pull it over my face, blinding me.

If my major foible is physical retardation, my major phobia is: *Manufacturer's Error.* When they say, 'We make these bolts to a tolerance of 400,000,' they mean that one of every 400,000 bolts fails. I'm convinced that's the bolt I'm going to get. Every time I think, 'Skydiving sure looks like a lot of fun!' it only takes a few seconds to remember that I'm bound to get the 1 in 500,000 parachutes that doesn't work. So there I was, high above the ship, teetering on a little rope, blinded by my own jacket, the wind and everyone else making me bounce up and down and swing back and forth, and all I could think was: *Manufacturer's Error.*

Kurt, working right next to me, said, 'Just look straight down over the beam, and you'll see the furling rope.' I said, '*No.*' He, meanwhile, spent lots of time playing around with his knots, getting them just so, meaning I couldn't get by and get below, which led to the classic conversation:

'Shut up.'

'No, you shut up.'

'No, you shut up.'

'No, you shut up.'

Finally, I made it back down, alive.

A *TWILIGHT ZONE* HOSTED BY SOMERSET MAUGHAM

Sailing across the South Pacific is just as completely romantic as our dreams, and it only took a week for all those randy Commonwealthies to start coupling up. I'd notice 'secret' touches and caresses here and there, and three times in two days, I was sitting around when various crew were talking, and one would say, 'Craig, you weren't supposed to hear that,' and of course, I didn't. One time as a joke I went up to Lydia, an English theater publicist, and said, 'Nats and I have been talking, and we've decided you should have sex with Albert,' but it was too late. She was already dating another crew member, while Albert himself had started pursuing Natalie with inappropriate ardor. Nats got to spend plenty of time, in fact, fending off crew, and she was mostly enjoying this, except when it came to Albert, who just wouldn't accept a no. It got to the point where, obviously, everyone on board was having sex except me.

The voyage crew included a group of 'mystery bachelors,' men who'd had tragic histories with women that they didn't care to discuss. Some of these men were on a mission every night to drink as much beer as possible, while discussing all the other times in their lives they'd gotten smashed, and vomited. They were like a crowd of giant teenagers, and when they came to our dress-up parties in skirts and makeup, it was obvious who shouldn't consider transvestitism as a career path. One night after getting drunk, the mystery bachelors split into sects, one taking over the deck, another commandeering the hold, both discussing who drank the most they ever saw in their whole lives, and how much did he vomit? I couldn't fall asleep, and I couldn't get away from them. My thoughts turned to suicide.

I was having coffee with Jo and Natalie the next morning when Jo, reading her *Lonely Planet*, suddenly announced: 'Sexually transmitted diseases are rampant in Fiji!'

I gave Natalie a look. 'That's why I'm keeping an eye on you. If I can't save you from the scourge of syphilis, maybe at least I can keep you from the heartbreak of chlamydia' (this was a complete joke, as Nats was maybe the most responsible twenty-year-old alive).

'Is that the one you have forever?' she asks.

'No, that's herpes.'

'It's the inflammation,' Jo offers.

'Oh. What Rose had,' says Nats.

'Rose? Does her mum know?'

'Of course.'

'That's what you get for pursuing roughtie-toughtie Maoris,' I joked.

'Actually, Samoans,' said Jo.

'He's a moog,' said Willie.

I was at the helm when the captain issued an order to turn starboard. Since all our steering so far had been keeping the ship on a straight course by watching the compass (harder than it sounds, with the wind and waves constantly pushing the boat around), this was really exciting, and Dad got a little jealous. The next day, we approached Levuka harbor on the island of Ovalau, our first stop in Fiji, and it was my turn to helm again. I kept postponing, letting others take the wheel, until finally, at just the right moment, I grabbed Dad and moved in. He got to turn port! Then the captain did an amazing thing; he let him helm all the way past the reef and into anchorage while the Doors sang from the galley: 'Who Do You Love?' His mission accomplished, Dad came up to me, trembling, he was so excited, and he said, 'That was the living shits!' and I said, 'What?' and he said, 'I mean, the living end!'

Looking at Ovalau from anchorage, we saw the tiny, ancient turn-of-the-century town of Levuka ringing the beach, backed by a ragged mountain and topped with an ominous black cloud. The front is the dry side, while the back is the wet, and that cloud means that, on the back half of this tiny land, it's raining. What immediately catches the eye, however, is the lurid neon-green cross of the Church of the Sacred Heart, erected by busy French Marists at the dead center of it all.

If cannibals are the number one target of missionaries worldwide, their preferred number two must be wayward nefarious dens of sin, and they found it all right here. Levuka was once the 'Wild East,' a major whaling port with sixty bars and Fiji's first 'European' visitors, escaped felons from Australia. It was the capital until 1882, when the state moved everything, even the pineapple cannery, over to

Suva on the central island of Big Fiji. For three years, the two largest Fijian cities communicated via carrier pigeon, but then in 1885, Levuka was decimated by a hurricane, not rebuilt, and allowed to slip into the mists.

Without luxe beaches, a civil service or much of any industry, Levuka has no regular tourists and no economic growth, and going there is like entering a *Twilight Zone* hosted by Somerset Maugham. Except for a tuna cannery (and a Bumblebee boat with a helicopter for spotting the herds), the island has been hermetically sealed since the turn of the century, and I loved it completely. The main Levuka buildings are all exactly the same as they were in 1885, many even retaining the nineteenth-century signage on their windows, like 'Milk Bar' and 'Photo-Studio-Deluxe,' and every street is laded with screaming bougainvillea, hibiscus, allamanda, poinsettia, poinciana, croton, plumeria and ixora trees.

We drove around the island in a Carina with an Indian guy named Bob-Murgan. In contrast to the big, brown Tongans, Fiji men look like Ozzie Aborigines, while the women greatly resemble Aretha Franklin in her giant-'fro period. Outside the major cities, everyone you see waves and shouts 'Bula!' (*hello*), so we had to wave 'Bula!' to everyone Bob-Murgan knew, which turned out to be *everyone*, while he gave a running commentary straight from *The Young and the Restless*: 'That farm's an Australian guy, with a Tongan wife, and three adopted kids from Samoa . . . That one's an English guy, with two Fijian wives, and an English one back home . . . There's the American resort, half finished, they're having legal troubles with the village and are in court . . .'

After passing through fields of cocoa beans and smelling their chocolate, we got hungry, and over a lunch of freshwater crayfish in coconut cream we met a family of five, the Alperts, who'd left the U.S.A. in 1992 to sail around the world together. Everywhere we went in the South Pacific we ran into yachties, Yanks, Brits, Kiwis and Ozzies who've sold their houses and left their businesses and thrown away most of what they own in order to wander around, aimlessly, in a boat. There are the ultimate run-away-from-homers, usually never staying anywhere for more than a year or so before sailing away, and far from seeming like a dream come true, the whole idea gave me the creeps. The Alpert yacht was lush and beautiful, but living with your two sisters and your parents for six years, in a thirty-foot room? Wandering around from place to place, that one room your only real home? Paring down everything you own, from clothes to books to CDs, to conserve space?

The parents were home-tutoring the kids, who were desperate to get off that damn boat and go to school. *Any* school. The eldest Alpert child was truly eloquent about their family's grand adventure: 'You know, at my age, you're trying to develop your own character, and I'm getting sick of making and losing friends so quickly.'

After a few rounds of snooker at the Ovalau Club, all the Sørenians ate dinner and then met up at the tiny, Indian-run Café Levuka, where the stereo was up full blast, the cops kept coming by, the manager just kept saying, 'But this is a private party!' and the Commonwealthies danced like love-drunk teens. The clientele included a dozen Chinese just off the tuna boat after months at sea (staring at Nats like they'd never seen a human female before), and a group of nefarious, gender-blurred Melanesians milling about (the kind of people you wouldn't exactly want to meet alone, late at night, in the middle of nowhere).

I got too sweaty and went outside to cool off, wandering across the street to watch the cops pounding *kava* with a big stick in a metal urn. They gave me a turn with the stick, watched my poor technique, and immediately took it back. At the café, a tailless shepherd kept trying to get in the club, and I told the little boy who owned him that he sure seemed like a good dog. 'Oh yes,' the boy said, 'Rusty is a good boy. He never bites people on the ankles or legs. He only goes for the throat, and he never lets go. I don't know why.' Then the boy yanked Rusty down the street by his ears while the dog screamed in pain and stared out with 'please don't eat me' eyes. Jo came out to the street, looked at us, and said, 'It appears I've lost my shoes.'

WE WANT *PACA-PACA*!

Just to the west and around the corner from Ovalau is Kandavu, a tiny island anchoring the fish-loving Great Astrolabe Reef, and centerpieced by the ultimate Fiji village. Set just back from the water, Ndravuni is a magnificent beach town of blue concrete houses with fieldstone porches and red corrugated-tin roofs set on tidy lawns, front yards filled with aubergines, macramé hammocks swinging between the palms, and a church pulpit draped by a needlepoint-it-yourself *Last Supper*. Even with the church and a giant stone tomb inscribed 'Go Ye Therefore and Preach the Gospel!' however, there were plenty of mysterious pagan things going on, like a tree stump raised on a mound, cut into the shape of an L, and painted blue, next to a set of carved-out logs filled with rocks and sticks. I guess they were spiritually covering all the bases. Up the road, in the village of Namuana, the women sing to giant sea turtles to come home for supper, but apparently this practice has all but died out, and we couldn't find anyone turtle-singing while we were there. Too bad; it's a great song:

> We, the women of Nambukelevu,
> Adorn ourselves with black ceremonial skirts.
> We assume an attitude of reverence.
> We paint ourselves with intricate markings.
> We disguise ourselves thus, Raunindalithe [meaning the turtle],
> That we may look upon you, O great one.

Dad hit town, and immediately had his hands grabbed by two squealing boys who dragged him off on a tour. The kids weren't old enough to speak much English, but they did know one English tune, so the three sang 'Happy Birthday!' over and over. Ozzie Jim ran into this trio and wanted to get a picture, so he mimed smiling by using his fingers to spread his lips apart, and the boys posed for him by using their fingers to spread their lips apart. One little girl, Lolei, kept following me, so I sang 'bula bula!' while doing the hula, but she kept following anyway. We wandered past yards filled with big, fat, healthy chickens, flower beds terraced with giant clamshells, pens of piebald just-born piglets, green-plaited baskets filled with fleshy-white yams and always, in the background, just out of reach, the ridiculous azure bed of the sea. There was a scuffling noise, and I looked up into the palm trees to see the world's most frightening arthropod, a coconut crab, whose claws are strong enough to cut through coconut (and that's really strong). When provoked, these enormous blue insectoid creatures glom on to whatever's there, and if you turn out to be the whatever, there's a choice: you can wait seven hours until the crab decides to let go, or lose a body part. A woman with a big net bag of what looked like grunion or sardines came by and asked, 'Ya got a ciggie, darlin'?'

I left the trail and wandered over to the beach, where big, white ghost crabs scurried away from my feet, and two women and a man were casting monofilament into the surf and pulling in tiny grunion one at a time. They saw me taking notes and asked, 'Are you keeping a field journal?' When I explained what I was doing, they said, 'We want *paca-paca!*' and I didn't know what that was, but I was pretty sure I didn't have any. Suddenly, there was a flurry in the water, and the women started screaming and screaming, and I didn't know what to do; maybe flee? Instead, I watched the man run back to the treeline, grab a big blue net, and race to the shore where, with a two-handed tennis swing, he swished through the surf to catch an entire school of grunion, along with a big, fat, tunalike fish, maybe thirty pounds, which flopped around on the beach. The women killed it by putting out its eye with a stick, and they were so wildly happy, leaping and screaming, that I thought: Maybe this is *paca-paca?*

That night, we went to a big *kava* ceremony hosted by the chief of Ndravuni's brother, Mike, in a communal room with inscribed cloth at the lintels and blinding fluorescent overhead tubes. *Kava* is the narcotic root of a pepper plant that is pounded into dust, tied up in an old sock, and swished through a three-legged wooden bowl full of water. When it looks muddy and fetid, it's ladled out to everyone in coconut cups, one at a time. If you drank a beer, took a tranquilizer and ate a Fizzic, you'd have the essence of this unique ritual. *Kava* ceremonies are supposed to be conducted in absolute silence, but Oceanians make an exception for their Anglo guests. Still, it's not exactly the most stimulating thing you've ever done on vacation.

All over the South Pacific, grog shops announce: *Fresh Pounded!*, and everywhere we went, there seemed to be an awful lot of *kava* drinking going on. The Fijians were very concerned, because American demand had thrown the grog market into massive inflation, doubling the price of root to $40 a kilo in the past two years alone. It's not unlikely that, should this trend continue and *kava* becomes increasingly valuable as an export, the ceremonies will falter, the addicts won't be able to afford their nightly guzzle, and Oceania will be awash in *kava* riots. We couldn't help but wonder: Just who in the U.S. is drinking all this damn *kava*? Then I had a thought – *New Age* – and this turned out to be true. Kurt found 'kavakava' as an ingredient in Celestial Seasonings' Sleepy Time herbal tea, Mary found it advertised as a 'supplement' in pill and powder form, and Dad decided that Oceania needed a new poem of love:

A mortar, a pestle, a root, a sweaty sock, and thou . . .

My *kava*-drinking buds that night were Georgie (already sullen and diffident, and we'd just gotten there) and Max (who catches sharks for the University of the South Pacific biology department). I got completely *kava*-plotzed, stupefied and disinterested in any kind of physical activity, including human speech. Lydia wanted to take a picture of Max drinking *kava*, but was too shy to ask, so I said, 'Max, this little shy girl wants a picture of you drinking, okay?' and he said, 'Tell the little shy girl it will be fine.' All night long, Max kept asking, 'How's the little shy girl? Is she getting enough *kava*?'

One big guy sat with all the girls in the back of the crowd, and I assumed he was a *fakaleiti* ('like a woman'), a popular Polynesian custom where, if a family doesn't include enough females, they raise a boy as a girl. The boy wears dresses and makeup and grows out his hair and works with the women, and may or may not grow up to be gay. This custom is so ingrained that one of the highlights of the King of Tonga's birthday party is the Miss Galaxy Contest, a 'transgendered' beauty pageant (with sewing, dancing and talent categories) that we sadly missed. This year, the patron was the king's granddaughter, the crowd was standing room only, and the winner was Natasha Pressland, who wanted to become a flight attendant and whose hobbies were 'dancing, praying and meeting people.' Fiji, too, had its own *fakaleiti* party called the Priscilla Festival, named after the movie *Priscilla: Queen of the Desert*, but tragically, we missed that as well. Just think of it: giant, football-player Tongans and ex-cannibal Fijians, parading around in national contest-winning drag, coming out of a culture that merges transvestitism, *kava* and Protestant fundamentalism. The more I tried to put all this together, the more I fell short, and the more I started thinking: *Oceania is just terrific*.

The *kava*, though, made me a little sad, since it reminded me of all the South Pacific traditions now gone forever. The pre-Methodist Fijian cannibals were obsessed with their hair, braiding, teasing and knotting it into dreadlocks and puffs, dying it white, yellow, red and striped, using human-hair extensions to make it even bigger, and having special headrests carved so their dos wouldn't be harmed while they slept. They painted their bodies and faces in every tint they could find, wore spiky jewelry carved from the teeth of sperm whales, and jousted at war, like medieval knights, with magnificent wooden clubs. Boys were only named after they'd killed someone, and meals would include parts of a captured warrior cooked and eaten, while he watched from a cage. Canoes were launched using live girls as rollers, and especially prominent captives were buried alive to hold up the foundation posts of new spirit houses. Inside those five-story-high grass huts, priests would wait beneath a giant piece of bark-cloth cascading from the ceiling for the spirits of the ancestors to slide down, into their mouths.

Back at the ceremony, Chris, a Brit with an ingratiating tenor voice, led the Commonwealthies in a weak round of Blake's 'Jerusalem' as a thank-you to the Ndravunians. The village, after drinking *kava* all night long, responded in turn with a staggering, four-part harmony of 'Isa Lei,' the mournful Fijian song of farewell. It was a mind-boggling a cappella wall of sound, as beautiful as any Ladysmith Black Mambazo effort, and they were ready right then and there to hit a recording studio.

Even in my *kava*-stupor, I now understood that Oceanians, at least the Tonga/Fiji branch, were something like Californians. When you first meet, they're always warm, friendly and smiling, but getting to the next level requires real strategy and serious effort. Between their Protestant fundamentalism and their antisocial *kava*, the Pacifists weren't really that interested in making contact with us.

This, of course, would have to change.

JUST DO IT!

The Protestant missionaries did plenty of obnoxious and offensive things when they showed up here in the 1800s, from getting traditional dancing banned by convincing everyone it led to pregnancy, to destroying all the *tiki* carvings as 'idols,' to slaughtering hundreds of thousands by infecting them with influenza, syphilis, smallpox and pneumonia. One of the most egregious Methodist accomplishments, however, was the bizarre written language they invented. If any speech could be transcribed in a straightforward, phonetic manner, it's the Polynesian mother tongue, but the missionaries decided instead to have a system where you'd have to know lots of arcane rules to be able to say anything. In Fijian, for example, the letter *b* is pronounced *mb*, *c* is pronounced *th*, and *q* is pronounced *ngg*, so the first chief to unite the islands into one Fiji is pronounced *thak-om-bau*, but missionary-spelled Cakobau, and the island of Beqa, where the firewalkers come from, is pronounced *benga*.

No one firewalks on Beqa anymore, but the island is rife with spectacular coral reefs, so we anchored in a narrow bay next to the town of Lalati, another tidy, bungaloid Fiji village. We wandered around town and immediately found something truly odd: a prickly pear cactus. Catherine asked our guide, Seru, 'Do you eat this?' He gave her that eye you give mental patients, and said, 'No, it's just for looking.' 'In the States, we eat this,' she insisted. I mentioned that it takes a great deal of work to skin cactus and boil down the pulp, and Seru thought it would be an excellent idea for Catherine to spend the night in Lalati, cooking it. Sadly, she demurred.

After meeting various Beqans, it was about four o'clock, and we were standing around, waiting for the little boat to show up to take us back to the big boat, when one of the chief's sons told us to go inside the big man's house. It turned out their *kava* ceremony, which we Larsenians were supposed to attend after dinner, was starting right now, and it wouldn't be polite for us not to join in.

Lalati's good Christian men begin their narcotic ritual by saying a benediction, which I asked my neighbor, Joseva, to translate. 'We are thanking Someone, we don't know who it is, for giving us this, and to make it strong,' he explained. 'It's someone up there, we don't know who.' It was just a small group and I was bored, so I decided to tell the men that the hot new song in Suva, the capital, was a big-band, jitterbuggy number, the story of what a man says to a woman at the end of the night: '*Vinaka . . . vinaka waka levu, vinaka, vinaka . . .*' (Thanks, thanks very much). They thought this was so funny that they sang it over and over, until it got to be really tedious. That night at nine, when the other Sørenites finally appeared, the perils of *kava* became clear. Kurt asked how many kids the chief of Lalati had, and no one could answer this question, not even the chief himself.

The next morning we had the entire village of fifty aboard for coffee, tea and cakes. There were some young women sitting around at the bow, doing nothing, so I went over to ask if their husbands had sung '*Vinaka! vinaka waka levu!*' to them last night. Indignant, they said no. I sang the song, and explained what it was for, and did a little jitterbug as accompaniment, and the Lalati women adamantly insisted that I keep dancing. I counteroffered: 'Only if you sing.'

While one girl went off to keep an eye on the local archreligious crone busybody so she wouldn't interfere with our fun, the women of Lalati sang every upbeat song they knew, while I danced the hakey-shakey, the rubber-squat, the panky-man and the limber-goose. In one village, my dancing had made the children scream with every new step, and now the women of Lalati tittered and cooed, like birds in love, singing beautifully, and spurring me on with cries of 'Just Do It!' 'Nike! Just Do It!'

Finally, I'd gotten what I came for.

We heaved up and set sail for Musket Cove and Plantation Island, upmarket resorts that are exactly what you find in Hawaii and the Caribbean and on the coasts of Spain and Greece: the *International Beach Resort*. Plantation was, like every IBR, painted aqua and peach, with open veranda restaurants offering a grill buffet, next to thatch umbrella tables overlooking pools, volleyball courts, cabanas and a host of sea toys, from popping windsurfers to jaunty Sunfish. The IBR is in fact the standard destination for almost everyone who comes to Fiji, but we'd been sailing around such out-of-the-way places that arriving here threw me into a little culture shock. After spending all that time in the outback, I now saw that mainstream

Fiji's about as Third World as Hawaii, with over a thousand Ozzies and Kiwis showing up every day for time-shares and cut-rate package stays, including all-you-can-eat breakfasts of spaghetti on toast.

That night, driving in on the rubber boat, a bowman swept a flashlight over the water to show hundreds of white fish leaping into the air. Musket Cove's owner, Dick, was longtime friends with the *Larsen* owners, so we made ourselves right at home, throwing back plenty of the resort's piña coladas, blended from fresh coconut cream and fresh pineapple juice, and each about the size of a baby. Dick then sent over a complimentary dozen and we polished those off. Everyone turned woozy and logy, trying not to think about the fifteen-minute walk back to the docks, when Catherine said, 'You know, what New Zealanders call ice cream, Americans call sherbet. Well, it's not exactly sherbet. Ice cream starts with cream, or a mix of cream and milk, or cream and eggs. It starts with a custard. Sherbet starts with fruit juice, and water, and some milk, or cream. No eggs. Well, maybe some. But it's not a custard. It's different. It's sherbet.'

Bilge puppy Baz had been talking about getting a haircut, and suddenly Jenna appeared behind him, brandishing a pair of rusty kitchen shears and an old blanket she'd gotten from the bar. Without a word, she wrapped the blanket around his neck and hammerlocked him with one arm, while snipping away with the other. It was really exciting and I sat there, glued to the seat, wondering: *Who will lose an eye?* She finished up and everyone went on home, intact, with Baz looking like a still-living Sid Vicious. He spent the next day wearing a cap until repairs could be made.

Across the lagoon from Musket Cove there was a whiff of white smoke rising from the island of Maleaolo. Jim, our resident agriculture expert, thought it was deliberate, either a slash-and-burn to make room for pasture, or a planned operation to safeguard against an out-of-control brushfire. Within an hour, the flames had spread across the hills, a wall of smoke rose up, and the entire island was engulfed, burning out of control. Dad's roommate, Rod, who has a time-share on the other side of the bay, said that the Maleaoloans did this every year, that they don't have crops for slash-and-burn, that they know nothing about preventive measures . . . that it just seemed to be done for no good purpose. When he was in the neighborhood, Paul Theroux had run into arsonists on Maleke, just up the Koro Sea, and I wondered if this was maybe the big new Fiji trend: 'I'm bored. Let's burn something!'

It was our last *Søren* party night, so the mystery bachelors were decked out in microskirts, lace evening gowns and muumuus. We drank rum punch while watching the flames stretch out into an orange glowing thread, a necklace of fire that rolled across the hills and destroyed a small world. Willie, who we could finally understand, said, 'I can't believe this is all coming to an end' . . . but he was talking about our voyage.

WHERE TO NEXT?

'That water's as flat as a plate of piss,' said Ozzie Jim the next morning as we motored to Viti Levu – Big Fiji. There was not one whisper of moving air, and there was visibility, in every direction, of sixteen miles. On this ship, for the first time in my life, I got to really *see* weather. Almost every day, the horizon was filled with queues of slowly moving black clouds, spilling flat sheets of rain. I'd sit bow-watch, and see a squall right in front of us, and think that at any minute we were going to get soaked, but instead the only showers that mattered were coming from the back, tracked in the winds that blew us across the South Pacific.

That afternoon, the sky turned half clear and half cloudy, and at one moment the sun hit at exactly the right angle. The port waters were Rinso blue, while starboard, the same ocean was gunmetal silver. Suddenly the wind gusted up, the boat began to rock, the spray flew over the surf and into our faces, and we were back to real 'white water' ocean-going. The dark, wet clouds caught up with us, we had to run for the oilskins, and I said to Dad, 'This must be the only vacation where you hope for serious rain, just to get the full experience.' We stood at the bow together, rising and falling, feeling the spray mix with the raindrops, thrilled and giddy.

We arrived at Suva, Fiji's capital, when the flame trees were in bloom, and went to eat at a seafood restaurant right on the wharf. It was a Saturday night, and the streets were teeming with people who'd bused in from the countryside to dance. After dinner, while everyone else was using the phones and bathrooms, I waited outside to watch the Suvans canoodling in their waterside park. Immediately, a giant transvestite in a bronze wig and microskirt appeared and said, 'Hi! Would you like to go for a good time?' I said, 'No. Thank you, though,' while in the tree next to us, a fruit bat giggled and squeaked. I was then approached by a traditional group of wandering Fijian minstrels, a quartet of men on guitars, banjo and ukulele performing mournful, *kava*-inspired ballads, just like the music you hear, drunk on margaritas, in bad Mexican restaurants. Thankfully, they moved on. Across the way, next to the ruins of the Victoria Grand Hotel, elderly gentlemen, all in starched whites, lawn-bowled.

On our last watch, Dad and Kurt were talking about how good it'd be to get back home, while I was thinking: *Where to next?* The *Søren* would be sailing on to the nation of Vanuatu, model for James Michener's Bali Hai, home of pigs bred to produce spiral tusks, land of giant-footed birds, megapodes, who bury their huge eggs to incubate in the sand of volcanoes, and jungle domains of never-seen-by-Anglos pygmy tribes. During World War II, a thousand Vanuatuans were hired away from home to work on U.S. military bases, and the men's stories, when they returned, evolved into the Jon Frum cargo cult. Many Vanuatu islands have renounced Christianity, kicked out the Presbyterians, and gone back to their traditional life of *kava* drinking, dancing and free love, because they believe by doing this, some day Jon Frum will return to rule over them and provide every material need. On one Vanuatu island, villagers build towers, tie liana vines to their ankles and jump off, their hair brushing against the yam fields and assuring a good harvest. When I thought about all I'd be missing, it was just too much. It was as if I'd never been anywhere.

At midnight, I looked up to see something I'd never seen before. There was the moon, fat and white, and ringed by a halo of all the colors in the world. In the sea, the slicing of the boat excited the plankton, which quivered and flashed, spreading a stream of watery fireflies in our wake. Behind our backs, tracked hard on the speed of the winds, those dark, wet clouds were coming.

SOURCES

Shana Alexander, 'Serengeti,' *National Geographic*, May 1986.

Natalie Angier, 'In Society of Female Chimps, Subtle Signs of Vital Status,' *The New York Times*, August 12, 1997.

Harvey Arden, 'Along the Grand Trunk Road,' *National Geographic*, May 1990.

John Bains and Jaromi'r Ma'lek, *Atlas of Ancient Egypt*, Facts on File, New York, 1980.

James Balog, 'A Personal Vision of Vanishing Wildlife,' *National Geographic*, April 1990.

Benjamin R. Barber, 'Jihad vs. McWorld,' *The Atlantic Monthly*, March 1992.

Carol Beckwith, 'The African Roots of Voodoo,' *National Geographic*, March 1985.

Rajesh Bedi, *Banaras: City of Shiva*, Brijbasi Printers, New Delhi, 1987.

Hans-Ulrich Bernard, *Amazon Wildlife*, APA Publications, Hong Kong, 1992.

Howard Blum, *The Gold of Exodus*, Simon & Schuster, New York, 1998.

Sarah Boxer, 'It Seems Art Is Indeed Monkey Business,' *The New York Times*, November 8, 1997.

Sarah Boxer, 'Writer with a Favorite Theme: Reconciliation of Opposites,' *The New York Times*, December 22, 1997.

Denis Boyles, *African Lives*, Weidenfeld & Nicholson, New York, 1988.

301

Denis Boyles, *Man Eater Motel*, Ticknor & Fields, New York, 1991.

John Brant, 'Daddy Dearest,' *Outside*, March 1996.

Stanley Breeden, 'Lord of the Indian Jungle,' *National Geographic*, December 1984.

James Brooke, 'Too Often, Cougars and People Clash,' *The New York Times*, September 3, 1997.

Susan Brownmiller, 'Shanghai Express,' *Travel & Leisure*, March 1997.

Elinor Burkett, '"God Created Me to Be a Slave,"' *The New York Times Magazine*, October 12, 1997.

Tim Cahill, 'Professor Cahill's Travel 101,' *Outside*, January 1997.

Robert Caputo, 'Journey Up the Nile,' *National Geographic*, May 1985.

Robert Caputo, 'Uganda: Land Beyond Sorrow,' *National Geographic*, April 1988.

Douglas H. Chadwick, 'At the Crossroads of Kathmandu,' *National Geographic*, July 1987.

Douglas Chadwick, 'Out of Time, Out of Space,' *National Geographic*, March 1991.

Mark Cherrington, 'In the Crosshairs,' *The Sciences*, January-February 1998.

Liesl Clark, 'Alive on Everest,' NOVA, www.pbs.org/wgbh/nova, December 15, 1997.

David Cohen, *A Day in the Life of China*, Collins, London, 1989.

Holland Colter, 'A Mute Asian Civilization That Speaks Eloquently,' *The New York Times*, February 20, 1998.

William Dalrymple, 'The River Goddess,' *Condé Nast Traveler*, September 1997.

Bhagavan Das, *It's Here Now (Are You?)*, Broadway Books, New York, 1997.

Basil Davidson, *Africa in History*, Touchstone, New York, 1995.

Dr Richard Dawood, 'Bad Medicine in China,' *Condé Nast Traveler*, September 1997.

Krishna Deva, *Khajuraho*, Brijbasi Printers, New Delhi, 1986.

Jared Diamond, 'Mr Wallace's Line,' *Discover*, August 1997.

Oria Douglas-Hamilton, 'Can They Survive?' *National Geographic*, November 1980.

Mike Edwards, 'Central Africa's Cycle of Violence,' *National Geographic*, June 1997.

Mike Edwards, 'When the Moguls Ruled India,' *National Geographic*, April 1985.

William S. Ellis, 'Shanghai,' *National Geographic*, March 1994.

Doug Fine, 'The Misty Future of Rwanda's Mountain Gorillas,' *The Washington Post*, April 30, 1995.

Allan C. Fisher, Jr., 'African Wildlife: Man's Threatened Legacy,' *National Geographic*, February 1972.

Dian Fossey, *Gorillas in the Mist*, Houghton Mifflin, Boston, 1983.

Dian Fossey, 'The Imperiled Mountain Gorilla,' *National Geographic*, April 1981.

Simon Freeman, 'Monkey Business in Borneo,' *The Guardian*, January 4, 1994.

Howard W. French, 'Sure Africa's Troubled, but There Is Good News,' *The New York Times*, June 15, 1997.

Fu Tianchou, *The Underground Terracotta Army of Emperor Qin Shi Huang*, New World Press, Beijing, 1984.

Biruté M.F. Galdikas, *Children of the Forest*, Little, Brown, New York, 1996.

Biruté M.F. Galdikas, 'Living with the Great Orange Apes,' *National Geographic*, December 1995.

Biruté M.F. Galdikas and Dr Gary L. Shapiro, *A Guidebook to Tanjung Puting National Park, Kalimantan Tengah (Central Borneo), Indonesia*, PT Gramedia Putaka Utama and the Orangutan Foundation International, Banjamarsin, 1994.

George Gerster, 'Fly of the Deadly Sleep,' *National Geographic*, December 1986.

Jeffrey Gettleman, 'Spell Bound in Java,' *Escape*, October 1997.

Ron Gluckman, 'The Americanization of China,' *Asiaweek*, June 28, 1997.

Nicholas Goldberg, 'Life Is Good for Uganda's Ruthless Ex-Dictator Amin,' *Newsday*, July 17, 1996.

Adam Gopnik, 'Is There a Crisis in French Cooking?' *The New Yorker*, April 21, 1997.

Nicholas Gordon, *Ivory Knights*, Chapmans, London, 1991.

Rick Gore, 'Ramses the Great,' *National Geographic*, April 1991.

Philip Gourevitch, 'Letter from the Congo: Continental Shift,' *The New Yorker*, August 4, 1997.

Philip Gourevitch, 'The Vanishing,' *The New Yorker*, June 2, 1997.

Editors, *Granta* magazine, *The Best of Granta Travel*, Granta Books, London, 1991.

William Greider, 'Planet of Pirates,' *The Utne Reader*, May-June 1997.

Joshua Hammer, 'After Rwanda,' *Outside*, April 1995.

Jeannette Hanby and David Bygott, *Ngorongoro Conservation Area: The Complete Guidebook*, David Bygott & Co., Karatu, 1992.

John Hemingway, *No Man's Land*, Dutton, New York, 1983.

Sean Henahan, *Female Hyenas and Male Hormones, A Strange Combination*, Access Excellence, May 1997.

Mark Hertsgaard, 'Our Real China Problem,' *The Atlantic Monthly*, November 1997.

Christopher Hitchens, 'District of Contempt,' *Vanity Fair*, March 1998.

Christopher Hitchens, 'There'll Always Be an India,' *Vanity Fair*, August 1997.

Jack Hitt, 'And of All the Plagues with Which Nature Is Cursed, Could It Be Me That's the Worst?' *Outside*, December 1996.

Thomas Fraser Homer-Dixon, 'On the Threshold: Environmental Changes as Causes of Acute Conflict,' *International Security*, Fall 1991.

Brendan Howley, 'Eating the Apes,' *Toronto Life*, December 1997.

Samuel P. Huntington, 'The Many Faces of the Future,' *The Utne Reader*, May-June 1997.

Tom Huth, 'Dreaming Bali,' *Condé Nast Traveler*, December 1997.

Elspeth Huxley, *The Flame Trees of Thika*, Penguin, New York, 1962.

Douglas Jehl, 'Massacre Hobbles Tourism in Egypt,' *The New York Times*, December 25, 1997.

Mark Jenkins, *To Timbuktu*, William Morrow, New York, 1997.

Richard Johnson, 'It's Title Torture for Chinese Flicks,' *The New York Post*, May 9, 1998.

Amanda Jones, 'The Look of Love,' *Escape*, January 1998.

Sebastian Junger, 'The Lure of Danger,' *Men's Journal*, April 1998.

Robert D. Kaplan, 'The Coming Anarchy,' *The Atlantic Monthly*, February 1994.

Robert D. Kaplan, 'Proportionalism,' *The Atlantic Monthly*, August 1996.

Timothy Kendall, 'Kingdom of Kush,' *National Geographic*, November 1990.

Stephen Kinzer, 'A Kinder, Gentler Tamerlane Inspires Uzbekistan,' *The New York Times*, November 10, 1997.

Stephen Kinzer, 'Nehru Spoke It, but It's Still "Foreign,"' *The New York Times*, January 27, 1998.

Nicholas D. Kristof, 'Across Asia, a Pollution Disaster Hovers,' *The New York Times*, November 28, 1997.

Nicholas D. Kristof, 'Why Africa Can Thrive like Asia,' *The New York Times*, May 25, 1997.

Reinhard Kunkel, *Ngorongoro*, HarperCollins, New York, 1992.

Howard LaFay, 'Uganda: Africa's Uneasy Heartland,' *National Geographic*, November 1971.

David Lamb, *The Africans*, Random House, New York, 1983.

Eugene Linden, 'Bonobos,' *National Geographic*, March 1992.

Eugene Linden, 'A Curious Kinship,' *National Geographic*, March 1992.

Kenneth MacLeish, 'Java – Eden in Transition,' *National Geographic*, January 1971.

Giovanna Magi, *Luxor*, Casa Editrice Bonechi, Florence, 1988.

Jerry Mander, 'The Case Against the Global Economy,' *Sierra*, 1996.

Charles C. Mann and Mark L. Plummer, 'The Butterfly Problem,' *The Atlantic Monthly*, January 1992.

Luis Marden, 'The Friendly Isles of Tonga,' *National Geographic*, March 1968.

Fred J. Maroon and P.J. Newby, *The Egypt Story*, The American University in Cairo Press/Chanticleer, 1984.

Desmond Bradley Martin, 'They're Killing Off the Rhino,' *National Geographic*, March 1984.

Peter Matthiessen, *The Cloud Forest*, Viking, New York, 1961.

Peter Matthiessen, *The Tree Where Man Was Born*, E.P. Dutton, New York, 1972.

Peter Matthiessen, *Under the Mountain Wall*, Viking, New York, 1962.

O. Louis Mazzatenta, 'China's Warriors Rise from the Earth,' *National Geographic*, October 1996.

John McCarry, 'Peru Begins Again,' *National Geographic*, May 1996.

James C. McKinley, Jr, 'Almost All the News in Kenya Is Turning Out Bad,' *The New York Times*, February 15, 1998.

Donald G. McNeil, Jr, 'How a Flightless Biped Dealer Feathered His Nest,' *The New York Times*, November 22, 1997.

Donald G. McNeil, Jr, 'Humans Answer Call to Be Their Cousins' Keepers,' *The New York Times*, February 24, 1998.

Donald G. McNeil, Jr, 'In Bushmanland, Hunters' Tradition Turns to Dust,' *The New York Times*, November 13, 1997.

Lawrence Millman, 'Redmond O'Hanlon in Trouble Again,' *Escape*, October 1997.

Bob Minzesheimer, 'Take a Literary Journey with Jan Morris,' *USA Today*, January 8, 1998.

Robert Mitton, *The Lost World of Irian Jaya*, Oxford University Press, Melbourne, 1983.

Matt Moffett, 'Peruvian Army Gets Lessons on Protecting the Vicuña,' *The Wall Street Journal*, June 13, 1997.

Karl Muller, *New Guinea*, Passport Books, Lincolnwood, 1993.

Seth Mydans, 'Indonesia Turns Its Chinese into Scapegoats,' *The New York Times*, February 2, 1998.

Seth Mydans, 'In Vast Forest Fires of Asia, Scant Mercy for Orangutans,' *The New York Times*, December 16, 1997.

Michael Nichols, 'Jane Goodall,' *National Geographic*, December 1995.

Redmond O'Hanlon, *Into the Heart of Borneo*, Vintage Departures, New York, 1987.

Redmond O'Hanlon, *No Mercy*, Alfred A. Knopf, New York, 1997.

Thomas O'Neill, 'Irian Jaya,' *National Geographic*, February 1996.

Charles Onyango-Obbo, 'Dictator Amin's Dream Returns to Haunt the Asians,' *The East African*, August 26–September 1, 1996.

P.J. O'Rourke, *All the Troubles in the World*, Atlantic Press, New York, 1994.

P.J. O'Rourke, 'The Great Mall of China,' *Rolling Stone*, December 25, 1997.

P.J. O'Rourke, 'Inside Tanzania,' *Rolling Stone*, June 12, 1997; July 10–24, 1997.

Editors, *Outside* magazine, *The Best of Outside*, Villard, New York, 1997.

Craig Packer, 'Captives in the Wild,' *National Geographic*, April 1992.

Athanasios Paliouras and His Eminence Damianos Archbishop of Sinai, *The Monastery of St Catherine on Mount Sinai*, Hiera Mona Sina–E. Tzaferi, Glyka Nera Attikis, Greece, 1985.

Colin Palmer, 'The Cruelest Commerce,' *National Geographic*, September 1992.

Robert Young Pelton, Coskun Arral and Wink Dulles, *Fielding's The World's Most Dangerous Places*, Redondo Beach, 1998.

Tony Perrottet, *Peru*, APA Publications, Hong Kong, 1991.

Tony Perrottet, 'Savannarama,' *Escape*, May 1997.

Constance Poten, 'A Shameful Harvest,' *National Geographic*, September 1991.

David Quammen, *Wild Thoughts from Wild Places*, Scribner, New York, 1998.

Santha Rama Rau, 'Banaras,' *National Geographic*, February 1986.

Johan Reinhard, 'Sacred Peaks of the Andes,' *National Geographic*, March 1992.

Jugoslovenska Revija and the Shanghai People's Art Publishing House, *China: All Provinces and Autonomous Regions*, Gallery Book/W.H. Smith, New York, 1989.

David Roberts, 'Age of Pyramids,' *National Geographic*, January 1995.

Joe Robinson, 'Latitude Adjustment,' *Escape*, October 1997.

Mary Rockefeller and Laurance S. Rockefeller, 'Problems in Paradise,' *National Geographic*, December 1974.

Jim Rogers, 'Land of Opportunity,' *Worth*, April 1996.

Mohammed Sale and Hour Sourouzian, *The Egyptian Museum Cairo Official Catalogue*, Prestel-Verlag, Munich, 1987.

George G. Schaller, 'Gentle Gorillas, Turbulent Times,' *National Geographic*, October 1995.

George Schaller, 'Secrets of the Wild Panda,' *National Geographic*, March 1986.

Cindy Schreuder, 'Debate Over Conservation of Mountain Gorilla,' *The Chicago Tribune*, June 13, 1995.

Ellen Ruppel Shell, 'Resurgence of a Deadly Disease,' *The Atlantic Monthly*, August 1997.

Philip Shenon, 'For Asian Nation's First Family, Financial Empire Is in Peril,' *The New York Times*, January 16, 1998.

Alex Shoumatoff, 'Mobutu's Final Days,' *Vanity Fair*, August 1997.

Meredith F. Small, 'Prime Mates,' www.nervemag.com, September 1997.

Linda Spalding, 'The Jungle Took Her,' *Outside*, May 1998.

Curt Stager, 'Africa's Great Rift,' *National Geographic*, May 1990.

Richard W. Stevenson, 'The Chief Banker for the Nations at the Bottom of the Heap,' *The New York Times*, September 14, 1997.

Alexander Stille, 'The Ganges' Next Life,' *The New Yorker*, January 19, 1998.

Oona Strathern, *Africa*, Passport Books, Lincolnwood, Illinois, 1995.

Gary Strieker, 'Endangered Apes Being Killed for Meat,' *CNN Online*, December 9, 1995.

E.M. Swift, 'What Big Mouths They Have,' *Sports Illustrated*, November 17, 1997.

Gary Taubes, 'A Mosquito Bites Back,' *The New York Times Magazine*, August 24, 1997.

John Taylor, 'Sorcery, Sunsets, Corpses and Whores,' *Esquire*, April 1996.

Jane Teas, 'Temple Monkeys of Nepal,' *National Geographic*, April 1980.

Paul Theroux, 'By Rail Across the Indian Subcontinent,' *National Geographic*, June 1984.

Paul Theroux, 'Cairo,' *National Geographic*, April 1993.

Paul Theroux, *The Happy Isles of Oceania*, G.P. Putnam's Sons, New York, 1992.

Paul Theroux, *Riding the Iron Rooster*, G.P. Putnam's Sons, New York, 1988.

Roger Vaughan, 'The Two Worlds of Fiji,' *National Geographic*, October 1995.

Jane Vessels, 'Koko's Kitten,' *National Geographic*, December 1995.

Betsy Wade, 'Dos and Don'ts for Park Safety,' *The New York Times*, October 19, 1997.

Wan Yi, Wang Shujoing and Lu Yanzhen, *Quin Dai Gong Ting Sheng Huo: Daily Life in the Forbidden City*, The Commercial Press, Hong Kong, 1985.

Stuart Cary Welch, *Indian Art and Culture, 1300–1900*, The Metropolitan Museum of Art/Holt, Rinehart & Winston, New York, 1985.

John Anthony West, *The Traveler's Key to Ancient Egypt*, Alfred A. Knopf, New York, 1988.

Paul A. Zahl, 'Seeking the Truth About the Feared Piranha,' *National Geographic*, November 1970.

THE WRECK OF THE WHALESHIP *ESSEX*

OWEN CHASE

In 1819, the whaleship *Essex* set sail from Nantucket for the South Pacific to hunt and kill sperm whales, among the largest and most powerful creatures in the ocean. The journey was to end in one of the most dramatic maritime disasters of all time – and one which became the inspiration for the climax of Herman Melville's *Moby Dick*.

On the morning of 20 November 1820, more than a thousand miles from the nearest land, the *Essex* was sunk, rammed by an enraged whale. Twenty sailors managed to scramble into three frail boats and took to the open sea.

Ninety crippling days of starvation followed. First Mate Owen Chase survived to publish his journal of these extraordinary events, but only by eating the flesh of his former shipmates . . .

'Even Melville could not better Chase's real-life account of shipwreck, camaraderie and cannibalism'
Mail on Sunday

'One of the classics of maritime adventure'
The Sunday Times

NON-FICTION / MEMOIR 0 7472 6363 9

More Non-fiction from Headline

THE GREATEST ADVENTURE

BERTRAND PICCARD and BRIAN JONES

'We took off as pilots, flew as friends, and landed as brothers' Bertrand Piccard

In March 1999 Bertrand Piccard and Brian Jones accomplished one of the great feats of human endurance: they were the first men to fly non-stop round the world in a balloon.

Their *Breitling Orbiter 3* balloon took twenty days to circle the globe, from Château d'Oex in Switzerland to the deserts of Egypt, breaking all previous records and placing Piccard and Jones firmly in the history books. They faced many problems that could have brought the balloon crashing to earth. Yet their courage and determination to succeed carried them on to victory.

In their epic account, Piccard and Jones relive many moments of high tension and drama as they bring their historic journey vividly to life. The flight was a triumph not only of technology but of the human spirit and will be an inspiration to anyone contemplating their own 'greatest adventure'.

'A great book' Chris Bonington

NON-FICTION / AUTOBIOGRAPHY 0 7472 6443 0